T0265786

MADE IN MANCHESTER

MADE IN MANCHESTER

A PEOPLE'S HISTORY OF THE CITY THAT SHAPED THE MODERN WORLD

BRIAN GROOM

**Harper
North**

HarperNorth
Windmill Green
24 Mount Street
Manchester M2 3NX

A division of
HarperCollins*Publishers*
1 London Bridge Street
London SE1 9GF

www.harpercollins.co.uk

HarperCollins*Publishers*
Macken House, 39/40 Mayor Street Upper
Dublin 1, D01 C9W8, Ireland

First published by HarperNorth in 2024

1 3 5 7 9 10 8 6 4 2

A catalogue record for this book
is available from the British Library

HB ISBN: 978-0-00-860852-1

Printed and bound in the UK using 100%
renewable electricity at CPI Group (UK) Ltd, Croydon

This book is contains FSC™ certified paper and other controlled
sources to ensure responsible forest management.

For more information visit: www.harpercollins.co.uk/green

CONTENTS

PROLOGUE

One night just before Christmas 1940, my mother, aged eight, was with her family at their house in Hulme, Manchester. She and her younger brother had been evacuated to leafy Altrincham in 1939, but like many children they returned home before bombing started in earnest. On 22 and 23 December Manchester was hit by an intense barrage of incendiary bombs and high-explosive devices in what became known as the Christmas Blitz. A bomb destroyed their house while they were in it but amazingly they survived. The raid happened so quickly that, although they had a cellar, there was no time to get into it, so the mum, dad and three kids – clutching the budgie's cage – dived under the kitchen table. It saved their lives. About a thousand others were not so lucky. Without that table I would not be around to write this book.

So this history has a personal resonance, though I hope it will appeal to a global audience. Manchester has been a notably international city at key periods since soldiers from across the Roman Empire arrived to build a fort at this damp location, aiming to control the tribes of northern Britannia. Manchester was in the forefront of the Industrial Revolution and became the 'shock city' of the 1840s, according to historian Asa Briggs. Its population had expanded sixfold in sixty years. The industrial city was a new phenomenon: visitors flocked to it from many countries, seeing in Manchester's experience a foretaste of the world's future. It was the centre of the global cotton industry and a hub of engineering and machine tool manufacture. No one knew whether all these changes would lead to prosperity or starvation. 'Certainly Manchester is the most wonderful city of modern times!' says the main character in Benjamin Disraeli's novel *Coningsby*.[1] To Friedrich Engels, who toured Manchester's miserable slums at night, it was 'hell on earth'.[2]

Manchester's story is one of birth, growth into Victorian grandeur, catastrophic decline by the 1980s and recent recovery. The eyes of the world are upon it once more as it has become a test case for how post-industrial cities can reinvent themselves. Manchester again finds itself controversial. To some, it exemplifies a smart, pragmatic way to use culture, leisure and knowledge-based business to build a twenty-first-century economy. Its burgeoning population is truly multinational, with more than a hundred and fifty languages spoken.[3] To others, 'Manctopia' or 'Manc-hattan', bristling with new skyscrapers that seem to spring up overnight, is a neoliberal playground for property developers and young middle-class graduates, while being also riddled with poverty and inequality. That sounds remarkably like *das Manchestertum* ('Manchesterism'), a term coined by German critics in the nineteenth century to symbolise selfish economic behaviour.

Manchester justifiably prides itself on its tradition of radicalism. This is the city where peaceful democratic reformers were crushed in the Peterloo Massacre. It was the main centre of working-class Chartism; the place where Engels and Karl Marx carried out research on what became the *Communist Manifesto*; the home of the militant Suffragette movement. 'Manchester is a city which has witnessed a great many stirring episodes, especially of a political character. Generally speaking, its citizens have been liberal in their sentiments, defenders of free speech and liberty of opinion,' said Suffragette founder Emmeline Pankhurst.[4] Yet it was also the home of a successful, employer-led campaign for free trade and economic liberalism.

It was dominated by the Conservatives in the late nineteenth century and between the twentieth century's two world wars.

Like my previous book *Northerners*, this work is a mixture of narrative history and chapters on social and cultural themes. It pays due respect to the city's multiple waves of immigration. Science/technology, sport and music each get a chapter to themselves, so important have these been in Manchester's history. 'If it stopped banging on about its football teams and its bands and its shops and its attitude, Manchester has something that it can be genuinely, enormously proud of, something that it should shout from the rooftops,' wrote Stuart Maconie in *Pies and Prejudice*. 'Manchester changed the world's politics: from vegetarianism to feminism to trade unionism to communism, every upstart notion that ever got ideas above its station, every snotty street-fighter of a radical philosophy, was fostered brawling in Manchester's streets, mills, pubs, churches and debating halls.'[5]

In *Made in Manchester*, figures from the city and its surrounding region are portrayed along with those born elsewhere who have played a part in its story. Notable people include scientists from John Dalton and Ernest Rutherford to the team that produced Baby, the world's first stored-program computer; industrialists such as Joseph Whitworth, whose standard screw threads laid the foundation of modern mass production; women's suffrage campaigners including Lydia Becker and Emmeline Pankhurst; writers such as Elizabeth Gaskell, Anthony Burgess and Shelagh Delaney; composers such as William Walton and Peter Maxwell Davies; and artists such as L.S. Lowry and Annie Swynnerton. Alongside these, the book attempts to describe the often agonisingly difficult lives of the city's ordinary people. It examines the growth of professional sport in the region, not just Manchester City and United, and popular entertainers such as Gracie Fields, Victoria Wood and Peter Kay. It describes Manchester's classical music history and its pop music scene, including the famous Haçienda club (once called the 'Halluçienda' in a slip of the tongue by a senior TV executive[6]) along with bands such as Joy Division,

New Order, The Smiths, Stone Roses and Oasis. Attention is given too to the city's rich but often ignored black music scene.

How am I defining 'Manchester'? The answer is, very loosely. The city of Manchester itself is a small, fat finger of land from Higher Blackley in the north to Woodhouse Park in the south, 44.6 square miles with a population of 549,000. Greater Manchester covers 493 square miles, has a population of 2.87 million and comprises ten boroughs: Bolton, Bury, Manchester, Oldham, Rochdale, Salford, Stockport, Tameside, Trafford and Wigan.[7] The book covers all these areas plus other places beyond its boundaries that look to Manchester as their nearest big city.

Identity can be a sensitive issue. Manchester has had city status since 1853 and Salford since 1926; in medieval times, Manchester was a village in Salfordshire, or the Hundred of Salford. Most of Manchester and all of Salford are in the historic county of Lancashire. In surrounding towns, variously situated in historic Lancashire, Cheshire and Yorkshire, a number of people were resentful that local government reorganisation in 1974 placed them under the new Greater Manchester County Council. Even after the county council was abolished in 1986, district councils saw advantages in continuing to work together. They formed a combined authority in 2011 in which some resources were pooled and various powers exercised jointly. Andy Burnham became Greater Manchester's directly elected mayor in 2017. But the change still rankles with some.

Personally, I have no difficulty in thinking of myself as a Stretfordian, Mancunian, Lancastrian and a northerner. I was born in Stretford Memorial Hospital on Seymour Grove in 1955 – one year before Ian Curtis of Joy Division and sixty-two years after flight pioneer John Alcock were also born in the same building, Basford House. My birth certificate says Stretford, Lancashire, but my home until I was almost five was nearby in Whalley Range, part of Manchester. We moved properly to Stretford for the rest of my childhood and then, when I was a teenager, to Sale in Cheshire, more recently part of Trafford. After several decades living away from the city, I moved in 2015 to Saddleworth in the historic West Riding of Yorkshire, now part of Oldham in Greater Manchester. Geographical identity is complex.

And what about that 'attitude', as Stuart Maconie calls it? Manchester has a reputation for boastfulness. Think of the Victorian phrase: 'What Manchester thinks today, England will think tomorrow.' This can be exaggerated, though. The phrase was as often as not uttered by outsiders rather than Mancunians and if anything more frequently in the form: 'What Lancashire thinks today, England will think tomorrow.' By the 1970s, when the city was in what seemed near-terminal decline, Mancunians were far from confident about singing their city's praises.

That did change with the emergence of Manchester's punk, post-punk and Britpop scene. Think of the 'swagger', the cocksure gait of 'proper Mancs' such as Liam Gallagher of Oasis and Ian Brown of Stone Roses. This perhaps smacked more of defiance than of boasting. Liam's brother Noel allegedly said: 'We like annoying people. It's a Manchester thing. It's a trait. We just like pissing people off.'[8] According to Manchester United star Eric Cantona: 'I feel close to the rebelliousness and vigour of the youth here. Perhaps time will separate us, but nobody can deny that here, behind the windows of Manchester, there is an insane love of football, of celebration and of music.'[9]

It did go a bit further, though. As Tony Wilson, the television presenter who co-founded Factory Records and the Haçienda, put it: 'Manchester became the centre of the universe. The best drugs. The best clothes. The best women. The best bands. The best club. Suddenly everyone wanted to be from Manchester; and if you were a Manc everyone wanted a part of you.'[10] T-shirts proclaimed: 'And on the sixth day God created Manchester.' Then there is the endlessly repeated phrase 'This is Manchester, we do things differently here,' frequently misattributed to Wilson but in fact written by Frank Cottrell-Boyce for the Tony Wilson character played by Steve Coogan in the 2002 film *24 Hour Party People*. It is derived from the first line of L.P. Hartley's *The Go-Between*: 'The past is a foreign country, they do things differently there.' Wilson did quote himself as having uttered a version of the phrase in 1976 in his movie tie-in book *24 Hour Party People*, a 'novelisation', but admits in the foreword that 'a lot of what follows is pure bloody fiction'.[11]

Manchester's reputation as a special place is something that needs to be earned anew with each generation.

1

BEGINNINGS

The rainy, sparsely populated spot near the Roman Empire's north-ernmost extreme must have seemed anything but glamorous to soldiers posted there to build and man a fort around 79 CE, attempt-ing to control tribes of northern Britannia. These Romans called their fort Mamucium (or something close). It was cosmopolitan, prefiguring the influx of foreigners attracted by nineteenth-century Manchester and also today's multinational city. Troops were recruited from across the empire. They might have been surprised to learn that, seventeen centuries later, this damp place would be at the centre of an Industrial Revolution regarded by many as the most transformative period in human history.

Inscriptions record some of the first known Mancunians.[1] There was Lucius Senecianus Martius of the Sixth Legion Valeria Victrix, who created an altar to the Goddess of Fortune. Others included Masovo, Cudrenus, Quintianus and Candidus, centurions in a cohort of auxiliaries from Frisia, in today's north Netherlands and north-west Germany, though we cannot be sure all were Germanic. Other detachments arrived from Austria, Hungary and possibly Spain. A soldier called Aelius Victor erected a stone altar to Rhineland goddesses. The fort was built on a sandstone outcrop above the confluence of the Irwell and Medlock rivers in an undulating glacial landscape between Pennine hills, the marsh and bog of south Lancashire and the Cheshire plain. In a landscape of oak and birch, other inhabitants included bears, wolves and boar – and probably Iron Age Britons, though hard evidence of where these lived is elusive.

Hunter-gatherers of an early human species are thought to have first roamed northern England at least half a million years ago in warm spells during the last Ice Age, though whether they visited the Manchester area is not known.[2] Firmer evidence comes from the Mesolithic period (c.9,500–4,000 BCE). Little has been discovered in Manchester city centre, however, apart from a few prehistoric artefacts from redeposited layers, meaning they may not originate from where they were found. In the wider city-region, Early Neolithic flints and Late Neolithic and Early Bronze Age stone axes and hammers have been found in the Bollin and Medlock valleys. Remains of a timber long house belonging to an Early Neolithic farming community were discovered at Oversley Farm, Ringway, during the building of Manchester Airport's second runway in the late 1990s.[3]

The Pennine region in the Iron Age was dominated by a tribe or confederation that the Romans called the Brigantes. Some suggest that the Manchester area may have been occupied by the Setantii, a possible Brigantian sub-group.[4] Cartimandua, Queen of the Brigantes, who collaborated with the Roman invaders, was ousted by her former husband, Venutius, a decade before Gnaeus Julius Agricola, governor of Britannia 78–84 CE, ordered the building of Mamucium. A statue of Agricola, who also came as close as anyone in history to conquering Caledonia, or Scotland, has pride of place over the main door of Manchester Town Hall.

Mamucium was built at a junction between the west–east route linking the legionary bases at Deva (Chester) and Eboracum (York) and another important route northwards to Luguvalium (Carlisle).[6] Scholars mostly favour the name Mamucium, though other variants exist, including Mammium; Mancunium is now thought less likely. Mamucium has been variously interpreted as coming from the

Brythonic *mamm* ('breast', as in breast-like hill), *mamma* ('mother', referring to a local river goddess) or even *maen* ('rock' or 'stone'). It became Mamecestre in the Middle Ages.[7]

Evidence of a one-time British population exists in placenames north and west of the city with Brythonic elements such as Eccles, Alt, Chadderton and Werneth. Later Anglo-Saxon settlements around Manchester are indicated by names like Chorlton, Clayton, Gorton and Moston. Danish settlements to the south and south-west are suggested in Cheadle Hulme, Davyhulme, Levenshulme and Hulme itself.[8]

The Romans stayed for about two hundred years or more. The first fort was made of stockpiled timber with defensive turf ramparts. It was square, covered about 3 acres and housed a 480-man auxiliary infantry unit. Later it was expanded a couple of times and then replaced by a larger stone construction in the third century. Non-Roman auxiliaries were paid half as much as legionaries, though after twenty-five years they gained Roman citizenship, which also included any wives and children.[9]

A civil settlement or *vicus* grew up outside the walls, made up of soldiers' families, traders, artisans and craftsmen, who set up furnaces and workshops alongside shops and brothels. There is evidence of Roman gods, including a possible temple of Mithras, popular with soldiers, and also Christian worship.[10] A word square discovered in the 1970s may be one of the earliest examples of Christianity in Britain: the anagram spells *pater noster*, the opening of the Lord's Prayer in Latin.[11] The *vicus* shrank dramatically or disappeared by the mid-third century, probably because the soldiers were needed elsewhere, and the Romans finally left Britain early in the fifth century.[12]

Roman Manchester has been largely destroyed, notably in the nineteenth century when the Rochdale Canal sliced across one corner of the site and the Manchester, South Junction and Altrincham Railway drove through the middle of the fort. The remainder of the fort lies under nineteenth-century buildings and roads.[13] The north gate was reconstructed in 1984. Castlefield, designated the UK's first urban heritage park in 1982, includes the terminus of the Bridgewater Canal – the world's first purpose-built industrial canal – and that of the world's first steam-powered inter-city passenger railway, Liverpool–Manchester.

After the Romans departed around 410, several hundred years of silence followed in which Manchester's occupiers left no written records and few artefacts. A legend holds that the castle was occupied by a giant called Tarquin until he was slain by Sir Lancelot du Lac, one of King Arthur's Knights of the Round Table, interpreted by some as a folk allegory for seizure of the Romano-British fort by Angles and their harsh treatment of local residents.[14] Manchester was on the fringes of the Anglo-Saxon kingdom of Northumbria, whose border with Mercia is thought to have been the Mersey. Later it was part of the Viking kingdom of York. A mysterious feature known as the Nico Ditch, which runs between Ashton Moss near Ashton-under-Lyne in the east and Hough Moss near Chorlton-cum-Hardy in the west, may be some kind of boundary marker.[15]

The *Anglo-Saxon Chronicle* records that Edward the Elder, Alfred the Great's son and ruler of Wessex, Mercia and East Anglia, in 923 reached the banks of the Mersey, built a fort at Thelwall and ordered a Mercian army to go 'to Manchester in Northumbria, to repair and to man it'.[16] Exactly what they repaired is unclear; it may have been the Roman fort.[17] By the Norman conquest, Manchester was part of the Royal Manor and Hundred of Salford. The whole Salford area, covering 350 square miles, was poor and sparsely populated. It has been estimated that the Hundred contained only about three thousand people and Manchester was a tiny village, surrounded by peat moss and rough moorland.[18]

Medieval Manchester was not an important town: the royal boroughs of Preston, Lancaster, Liverpool and Wigan were more prominent. The settlement was now on a rocky outcrop above the confluence of the Irwell and Irk, almost a mile north of the Roman fort. Manchester merited one entry in the 1086 *Domesday Book*: 'The church of St Mary and the church of St Michael held in Mamecestre one carucate of land quit from every due except geld [tax].'[19] St Mary's was the Anglo-Saxon forerunner of the cathedral, but the reference to St Michael has puzzled historians. Some think it refers to a church in Ashton-under-Lyne, while others are uncertain. Salford was the administrative centre and Manchester was the ecclesiastical centre, with a huge parish. New chapels were established by the Longford family at Didsbury in the thirteenth century, the Traffords at Stretford in the fourteenth, and by others at Chorlton, Denton, Blackley, Gorton, Newtown and Birch in the sixteenth century.[20]

William the Conqueror assigned the land between the Ribble and the Mersey, among other large estates, to Roger de Poitou, son of Roger of Montgomery, a cousin of William who had fought at Hastings. Roger forfeited the land briefly under the Conqueror for unknown reasons and later lost it for good by taking part in a rebellion in 1102 against Henry I. In the meantime Roger had kept the manor of Salford for himself but granted other lands in the Hundred to five knights in return for service. One of them, Nigel, received land soon to be known as the Barony of Manchester. Thus Salford and Manchester were sundered administratively, never again to be reunited. Salford became the possession of the sovereign as Duke of Lancaster in 1399. The two cities have at times been uneasy neighbours. In the Edwardian era, for example, a dispute between the tramway committees meant that travellers crossing the boundary had to walk several hundred yards to catch a different tram. They could blame Roger de Poitou.[21]

Nigel disappeared from the historical record and the barony came into the hands of Albert de Gresle or Grelley before the end of the eleventh century. The Grelleys were lords of the manor of Manchester for almost two hundred years. Albert's son Robert was one of the northern barons who made King John sign Magna Carta in 1215 and fought against him when he failed to keep its terms. Robert was the first lord of the manor to live in the town. He brought in skilled craftsmen to build a stone manor house, part of which may survive in the stonework of Chetham's School of Music. The medieval town also had a castle, probably a motte and bailey structure, which seems not to have been in use beyond the fourteenth century. One surviving feature is the Hanging Bridge, partly visible from the cathedral's south entrance, and the Hanging Ditch (from *hangan*, or hollow, rather than executions); it was dug apparently to surround the medieval town and eventually became filled by rubbish.[22]

The early manor was agricultural, but by the thirteenth century it was becoming more urban. A weekly Saturday market had been established. Henry III in 1227 granted Robert Grelley the right to hold an annual three-day fair, which took place on 20–22 September at Acresfield, the site today of St Ann's Square. The fair had a long life; it continued when the square was created and eventually relocated to Shudehill and then Campfield in the Castlefield area, before it ceased in 1876.[23]

Textile industries were becoming established, possibly from Roman times, and Flemish weavers may have settled in the Manchester area by the fourteenth century.[24] Residents were no longer villeins, tied to working for the lord of the manor, but had become burgesses, free men with the right (subject to certain conditions) to sell up and move on if they chose. Lords could make more money from a town's markets and fairs than they could from a villein's service. There was little sign of the town flourishing, however. Life was short and harsh. There were plagues and poor harvests. Manchester was badly hit by the Black Death: the chapel yard at Didsbury was consecrated to bury its victims in 1352.[25]

There were two courts: the Portmoot, covering the town, and the baronial court – Curia Domini – with wider powers. Instruments of justice included the pillory, ducking stool and gallows. One quirk was that the maximum fine for wounding someone on a Sunday was twenty shillings, compared with one shilling on a weekday.[26] Thomas Grelley, eighth baron, granted the town its first charter in 1301, based on one granted to Salford in about 1230; the Manchester version largely confirmed rights and privileges that burgesses already held. While single women could not be burgesses, many were engaged in trade. Wives could represent their husbands in court if the husband were absent on business. The charter laid down regulations about prices fixed by the lord for the sale of bread and beer and an obligation to grind corn at the lord's mill and bake bread at his oven.[27]

Thomas Grelley sold the manorial rights in 1309 to John la Warre, his brother-in-law from Gloucestershire. John's grandson Roger, tenth baron, was taken to court in 1359 by Henry, Duke of Lancaster. Jurors at Preston ruled that Manchester was not a borough, with significant powers and independence, but merely a market town – a situation that was to persist until the nineteenth century, despite enormous growth. According to historian Alan Kidd: 'This judgment represented a successful attempt by the manorial lord to prevent the town achieving self-government.'[28]

Thomas la Warre, who became the twelfth lord in 1398, was already rector of the parish of Manchester. He won licences from the Pope and Henry V to transform St Mary's into a Collegiate Church and it was rebuilt in the perpendicular style from 1422. Like other parishes, Manchester had suffered from absentee rectors. Thomas sought to tackle clerical abuses by giving the site of his manor house to establish a College of Clergy in 1421. It is now home to Chetham's School of Music, a fine medieval building. The Collegiate Church became Manchester Cathedral in 1847. It was damaged in the 1940 Manchester Blitz and again in the 1996 IRA bombing.[29]

Between the fifteenth and eighteenth centuries, Manchester developed into a significant regional capital. Tudor Manchester was still a small settlement, just a few streets centred around the Collegiate Church, although John Leland, who travelled all over England as the King's Antiquary, described it around 1540 as 'the fairest, best builded, quickest and most populous town of all Lancastershire'. Leland recorded that a lot of 'Irish yarn' was bought by Manchester men in Liverpool, probably referring to flax, used in making linen.[30]

By Elizabethan times, Manchester was a manufacturing and marketing centre for woollens and linens. Goods were sold throughout the provinces and on London markets. Most production was carried out by independent weavers working in their own homes, who bought their own raw materials and sold direct to merchant clothiers. In 1552, a parliamentary act regulating the manufacture of woollen cloth referred to 'Manchester cottons' (actually a form of woollen cloth), 'Manchester rugs' and 'Manchester frizes'. Factors that encouraged the industry's growth included Manchester's location at the confluence of several rivers and proximity to Liverpool for imports of raw material. Lack of a corporation and craft guilds may also have helped: newcomers were not kept out. The absence of restrictions also enabled the linen industry to adapt to cotton. Once a town developed a specialism, it attracted people with suitable skills, established a reputation for particular products and developed a merchandising network.[31]

By Elizabeth's reign, Mancunians had home comforts such as chimneys and glass windows. People slept on beds with pillows and mattresses, rather than straw pallets and wooden bolsters. In 1515, Hugh Oldham, Bishop of Exeter (brought up in Manchester), founded Manchester Grammar School, one of England's first free grammar schools for boys. He aimed to remedy the fact that Lancashire boys, in his view, 'having pregnant wit have been for the most part brought up rudely and idly and not in virtue or cunning or good manners'. The school was endowed with rentals from property and with the income from three mills; it occupied premises in Long Millgate. It moved to Rusholme in 1930, but still retains the bishop's badge and his motto, *Sapere aude*.[32]

While religious life for many centred on the Collegiate Church, Manchester became a centre of Puritanism, partly influenced by local young people educated at Protestant colleges in Oxford and Cambridge who returned to practise as clergy. In 1588, Robert Waldegrave set up a mobile printing press on Oldham Road and began producing the Martin Marprelate tracts, viciously satirical attacks on the Church. The press was destroyed and Waldegrave fled to Scotland.[33]

In these turbulent times, the College of Clergy was dissolved in 1547, re-established by Mary in 1557, dissolved again on Elizabeth's accession in 1558 and again re-established as a Protestant institution in 1578.[34] One of Manchester's strangest episodes was the appointment of John Dee, alchemist, mathematician, astrologer and scientist, as warden of the college, known as Christ's College, in 1595. Some think he may have been the model for Prospero in Shakespeare's *The Tempest*. He advocated turning England's imperial expansion into a 'British Empire', a term he is credited with coining. He tried to talk to angels, who he thought would reveal the divine language that God had used to create the universe. The Collegiate Church was in disrepair, college buildings had been sold and lands leased to local gentry on terms mired in litigation. Dee struggled to exercise control over Puritan fellows who despised him. He was forced to borrow and had barely enough money to feed his family and servants. After his wife died of plague in 1604, Dee left Manchester to return to London, but remained warden until his death in 1609.[35]

The town's manorial rights passed through several hands and were bought for £3,500 in 1596 by Nicholas Mosley, London representative of a wealthy family of Manchester clothiers. He became Lord Mayor of London and built Hough End Hall on the site of his father's house in Withington, Manchester. The Mosleys were lords of the manor until their descendant, Sir Oswald Mosley, sold the rights to the Corporation of Manchester for £200,000 in 1846.[36]

Sir Nicholas governed through the manorial court called the Court Leet, which met twice a year. As Manchester grew, wandering pigs became such a nuisance that the court appointed a public swineherd, who 'assembled his charges with a horn in the morning and led them out to the lord's waste at Collyhurst', where he kept them till evening. Townsfolk paid the swineherd a penny quarterly for every pig. Another nuisance was gangs of men and boys 'using that unlawful exercise of playing with the football in the streets of the said town, breaking windows and glass at their pleasures'. Football, ever divisive, was to play a big part in Manchester's history.[37]

2

CIVIL WAR TO GEORGIAN BOOM TOWN

Shots rang out on 15 July 1642 in a skirmish between royalists and parliamentarian militia outside Manchester's Eagle and Child tavern. Richard Percival (or Parcival), a linen weaver from Kirkmanshulme, a hamlet east of the town, attacked one of the royalists, who were leaving a banquet. Percival was shot dead, making him the first attested casualty in England's seventeenth-century civil wars. Three wars over a decade (1642–6, 1648–9, 1649–51), along with parallel conflicts in Scotland and Ireland, were traumatic events.[1]

Shortly after that skirmish Manchester, a parliamentarian stronghold, became briefly and unsuccessfully besieged by royalists, bringing the town to national attention. Had it fallen, the war might have taken a different course. The town, with a population estimated at just over three thousand, was emerging as a regionally important textile and trading centre.[2] Growing pains included overcrowding, mountains of manure and repeated outbreaks of plague. As Manchester grew in importance, it became embroiled in the era's religious and political conflicts.

Central and western Lancashire were among Charles I's strongest areas of support. Towns such as Preston, Warrington, Wigan and Salford sympathised with the king, while Manchester, Rochdale and Bolton were for parliament.[3] The most influential local royalist leader was Lord Strange (James Stanley, heir to the Earl of Derby). Both sides searched frantically for arms and gunpower, though Strange failed to seize Manchester's ten barrels of powder, which had been moved to secret locations. It was Strange who led a royalist entourage to the Eagle and Child.

In August, King Charles raised his standard at Nottingham, starting the war, ignoring Strange's advice to raise it at Warrington.[4] Strange, impeached for high treason by the House of Commons, set about raising troops. Defensive preparations in Manchester were led by Robert Bradshaw and William Radcliffe. However, the town lacked walls and gates, making it vulnerable to attack. It hired a German military engineer named Johann Rosworm, who had served in the Low Countries and Ireland during the Thirty Years War. Chains and bars were stretched across the streets to prevent a cavalry charge and iron gates built across the approaches to Market Street.[5]

The attack came on Sunday morning, 25 September, with two thousand infantry, three hundred cavalry and six pieces of artillery. Familiar bell chimes were sounded in reverse by defenders to warn the populace. The royalists, who approached from Salford, were repulsed at Deansgate and the Old Bridge over the Irwell. They were fought off again on Tuesday, though defenders fretted that they were running short of ammunition. On Thursday, Captain Standish, one of the royalist leaders, was killed in another assault on the Old Bridge. Coincidentally, Strange's father died elsewhere that day, so he became the seventh Earl of Derby. The royalists gave up on Saturday after deluges of rain all week and retreated following a brief exchange of prisoners. The siege had been poorly led and uncoordinated. The royalists were estimated to have lost two hundred and twenty men, while the townspeople lost just nineteen.[6]

Parliament gave a vote of thanks. Had Manchester fallen, the whole of Lancashire might have come into royalist hands. The war caused poverty and unemployment, however, with the town bearing the cost of supporting its garrison until parliament decided it should be paid for by sequestrating royalist estates. Distress was so bad that collections were made for its relief in churches around the country. In 1644, Prince Rupert, the king's nephew, passed by Manchester and sacked Bolton, known as the Calvinist 'Geneva of the North'. After that battle, up to a thousand parliamentary soldiers and civilians were killed in one of the war's worst massacres. The Earl of Derby was later tried for treason and beheaded at Bolton for his part in it. Meanwhile an outbreak of plague in Manchester in 1645 killed hundreds.[7]

The end of the first Civil War solved little because the winners were divided between the army, which championed independent or separatist religious views, and parliament, which favoured presbyterianism (assemblies of elders replacing bishops in the Anglican Church) – a division that also gripped Manchester. This was an era of unorthodox political and religious sects. Gerrard Winstanley, leading theorist of the Diggers, had been born in Wigan in 1609, the son of a mercer or cloth trader. He became a merchant tailor in London, but was bankrupted by the Civil War. In 1649 Winstanley and followers took over common land at St George's Hill in Surrey to grow and distribute food, but landowners sent armed men to attack them. Eventually the colony was abandoned.

After a second war between the king and parliament, the Commonwealth was proclaimed in Manchester's Market Place on 6 February 1649. All church property was seized, including the Collegiate Church. Warden Richard Heyrick, a presbyterian, refused to leave his post. He was arrested on suspicion of sympathy with the exiled Stuarts and narrowly escaped the death sentence, before being released on payment of a fine. After reinstatement, he was instrumental in establishing a presbyterian system throughout Lancashire, though this lasted only until 1653.[8]

Oliver Cromwell rewarded Manchester's loyalty by granting the town its first member of parliament. Burgesses chose Colonel Charles Worsley, who had been commander of Cromwell's own infantry regiment. His family lived in Platt Hall, in Platt Fields, where the parliamentary mace was brought after Cromwell ordered removal of 'that bauble' from the Commons. After five months, parliament made Cromwell lord protector (dictator) and was dissolved. Worsley was promoted to major-general in charge of Lancashire, Cheshire and Staffordshire. A keen Puritan, he boasted of closing numerous alehouses. He was tipped as a possible successor to Cromwell until he suddenly died, aged thirty-five, in 1656. His statue is on the Albert Square/Princess Street corner of the town hall. By the Restoration, Manchester had lost its representation in parliament. It would be almost two hundred years before it was restored.[9]

During the Commonwealth, Chetham's Hospital, a charitable school for boys, and Chetham's Library, the oldest free public reference library in the English-speaking world, were created. These were provided for in the will of Humphrey Chetham, a leading merchant, who was born at Crumpsall Hall and studied at Manchester Grammar School. He died in 1653 and set up a £7,000 foundation for forty poor boys to be clothed and educated from age six to sixteen, after which they would be apprenticed. He insisted they should be 'children of honest, industrious and pains-taking parents, and not of wandering, or idle beggars, or rogues'. They should not be bastards, lame, infirm or diseased and he was specific about where they were to come from: 'fourteen from Manchester, six from Salford, three from Droylsden, two from Crumpsall, ten from Bolton-le-Moors, and five from Turton'. The school opened in 1656 in a building that was formerly home of the warden and fellows of the Collegiate Church.[10]

Chetham provided £1,000 'for, or towards a library, within the town of Manchester, for the use of scholars, and all others, well affected, to resort to'. The Civil War nipped in the bud a project to create a university at Manchester. This scheme, broached in 1640, had support from Lord Strange; his Manchester residence, the Old College, was suggested as a suitable site. In fact Manchester was not to get a university until the nineteenth century.[11]

By the Restoration in 1660, even parliamentarian Manchester was so weary of conflict and bitterness that it celebrated Charles II's coronation heartily. There was a military procession, a public dinner, church services, fireworks, bonfires and the public water supply was made to run with wine. William Heawood, steward of the Court Leet, wrote to a London relation: 'The Gentlemen & Officers drunck his Majesties health in Claret running forth at three streams of the said Conduit, which was answered from the Souldiery by a great volley of shot, and many great shouts, saying "God save the King"; … during the time of dinner, and until after Sun-set, the said Conduit did run with pure Claret, which was freely drunke by all that could, for the crowd came near the same.' Heyrick hailed the Restoration in a sermon and accepted the restored Prayer Book.[12]

In London, Marple-born lawyer John Bradshaw had in 1649 been appointed lord president of the High Court of Justice, an unprecedented tribunal set up to try Charles I, after which the king was beheaded. That made him the only English person ever to hand down sentence of death on his sovereign. Although he was dead by the time of the Restoration, Bradshaw's body was brought up from Westminster Abbey, along with that of other regicides including Cromwell, and hanged in its coffin at Tyburn.

Manchester's growth accelerated in the century after 1660 when its population more than quadrupled in size. Elizabethan Manchester was already a manufacturing and marketing centre for woollens and linen. After 1600 came the rise of the Lancashire cotton industry. Cotton was first introduced through manufacture of fustians, a linen and cotton mix that spread rapidly through east Lancashire, notably in Bolton, Blackburn and Oldham as well as Manchester. Manchester was also notable for smallware manufacture (ribbons, tapes and buttons etc.) and silk weaving, but it was trade in cotton products that took off. By 1750 pure cottons were being produced.[13]

During the eighteenth century Manchester became a nationally significant town despite its antiquated system of local government, lacking a borough corporation. Daniel Defoe called it 'one of the greatest, if not the greatest mere village in England', echoing comments by Bishop Nicholson of Carlisle and William Stukeley, an

American visitor. Defoe also complimented the town on its child labour, 'the smallest children being all employed, and earning their bread'. Merchants became wealthy from the 'putting-out' system in which they supplied yarn for spinning and weaving in workers' homes and then had the products finished and took them to market.[14]

Political and religious divisions became even more entrenched, though reactions in Manchester appeared initially muted when Catholic James II briefly succeeded Charles II, before being replaced by William of Orange in the Protestant 'Glorious Revolution' of 1688. A significant minority in Britain refused to accept William and Mary as sovereigns, instead believing that monarchs were appointed by divine right. Over the next six decades Jacobites pressed for restoration of James and his heirs. Stronger feelings emerged over the 'Lancashire plot' of 1694, in which eight members of the gentry were tried in Manchester for allegedly planning to murder or overthrow William and Mary and reinstate James II. Chief witness John Lunt claimed he was issuing commissions from James to Lancashire Jacobites, including the accused, preparatory to an uprising. Defence witnesses described Lunt as a scoundrel, bigamist and highwayman. The jury quickly found the defendants not guilty, causing celebrations in Manchester.[15]

In the same year, Manchester's first nonconformist chapel opened. Henry Newcome, a presbyterian preacher, was forced by the Act of Uniformity in 1662 to sever links with the Collegiate Church. After some clandestine preaching, he obtained a licence to preach in a barn in Shudehill and by 1694 – the year before he died – the Dissenters' Meeting House opened on Cross Street. Cross Street Chapel was to play an important role and later became Unitarian. Other Protestants who supported the 1688 revolution became discontented with the Tory clergy at the Collegiate Church. A separate church was founded by Lady Ann Bland, a 'low-church' Anglican who was Sir Edward Mosley's daughter. St Ann's Church was consecrated in 1712 in what was to become St Ann's Square.

Bland had a Tory rival, Madame Drake. Bland wore orange to irritate Drake while the latter wore tartan to annoy Bland.[16]

Manchester divided between the congregation of the Collegiate Church, which was Tory and sympathetic to the Stuart cause (whose supporters met at the Bulls Head Inn, later destroyed in the 1940 Blitz), and that of St Ann's, which sided with the Whigs (whose secular base was the Angel Inn). Tories held offices as justices of the peace, churchwardens or officers of the Court Leet, while Whigs and dissenters included many rising manufacturers and merchants. The two churches even spawned rival dancing groups, sporting as emblems the Stuart tartan and an orange blossom respectively. It is not easy to explain why a town once largely parliamentarian now had many Jacobite sympathisers. Part of this may have been down to younger sons of the landed gentry becoming apprenticed to Manchester merchants and manufacturers and then receiving family money to set them up in business. It may also have been more broadly that, in growing rapidly, the city was importing people with more conservative rural attitudes.[17]

On 10 June 1715, the birthday of exiled James Edward Stuart, who was the 'Old Pretender' and son of James II, a mob led by a blacksmith named Tom Syddall attacked Cross Street Chapel, smashing doors and windows and setting it on fire. Syddall was arrested and imprisoned in Lancaster Jail, until Jacobite forces released him in the 1715 uprising, in which an army invaded from Scotland. James was told he had been proclaimed as James III in Manchester and that fifty troops had been raised in the town to support him, but the rebels were forced to surrender at Preston. Syddall was captured and he and four others hanged in Manchester, where his severed head was displayed on the Market Cross.[18]

In 1745, Charles Edward Stuart, the 'Young Pretender', led a rising to gain the British throne – now occupied by George II – for his father, the Old Pretender. Invading from Scotland with an army of 6,000, he picked up little support before he reached Manchester.

Many residents left ahead of Charles's arrival. The first invaders to enter were Sergeant Dickson, a girl and a drummer (giving rise to a legend that Manchester had been taken without resistance by a sergeant, a drummer and a whore). Charles entered to cheers and the sound of church bells. Local people made a show of enthusiasm, but few signed up. Whereas the Jacobites hoped for more than one and half thousand volunteers, eventually a Manchester regiment of two to three hundred was formed, led by Colonel Francis Towneley, who was from a Lancashire Catholic family. Manchester had also hedged its bets by subscribing nearly two thousand pounds for a troop of soldiers loyal to George II to be commanded by the Earl of Derby. An epigram attributed to Manchester poet John Byrom (though he claimed to have heard it from someone else) reflected those who had confused loyalties:

> God bless the King! (I mean our faith's defender!)
> God bless! (No harm in blessing) the Pretender.
> But who Pretender is, and who is King,
> God bless us all! That's quite another thing!

Charles turned back at Derby, fearing that three large Hanoverian armies were approaching. He stopped for a day in Manchester, where crowds stoned and threatened him. His soldiers responded by looting. Charles fined the town £5,000 and took a hostage against payment. He was persuaded to reduce the fine by half and the money was raised. Charles gave a written undertaking to repay the sum as soon as 'the Country is in quiet and Tranquility under our royall Government'. Heading north, Charles paused at Carlisle and gave the Manchester Regiment the hopeless task of meeting Cumberland's pursuing army. Eventually they had no choice but to surrender. Towneley and others were hanged, drawn and quartered, including Thomas Sydall, son of the earlier Thomas Sydall. While St Ann's congregation gave thanks for their deliverance, unruly elements attacked the houses of widow Sydall and other Jacobite sympathisers.[19]

Manchester was developing apace. Its first Exchange, a two-storey brick and stone building, was built by the lord of the manor in 1729. The lower part was open and used as a market hall, while upstairs there was a room where the courts met and theatrical performances were held.[20] The town became a centre for nonconformists. The first Methodist services took place in a room overlooking the Irwell near Blackfriars Bridge. Soon they built their first chapel, at Birchin Lane, off the High Street.[21] In 1772, the population was estimated at just over twenty-two thousand; all parts of the town were still within five minutes' walk of the Exchange.

Among notable residents was Doncaster-born Elizabeth Raffald, who ran a shop in Market Place selling 'Cold Entertainments, Hot French Dishes, Confectionaries, &c' and published a cookery book, *The Experienced English Housekeeper*. She also published the town's first business directory (and may possibly have invented the Eccles cake.)[22] Running the King's Head Inn in Salford proved more difficult: she and her hard-drinking husband got into financial difficulty. Her recipes have been copied by writers including Isabella Beeton in *Mrs Beeton's Book of Household Management* and admired by modern cooks including Elizabeth David and Jane Grigson.

By the first census in 1801, Manchester's population was above seventy thousand. A growing number of Catholics led to the opening of St Mary's Church, nicknamed the 'hidden gem', in Mulberry Street. The first reference to a Jewish congregation was in the 1750s, with an improvised synagogue in an upper room at Infirmary Yard, off Garden Street, Withy Grove. It moved in 1806 to a room at Ainsworth's Court, Long Millgate.[23]

An Act of Parliament in 1765 provided for cleansing, lighting and fire engines. Police Commissioners (in fact general administrators) were created in 1792. At first they were ineffective at tackling problems such as a dire shortage of water supply. There was favouritism and bribery, though things changed after criticism and actions were taken including building brick sewers and opening soup kitchens for the destitute. Much of the credit was due to Charles Brandt, a

German-born merchant who became boroughreeve (chief municipal officer) and treasurer.[24] Feeding the growing population was a serious problem, provoking frequent riots in response to shortages. In the 'Shudehill fight' of 1757, four people were killed. In 1800, one Hannah Smith was hanged for encouraging people to steal potatoes from a cart; she also led a mob against a dairy cart and was later seen selling stolen butter.[25]

Manchester Infirmary, along with a dispensary and a lunatic hospital and asylum, were founded by charitable initiatives. The infirmary was initially in Shudchill, then Piccadilly from 1755 (demolished in 1910). The first purpose-built Sunday school opened in about 1782, after which Sunday schools expanded rapidly. Meetings to discuss science at the home of scholar Thomas Percival led to the creation of Manchester's Literary and Philosophical Society in 1781. Manchester Academy, also known as New College (a successor to Warrington Academy) opened in 1786, providing higher education for nonconformists, though it led a peripatetic existence: it moved to York, back to Manchester, then to London and finally became Manchester College, Oxford. Manchester Circulating Library began in 1757 and the Portico, a library and reading room, in 1806. The Portico's first secretary was Peter Mark Roget, a physician at the infirmary, later better known for his Thesaurus. The first permanent theatre opened in Marsden Street in 1753, replaced in 1775 by the Theatre Royal in Spring Gardens, later moved to Fountain Street.[26]

Manchester's burgeoning commercial life led to development of transport, with roads, packhorse routes and canals converging on the town. Coach services expanded. James Ogden, an author who began working life as a fustian cutter, wrote in 1783: 'The large and populous town of Manchester has now excited the attention and curiosity of strangers, on account of its extensive trade and the rapid increase of its buildings, with the enlargement of its streets.'[27] The stage was set for a momentous role in the industrial age.

3

THE RISE OF COTTONOPOLIS

It was Preston-born Sir Richard Arkwright, abrasive genius of the Industrial Revolution, who gave Manchester its first cotton-spinning mill in 1781. It was a source of wonder: the erection of the mill chimney at Miller Street near Shudehill attracted crowds daily who stared in awe at its height.[1] By 1800 there were dozens of such chimneys. Manchester was on its way to becoming Cottonopolis, the centre of an industry reshaping the world.

The factory's arrival symbolised a shift from home-based work to a world in which machines produced yarn and cloth in previously unimaginable quantities. Never before had such a global industry been built more than two thousand miles from its nearest source of raw materials. Factories created a new urban environment and new ways of working and living, ultimately helping to generate sustained economic growth along with wealth, inequalities and some dire social conditions. Manchester's population grew from below 10,000 in 1700 to an astonishing 303,000 in 1851.[2]

Visitors beat a path to observe the first major industrial centre, evoking admiration and revulsion. 'It is one of the most flourishing places in the kingdom, large, opulent, well built', wrote Percival Barlow in his *General History of Europe* (1790). Yet John Byng, later Viscount Torrington, visiting in the same year, found it a 'great nasty manufacturing town … a hole where the slave working and drinking a short life out, is eternally reeling before you from fatigue or drunkenness'. Diarist Anna Walker in 1789 said it was 'a Dull, Smoky, Dirty Town … from whence the Black Soot rises in clouds to Overspread the surrounding Country'.[3] Industrial pollution was to have long-lasting consequences for health and the environment.

Cotton production was becoming concentrated in Manchester by about 1750, giving it a head start to capitalise on the popularity of cotton fabrics, which were more comfortable to wear and easier to wash than woollens and could be dyed and printed with relative ease. Factors that aided Manchester included existing textile skills and commercial expertise. It had rivers to provide water power and was close to sources of coal for steam engines. It had no craft guilds and few regulations aimed at keeping newcomers out. It was an 'open town, destitute of a corporation and unrepresented in parliament', which was 'probably to its advantage', wrote physician and author John Aikin in 1795.[4]

It was also close to Liverpool, giving easy access to a growing supply of cheap, slave-grown cotton from the West Indies and the US, as well as an outlet for exports. Manchester was to play an important role in the campaign to abolish slavery, but benefited from it up to the American civil war. Transport links were improving. The Mersey and its tributary, the Irwell, were made navigable by the Irwell and Mersey Navigation, completed in 1736, establishing a water route from Liverpool enabling seagoing vessels of up to fifty tons to sail into Manchester via eight locks. Manchester's first wharf opened at the bottom of Quay Street.[5]

Francis Edgerton, third duke of Bridgewater, opened Britain's first purpose-built industrial canal in 1761 between Manchester and his coalmines at Worsley (later extended to Runcorn and Leigh), with the aid of his chief engineer, Staffordshire's James Brindley. The Barton aqueduct, which carried the canal over the Irwell, was an engineering marvel. The Bridgewater Canal halved the price of coal in Manchester and sparked off canal mania, though it took the duke decades to make a return on his investment. The connection of the canal to Altrincham, Sale and Timperley in 1865 stimulated market gardening there and warehousing at Broadheath. Other canals followed: the Ashton in 1796, the Rochdale – the first trans-Pennine canal – in 1804, the Manchester, Bolton and Bury completed in 1808.[6] Improvements to notoriously bad roads were also important. The road to Buxton became the North West's first turnpike by a 1724 Act, easing travel on the route to London via Stockport and Derby. Turnpike trusts charged tolls in return for maintaining roads. Other turnpike roads linked Manchester with nearby towns. Stagecoach services expanded. By the turn of the century, the four and a half days it had taken a 'Flying Coach' to reach London in 1754 was down to an average thirty hours and occasionally less than twenty.[7]

Inventors were mostly not Manchester-born, though some were from surrounding towns. John Kay, a farmer's son from Bury, patented his flying shuttle in 1733 – a wooden tool that automatically threw the weft thread back and forth across a loom where previously it had been passed by hand, thus doubling weavers' productivity. By the 1760s it was widely used but Kay fought unsuccessful legal battles against weavers who refused to pay royalties. He died in poverty in France.[8] Kay's invention raised demand for cotton yarn, solved by breakthroughs in spinning. James Hargreaves, an illiterate handloom weaver from near Blackburn, is credited with inventing the spinning jenny – a Lancashire term for an engine – in 1764. Spinners, fearing it would put them out of work, twice broke in and destroyed his jennies, but by the late 1780s about twenty thousand were in operation.[9]

A former barber and wig-maker, Richard Arkwright patented the spinning frame in 1769, also known as the water frame after it was adapted to use water power. It consisted of four rollers that drew out cotton strands before a spindle twisted them into thread, which allowed for continuous spinning. In 1779, Bolton's Samuel Crompton combined elements of the jenny and water frame to make a complex machine called the mule (so called because it was a hybrid, in the way that a mule is the result of crossbreeding a female horse with a male donkey). This produced yarns that rivalled India's finest and it became the world's dominant spinning machine for 150 years. Crompton, who played violin at Bolton's theatre, had little talent for business and never managed to cash in.[10]

Arkwright, shrewd and with a streak of arrogance, was one of the few inventors to become wealthy, renowned not only for the water frame but above all for his role in creating and spreading the factory system. He also displayed political skills. The 1721 Calico Act, aiming to protect British woollen textiles, had banned the purchase of printed calicoes made from Indian white goods and restricted the printing of all-cotton British cloths, though cotton-linen fustians were exempt, as confirmed by the 'Manchester Act' of 1736. When Arkwright sought to export his printed calicoes he found they were subject to twice the excise duty levied on fustians. In 1774 he persuaded parliament to pass an act that removed restrictions on home-made cotton textiles while continuing them for Indian cloth. British cloth would have three blue threads in the selvage and would be stamped 'British Manufactory'. The result was a massive influx of investment into the British cotton industry.[11]

Arkwright's Manchester spinning factory – along with others he built in Derbyshire, Nottingham, Staffordshire and Scotland – followed the success of his Cromford mill in Derbyshire. His mill at Birkacre, Chorley, was destroyed in anti-machinery riots and he lost legal battles against spinners who infringed his patent, but this did not stop him amassing a fortune estimated at up to half a million pounds.[12] Arkwright appears initially to have tried to use a steam engine to drive his Manchester water frames, but by 1789 the mill was water-powered, with steam pumping water to the wheel. Within a few years, problems of driving cotton machinery by steam were resolved. The first purpose-built steam-powered mill was erected by Peter Drinkwater in 1789 in Auburn Street, off Piccadilly. Drinkwater was a fustian putting-out merchant who had turned mill owner. His mill used a rotary beam engine made by Boulton & Watt of Birmingham and soon employed about five hundred people. By 1816 there were eighty-six steam-powered mills in Manchester and Salford.[13]

The main cluster was in Ancoats, north of the town centre, and included huge factories of the Murray brothers and McConnel & Kennedy. Another cluster was south of the centre along Oxford Road and Cambridge Street by the River Medlock. Further zones were created alongside the Rochdale and Ashton canals to the east and in the Irk Valley to the north. Adam and George Murray, James McConnel and John Kennedy were all Scots. McConnel & Kennedy, the largest mill complex, employed almost 1,600 people by 1836. Fortunes could be made, though fiercer competition by the mid-1820s may have spread profits more thinly. Risks were high. Percival Barlow wrote in 1790: 'The manufacturers of Manchester live like men of fortune, which indeed they are, though there have lately been a great many capital failures in that place.' (He added for good measure: 'The women of Manchester and indeed all Lancashire are esteemed handsome.')[14]

Weaving proved more difficult to mechanise than spinning. Edmund Cartwright, a Wakefield-educated Anglican vicar, created the first power loom in the 1780s, but his machines were fraught with problems. Gorton master spinner Robert Grimshaw opened a weaving factory at Manchester's Knott Mill in 1790, using thirty of Cartwright's looms, but it burned down within weeks of opening. It is uncertain whether this was an accident or arson inspired by hand-loom weavers' fears. The 'dandy loom' patented by William Ratcliffe of Stockport in 1802 was an improvement, but power looms did not overtake handlooms until the 1840s.[15]

Despite all this, Manchester was never predominantly a manufacturing town – a 'warehouse town' is more accurate. Warehouses absorbed more than 48 per cent of property asset investment by 1815 compared with 6 per cent in factories. The number of cotton mills peaked at 108 in 1853. The last was built in Miles Platting in 1924 and fewer than thirty mills have survived into the twenty-first century.[16] Bolton surpassed Manchester as a spinning town by the 1850s and Oldham by the 1860s, while Manchester developed as the industry's commercial and financial centre.

Manchester's first bank – Byrom, Allen, Sedgwick and Place, also known as Manchester Bank – opened in 1771 but failed in 1788, when its premises were taken over by Heywood's Bank.[17] Many banks were founded over the next century. Before the banking system developed, industrialists relied on finance from other business people or family, social and faith networks. Nathan Mayer Rothschild, of the Rothschild banking dynasty, established a textile trading and finance business in Manchester in 1798 at the age of twenty-one before moving to London and founding N.M. Rothschild.[18] A new Exchange, opened in 1809 (on the corner of Exchange Street, looking on to the Market Place), proved popular with the business community. Modelled on the example of Lloyd's Coffee House in London, it had a post office, news room and dining facilities and boasted that 'every article of political and commercial intelligence is to be procured for their perusal'.[19]

Cotton aided development of other industries, notably engineering and chemicals. There were continuous improvements in textile machinery and power systems. In the view of historian Roger Osborne, Manchester had replaced Birmingham as the centre of British engineering by 1820. Salford's Bateman & Sherratt competed with Boulton & Watt to meet demand for steam engines. Manchester attracted young engineers such as Welsh-born Richard Roberts, who made machine tools and improved the design of textile machines, notably Crompton's mule. Scots-born William Fairbairn's business undertook all the ironwork in the construction of mills (including Titus Salt's woollen mills at Saltaire near Bradford), along with steam engines, water wheels and locomotives. James Nasmyth, another Scot, opened a foundry at Patricroft, Eccles, and invented a steam hammer. German-born Charles Beyer and partner Richard Peacock built a railway works in Gorton, making locomotives for countries from Belgium to Australia.[20]

Manchester became a centre for machine tools, notably thanks to Stockport-born Joseph Whitworth, who established his works in Openshaw in 1833. He created a standard system of screw threads that remained in place in much of the world until after the Second World War. Before him, there were no standard measures for nuts and bolts. Standardisation allowed components to become interchangeable, enabling mass production. Letter-writer Jane Carlyle said he had 'a face not unlike that of a baboon; speaks the broadest Lancashire; could not invent an epigram to save his life; but has nevertheless "a talent that might drive the Genii to despair" and when one talks with him, one feels to be talking with a real live man, to my mind worth any number of the Wits that go about'. Whitworth bequeathed much of his fortune to the people of Manchester, with the Whitworth Art Gallery and Christie Hospital partly funded by his money.[21]

Engineering became important to other towns. Platt Brothers of Oldham was the world's largest textile machinery manufacturer. Other large employers included Howard & Bullough (Accrington) and Dobson & Barlow (Bolton). Salford was a centre for engineering and ironworks.[22]

Many Manchester industrialists were nonconformists. Barred from parliament, military and civil service before 1829, dissenters made their way as artisans and merchants. Methodism, at its nineteenth-century peak, was to become the dominant faith of much of northern England. Several manufacturers in Manchester were Unitarians, including McConnel and Fairbairn. Unitarians believe that God is one entity rather than a trinity; it was an optimistic religion with a faith in progress. Samuel Oldknow, however, a Unitarian who wove muslins or fine fabrics, saw his Manchester, Cheshire and Derbyshire-based empire crumble in the 1790s and he died owing the Arkwright family and others more than £200,000.[23] Remains of his Mellor Mill at Marple have been excavated and opened to public view.

At the wilder end of nonconformism, Manchester-born Ann Lee, daughter of Quakers, became 'Ann the Word', leader of a sect known as the Shakers, so called because they worshipped by ecstatic dancing or 'shaking'. She and her followers emigrated to upstate New York in 1774 after she had been arrested several times for breaking the Sabbath and blasphemy. Followers believed her to be the 'second coming' of Christ in female form.

Manchester drew in migrants, initially from rural Lancashire and Cheshire and later from Ireland, Scotland and other parts of England. Availability of work for young people of both sexes encouraged early marriage and an increased birth rate, though this was accompanied by an alarmingly high death rate.[24] While many found better opportunities than they had in the countryside, factory work and its irksome discipline was a shock. Workers faced a day of fourteen hours or more in hot, humid conditions, unable to leave the machine except at designated meal breaks, even for a toilet break; some employers sent a bucket round three times a day so workers could relieve themselves at their posts.[25]

Children were often beaten to keep them awake and worked long hours in unnatural postures that could cripple them for life. A mill in Pendleton, Salford, owned by William 'Black' Douglas, was nicknamed the 'Cripples Factory'. William Swanton, an overseer at Eccles' mill, Wigan, admitted he had attached 14 lb cast-iron weights to nine-year-old throstle spinner Ellen Hooton's back and shoulders to prevent her from running away. This was with the knowledge of her mother Mary, who did not get on with Ellen – perhaps because Ellen would rather run away than earn money for the family – and told the overseer 'he might do anything' with her daughter, even have her for himself.[26]

The early factory system relied heavily on women and children, seen as cheaper and easier to manage than men. Jobs done by women or girls included those of 'tenters' or 'stretchers', who worked carding machines that straightened cotton fibres ready for spinning. Factory work was widely held to undermine the morals of its female labour force. One witness told an 1833 Factory Commission: 'It would be no strain on my conscience to say that three-quarters of the girls between fourteen and twenty years were unchaste.' Women faced predators. Some mill owners were alleged to offer the sexual favours of female workers to important visitors. Those working night shifts could face unwelcome personal attention from an overseer.[27]

Not all Manchester mills exploited workers. Drinkwater employed twenty-one-year-old Welshman Robert Owen as his manager in 1792, who operated an enlightened regime. Owen became an active member of Manchester's Literary and Philosophical Society, meeting men such as Dr Thomas Percival, an early advocate of factory reform. Owen later carried the principles he learned into his model community at New Lanark, Scotland.[28]

By 1800, rapid industrialisation was leading to a sharp decline in housing standards. Aikin noted in 1795 that 'in some parts of the town, cellars are so damp as to be unfit for Habitations'. Poet Robert Southey, visiting in 1808, observed: 'The dwellings of the labouring manufacturers are in narrow streets and lanes, blocked up from light and air … crowded together because every inch of land is of such value, that room for light and air cannot be afforded them.' Richard Holden, a visiting attorney from Rotherham, wrote: 'The town is abominably filthy, the Steam Engines pestiferous, the Dyehouses noisome and offensive and the Water of the River as black as ink or the Stygian Lake.' This led to appalling slum conditions by the 1830s.[29]

Industrial development continued. Three waterways linked Manchester and Liverpool by the 1820s but demand was outstripping capacity. The prime mover in building a railway between the towns was a Liverpool merchant, Joseph Sanders, backed by Manchester merchants. Their proposal was opposed by canal interests, who denounced the scheme as wild and impractical; they claimed it would stop cows grazing, hens laying, kill passing birds, make horses extinct and slaughter passengers when boilers exploded.

George Stephenson, builder of the Stockton and Darlington Railway, was hired as engineer. A first attempt to get parliamentary approval in 1825 failed, in part because of errors in Stephenson's survey; he was hampered by having to conduct parts of it by stealth over opponents' land, sometimes at night.[30] A second attempt succeeded the following year and construction began. The thirty-five-mile line included Wapping Tunnel beneath Liverpool and crossed Chat Moss peat bog using brush floats. A trial was held at Rainhill in 1829 to decide whether locomotives were suitable – as opposed to having stationary engines pulling wagons via cables – and if so which were the best. The contest was won by George and Robert Stephenson's *Rocket*, which pulled thirteen tons at an average twelve miles per hour and a top speed of thirty. The Stephensons were given the contract to produce locomotives for the first inter-city railway.[31]

The Liverpool and Manchester Railway opened on 15 September 1830 when a crowd of about fifty thousand gathered in Liverpool to watch eight trains depart for Manchester. Guests included the Duke of Wellington, prime minister, though he was not a railway enthusiast ('They encourage the lower classes to travel about'). The occasion was marred by tragedy when, after a train stopped to take on water, Liverpool MP Walter Huskisson stepped down on to the parallel track and was hit by a passing locomotive. He was taken to the nearest place on the line, Eccles, but died later that day. When Wellington's train reached Manchester, the town's radical tendencies were on show. Each loyal cheer was countered by hisses and booing and cries of 'No corn laws' and 'Remember Peterloo'.[32]

The railway, built mainly to carry goods, was a surprise hit with passengers. Whereas stagecoaches had carried about fourteen thousand people a year between Liverpool and Manchester, the railway conveyed more than four hundred and forty-five thousand passengers in its first year. Routes to Birmingham and London opened later in the decade. Stockport's famous viaduct, 1,792 feet long and 111 feet high, opened in 1840. Later came lines to Leeds and Sheffield involving ambitious Pennine tunnels.[33] Liverpool Road Station, terminus of the Liverpool and Manchester Railway, is now part of the Science and Industry Museum. Its classical frontage, a grade-one-listed building, looks more like a Georgian townhouse than a station, largely because no one knew what a station should look like.[34] Soon stations ringed the city centre, though there was a lack of through-lines because the centre was crowded with factories, houses, shops and warehouses – still problematic today. Lines were built to other cotton towns. Suburban lines shaped the conurbation's growth.

John Greenwood, a Pendleton tollkeeper, created one of the world's first horse-drawn bus services in 1824, linking the centre with suburbs such as Pendleton, Ardwick and Cheetham Hill. By 1850 there were sixty-four such services.[35] Long-distance coaches disappeared quickly, unable to compete with railways. Canals declined more slowly. Railways created an opportunity for entrepreneurs such as George Bradshaw, a Pendleton-born Quaker. After first publishing maps of canals, his Manchester company in 1839 published the world's first compilation of railway timetables, *Bradshaw's Railway Time Tables and Assistant to Railway Travelling* – unpopular with railway companies, which found themselves tied to running services on time.

Manchester's growth was to become even more explosive in the nineteenth century's early decades.

4

RIOTS AND RADICALS

John Lees, a cotton mill owner's son from Oldham, had been in the heat of battle during Wellington's victory over Napoleon at Waterloo. Four years later, defying his father's wishes, he went to a rally for political reform at St Peter's Field, Manchester, on 16 August 1819. Lees was beaten by special constables and suffered sabre wounds from the cavalry on his back and elbow. He told a friend that 'at Waterloo there was man to man, but at Manchester it was downright murder'. Lees died three weeks later, aged twenty-two. Blood poured from his mouth when his body was lifted into the coffin.[1]

An estimated eighteen died of injuries received on that day and almost seven hundred were seriously injured in what became ironically dubbed the 'Peterloo Massacre'.[2] Many were women and some were children. It was arguably the most important day in Manchester's history. The reform movement suffered a severe setback in the short term, but Peterloo's legacy helped to pave the way for the Reform Act 1832, which enfranchised Manchester, Salford and other industrial towns of the North West.

Manchester prides itself on its radical heritage. It was prominent in the working-class Chartist campaign for universal male suffrage. Karl Marx and Friedrich Engels began research that led to the Communist Manifesto at Chetham's Library. The Trades Union

Congress first met in the city in 1868. The Suffragette movement was founded by Manchester's Emmeline Pankhurst. Yet Manchester was also home to a successful, employer-led campaign for free trade, a key aspect of economic liberalism, which might seem contradictory. What was once a minor provincial town was now at the centre of social, political and economic currents sweeping the world.

The period 1790–1850 in Britain was turbulent, with protests in the rural south as well as the North. There were French and American wars, explosive population growth and food shortages caused by climatic disruption and poor harvests. People faced being displaced from their old livelihoods by factories. There were stresses of urbanisation and diseases such as tuberculosis, typhus and cholera. At the time, no one knew whether all this would lead to increased prosperity or starvation. Manchester was in the thick of it, not helped by the cotton industry's boom-and-bust pattern. Its population more than quadrupled between 1801 and 1851.[3]

The French Revolution of 1789 exacerbated tensions between Manchester's Tory-Anglican and Whig-nonconformist factions. Few members of the gentry lived in the town, but middle-class Tory manufacturing and merchant dynasties such as the Birleys and Peels often intermarried with county society and employed younger sons of gentry families in their warehouses. Between the 1790s and 1830s Tories ran the town, controlling bodies such as the Police Commissioners and Court Leet. Many belonged to a drinking club founded at John Shaw's Punch House (now Sinclair's Oyster Bar). The Whig faction was dominated by Unitarian families who worshipped at Cross Street and Mosley Street chapels, including the Heywoods, Percivals, Philipses, Hibberts, Potters and Gregs. Nonconformists were not only barred from universities and professions but also excluded by convention from marriage into landed society. They campaigned against the Test and Corporation Acts, which denied them civil rights, finally repealed in 1829.[4]

William Pitt the Younger introduced repressive measures such as the Seditious Meetings Act, restricting the right of individuals to assemble, and suspended *habeas corpus*, which protected citizens from arrest without trial. Radicals led by Thomas Walker, merchant and former boroughreeve, formed the Manchester Constitutional Society in 1790 to campaign for parliamentary reform and created the *Manchester Herald*. Tory loyalists, who had formed the Church and King Club, staged riots in 1792 in which a mob attacked dissenters' chapels, wrecked the *Herald's* offices and for three nights besieged Walker and others in their homes, breaking windows and threatening violence. Magistrates and constables simply stood by. Walker and friends, who had used firearms to defend themselves, were arrested and tried at Lancaster Assizes for conspiracy to overthrow the constitution and aid the French. He was acquitted.[5]

All this subdued any impetus towards reform. Patriotism got the upper hand. The darkening of the French Revolution strengthened patriotic sentiment. Publicans put up signs saying 'No Jacobins admitted here'. When a French invasion seemed to be threatened in 1804, Manchester mustered 5,800 volunteers to resist. Reform societies were made illegal and many reformers were forced underground into republican organisations such as the Society of United Englishmen, which claimed hundreds of members in Manchester before being proscribed in 1798. Despite suppression of political dissent, however, the era of 'church and king' populism was coming to an end, being undermined by food shortages, political alienation and industrial unrest, particularly among weavers. Magistrate Thomas Butterworth noted in 1800: 'The public eye is daily saluted with sedition in chalk characters on our walls. And whether the subject regards Bread or Peace – "NO KING" introduces it.'[6]

Food supply continued to create problems, causing periodic riots. Rioting, however, was less effective in restraining prices than it had been when justices of the peace had a role in setting them. Manchester's last food riot took place in 1812. By then, the focus had shifted towards trade unions' effort to raise wages, which met fierce opposition from employers and government. The anti-union Combination Acts of 1799 and 1800 were directed specifically against Lancashire's textile unions. Even after these were repealed in 1824, unions faced a hostile climate.[7]

The strongest trade unionists in Manchester were mule spinners. Mules were exclusively operated by men; spinners had authority over women and children, who performed tasks such as repairing broken threads and cleaning machinery. Spinners' unions were formed in Manchester and Stockport in 1792. There were strikes in 1795 and at the century's end. For a time the Manchester union had some success, but a rolling strike in 1810 by a federation of Lancashire spinning unions failed. Economic depression after the Napoleonic wars further eroded wages. Spinners suffered wage cuts of up to a third in 1816. The union staged a strike in 1818, bringing out 20,000 workers. There was violence against 'knobsticks' (blacklegs). Soldiers fired on the strikers, killing one spinner and wounding several. Union leaders were imprisoned and activists blacklisted.[8]

Many protests came from self-employed workers such as hand-loom weavers whose livelihoods were threatened by factories. Weavers' piecework rates dropped by more than half between 1805 and 1819 and many had little or no work.[9] The Luddite insurgency began in 1811 among Nottinghamshire hosiery workers, led by a probably mythical Ned Ludd, and spread to Yorkshire and Lancashire. Several protesters were killed in an attack at Middleton, north of Manchester, on the mill of Daniel Burton, an early power loom adopter. The Luddites failed to halt the spread of power looms. While Manchester was not a centre of Luddism, it was such a hotspot for unrest that 2,000 troops became permanently stationed there. A riot broke out in April 1812 when conservatives planned a meeting to congratulate the Prince Regent on retention of a Tory ministry opposed to reform. The meeting was cancelled for fear of disruption, but too late. Thousands gathered outside the Exchange Hall and broke windows and furniture before the army dispersed the crowd.[10]

Peace in 1815 after twenty-three years of almost continuous war brought even greater hardship. Demobilised soldiers returned home to unemployment. The eruption of Mount Tambora in Indonesia in 1815, the largest volcanic explosion known to history, darkened skies and created the worst European food shortages for more than a century in 1816–17. Reformers campaigned for universal male suffrage and annual elections, while the government intensified repression, employing a network of paid spies. Hampden Clubs – radical campaigning and debating societies – became popular in the North, with about forty in the Manchester region, claiming membership of 8,000.[11] *Habeas corpus* was suspended again and acts passed to prevent public meetings and extend the law against sedition.

Parliamentary reform was a key radical demand. Rapidly industrialising towns such as Manchester and Salford had no dedicated MP, but shared MPs with Lancashire. Those entitled to vote were mostly rich landowners, about 15 to 16 per cent of adult males in England and Wales, down from 24 per cent a century before.[12] A petition to parliament for universal male suffrage gathered three-quarters of a million signatures in 1817 but was rejected by the Commons. Reformers also wanted to repeal the corn laws, which excluded imports of grain until the price reached near-famine levels. The government had introduced these in 1815 to protect landowners from loss of government contracts to feed the armed forces, but this raised the price of bread. With bread a luxury, the main working-class subsistence was oatmeal, potatoes and turnips.[13]

In March 1817, thousands gathered on St Peter's Field to support a march to London by 'Blanketeers' (each carrying a blanket to sleep in), aiming to petition the Prince Regent for urgent help for the cotton industry and to protest against parliament's resistance to reform. Among organisers was John Bagguley, a young working-class radical who had called for the royal family to be arrested if reform were not forthcoming. The meeting was broken up and leaders imprisoned. Cavalry trampled some and wounded others with their swords. One bystander was killed. Most marchers were stopped at Stockport. Shortly afterwards, authorities raided a secret meeting at Ardwick Bridge, claiming to have uncovered an 'Ardwick Plot' to make 'a Moscow of Manchester', setting it alight as a signal for revolt, referencing the devastating fire during Napoleon's occupation of Moscow.[14]

Around this time women in Lancashire and some in Yorkshire began organising reform societies, regarded as the earliest organised female activity in British politics. Female societies were established in places such as Stockport, Blackburn, Leigh, Rochdale, Royton, Leeds and Manchester. The first was in Blackburn in June 1819 under the leadership of Alice Kitchen. Female suffrage was not yet on the agenda, but if all adult males could vote, at least families would be represented. Activists attracted opprobrium as 'female Viragoes' in newspapers and via satires and caricatures. Susannah Saxton, secretary of the Manchester Female Reform Society and wife of a printer and bookseller, urged people to 'unite with us as speedily as possible; and to exert influence with your fathers, your husbands, your sons, your relatives and your friends, to join the Male Union for constitutionally demanding a Reform in their own House, viz. The Commons House of Parliament; for we are now thoroughly convinced, that for want of such timely Reform, the useful class of society has been reduced to its present degraded state.'[15]

The famous meeting at St Peter's Field on 16 August 1819 followed mass or 'monster' meetings at Oldham, Stockport, Ashton and Rochdale as well as Manchester. On 8 January, some eight thousand people had met on the field to hear reformers' leader Henry 'Orator' Hunt – a Wiltshire farmer – urge them to approve a declaration to the Prince Regent that 'the only source of all legitimate power is in the People', derived from the Rights of Man philosophy of the French and American Revolutions.[16]

Hunt, invited back for the August event, was addressing mass meetings across the country. His intentions were peaceful, though some saw his speeches as inflammatory. When he heard that preparations involved drilling on the moors with pikes and even firearms, he demanded that those involved 'cease playing at soldiers' and come 'armed with no other weapon but that of a self-approving conscience'.

On the morning of the meeting, bands of men, women and children arrived from surrounding towns behind banners and flags, with few pikes or firearms in evidence. Banners called for 'Universal Suffrage', 'No Corn Laws' and 'Parliaments Annual'; those saying 'Liberty or Death' perhaps appeared more provocative. The crowd probably numbered forty to fifty thousand. Sir John Byng, commander of northern forces, was absent at a horse-racing meeting, leaving relatively inexperienced Lieutenant-Colonel Guy L'Estrange in charge of 1,500 soldiers consisting of the Fifteenth Hussars and the volunteer Manchester and Salford Yeomanry and Cheshire Yeoman Cavalry. The Manchester and Salford Yeomanry, comprised of local manufacturers, merchants, shopkeepers and publicans, had been formed just two years earlier and were poorly trained.[17]

Hunt's party included female reformers dressed in white, notably Mary Fildes, president of the Manchester Female Reform Society, daughter of a Stockport bookkeeper, who was waving a banner. They received some abuse from bystanders, including other women. Hunt, wearing his distinctive white hat, received a roar from the crowd as he stood to speak. Magistrates, interpreting this as a potential insurrection, claimed they read the Riot Act twice, though no independent witnesses confirmed this. The magistrates ordered Hunt and his party to be arrested, but Deputy Constable Joseph Nadin said special constables needed military support. First to arrive were the Manchester and Salford Yeomanry, led by their second-in-command, Tory cotton master Hugh Birley, previously involved in a violent altercation with his workers during a dispute. The magistrates sent the Yeomanry in to accompany Nadin as he made arrests.[18]

The first victim was two-year-old William Fildes – no direct relation to Mary – accidentally run down and mortally injured as the Yeomanry entered the field. They cut a path to the hustings with sabres drawn. Arrests were made, but the Yeomanry began to panic as they became separated from each other and struck out with their swords. They tried to seize flags and banners, 'cutting most indiscriminately to the right and to the left to get at them', according to

John Tyas of *The Times*. Women appeared to have been targeted. One victim, Margaret Downes, was 'dreadfully cut in the breast' and assumed to have died, though there is no firm record. According to witnesses, Mary Fildes was beaten by constables and cut across her upper body by a soldier. She escaped and laid low for a fortnight to avoid arrest. Hunt was led away, shielded behind Nadin.[19]

As the Hussars arrived, L'Estrange shouted up to William Hulton, the magistrates' chairman: 'What am I to do?' Hulton replied: 'Good God, Sir, don't you see how they are attacking the Yeomanry? Disperse the mob.' The field was cleared in ten minutes. Although the Hussars reportedly used just the flat of their swords, the main exit route was blocked and many were trampled and crushed in the panic. Sixty-year-old Margaret Goodwin recognised a member of the Yeomanry riding towards her. She cried out: 'Nay, Tom Skelmerdine, thee wilt not hurt me, I know!', but he rode her down and cut her about the head with his sabre. Mary Heyes, a mother of six who was pregnant with her seventh child, died after being trampled by a horse. One Hussars officer was heard trying to restrain his own men and the Yeomanry, saying: 'Gentlemen! gentlemen! for shame! Forbear! The people cannot get away.' Weaver and writer Samuel Bamford, who was in the crowd, reported: 'Several mounds of human beings still remained where they had fallen, crushed down and smothered. Some were still groaning, others with staring eyes were gasping for breath, and others would never breathe more.'[20]

There was further violence that evening in New Cross before uneasy calm was restored. More than one in three of those injured at St Peter's Field were handloom weavers, along with shoemakers, hatters and tailors; only about one in twenty were factory workers. There were Waterloo veterans on both sides. The name 'Peter-loo' was coined five days after the massacre by James Wroe, editor of the radical *Manchester Observer*, ironically comparing the attacks on unarmed civilians to the brutality of the battle against Napoleon.

Lord Sidmouth, home secretary, conveyed the Regent's thanks to the magistrates and military for their 'prompt, decisive, and efficient measures for the preservation of public peace'. Hunt was jailed for thirty months. Legislation known as the Six Acts was passed to suppress radical meetings and publications. The *Manchester Observer* closed in 1821 after arrests and heavy fines. However, John Edward Taylor, Quaker, cotton merchant and journalist, established the *Manchester Guardian* earlier that year, less radical but committed to liberal reform. While the government congratulated itself on having seen off a threat, Manchester had given a lead that was to culminate in the Reform Act.[21]

In Manchester, power had started to shift from the Tories. The 1832 Act increased the national electorate to about 20 per cent of adult males and enfranchised towns including Manchester (for the first time since 1660), Salford, Bury, Bolton, Rochdale, Oldham, Ashton and Warrington. But it did not widen the social mix: it created uniform voting qualifications based solely on ownership or occupation of property, including householders who paid a yearly rental of ten pounds or more, strengthening the influence of land-owners and wealthy urban elites. Two Whig MPs, Mark Philips and Charles Poulett Thomson, were elected for Manchester, and another, Joseph Brotherton, in Salford. William Cobbett, Independent Radical, came bottom out of five candidates in the Manchester election. Manchester's Whig members were returned in 1835 and again in 1837 when William Ewart Gladstone, standing as a Tory, came bottom.[22]

Whigs won the 1832 election nationally by a landslide and passed further measures including the Municipal Corporations Act 1835, enabling towns such as Manchester and Salford to opt to acquire an elected borough corporation. Manchester was still governed by five separate bodies: the Court Leet; churchwardens and overseers; police and improvement commissioners; surveyors of highways; and justices of the peace. It had different police forces for day and night. A young calico manufacturer, Richard Cobden, led campaigners for change. 'Peterloo could not have happened if your borough had been incorporated,' he said.[23]

Opposition to an elected corporation came from Tories, who feared losing to Whigs, and radicals who felt the 1832 reforms were inadequate and objected to the Poor Law Amendment Act 1834, which cut spending on poor relief and introduced workhouses. There were petitions for and against an elected corporation. The one against had three times as many signatories, but Captain Jebb, the civil servant advising the Privy Council, weeded out dubious signatures and a charter was granted to create the new borough. Tories, claiming the outcome had been manipulated, boycotted the first elections in 1838 (Salford was incorporated in 1844). The two sides backed different appointees as borough coroner, who even started carrying out rival autopsies of the same bodies as a consequence. There were years of legal wrangles before Manchester's charter was finally established in law in 1842. In 1846 Sir Oswald Mosley, lord of the manor, sold his manorial rights to the borough for £200,000, exactly 250 years after his ancestor Nicholas bought them for £3,500.[24]

The new corporation in 1842 adopted a coat of arms showing a shield of red and gold, bearing the image of a ship, supported by an antelope and a lion and crowned by a globe covered in bees. The shield was taken from the medieval lords of Manchester; the ship represented trade and enterprise; the antelope and lion were from the arms of King Henry IV, a Lancastrian. At the foot was the motto, *Concilio Et Labore*, meaning 'by counsel and work', from the biblical book of Ecclesiasticus. The bees symbolised industriousness.

Trade unions had become legal with repeal of the Combination Acts in 1824. John Doherty, an Irishman who had been imprisoned for union activities, was elected secretary of the Manchester Cotton Spinners' Union in 1828. His attempt to create a Grand General Union of Cotton Operatives of the United Kingdom collapsed in 1830 after a call for a general strike failed. His National Association for the Protection of Labour, a would-be union for all trades, lasted only two years. The Manchester Spinners lost members and influence as a result.[25]

Disillusion with the 1832 Act and anger about the Poor Law spurred creation of the Chartist movement, which began in 1837 when the London Men's Working Association issued a six-point charter calling for universal manhood suffrage, secret ballots, annual elections, equal electoral districts, payment for MPs and abolition of the minimum property requirement for MPs. Agitation for the charter in Manchester began with formation of the Manchester Political Union in 1838. The MPU organised a meeting at Kersal Moor in Salford at which at least fifty thousand people heard Joseph Rayner Stephens, a Methodist preacher, describe Chartist demands as a 'knife and fork question', appealing to hard-pressed workers. A petition sent to parliament was rejected.

The following year the National Charter Association, viewed as the world's first prototype working-class political party, was formed at the Griffin Inn, Ancoats. Rejection of a second petition in 1842, along with a depression in factory districts, prompted a meeting on Mottram Moor that resolved that all labour should cease until the charter became law. In the 'plug plot' riots that year, tens of thousands of strikers forcibly closed down factories by removing plugs from steam engines. *The Times* reported that two thousand soldiers and six pieces of artillery were on the streets of Manchester. Two policemen were killed, but there was no repeat of Peterloo.[26]

The Chartists' emphasis switched to London, which they found hard to win over with its size and occupational diversity. They lost momentum in 1848 when leaders organised a rally on Kennington Common, on the wrong side of the Thames, and decided not to defy a police ban on a procession to parliament. Several hundred Chartists were arrested in London and the North, leading the movement to collapse. Ernest Jones, a barrister, poet and friend of Marx and Engels, had become the Chartists' most eloquent spokesman; he was arrested in Manchester and imprisoned for two years for sedition and unlawful assembly. After release he struggled to rebuild the divided movement. He returned to his practice as a barrister and was on course to become a Liberal MP for Manchester when he died suddenly at age fifty in 1868.[27]

In the short term Chartism was a failure, though by 1918 all the charter's points had been achieved except annual general elections. The Anti-Corn Law League, founded by employers championing free trade, by contrast achieved its objective within a decade. Manchester's global influence was to owe as much to the 'cottono-cracy' as to radicals or workers.

5

SHOCK CITY OF
THE 1840S

It is hard to overstate how fascinated the world was with Manchester in the 1840s. It seemed a foretaste of the future. 'All roads led to Manchester … the shock city of the age,' wrote historian Asa Briggs.[1] As the first major industrial urban centre – though not formally designated a city until 1853 – it was radically different to what had come before. All things seemed possible: new ideas, new industrial processes, new social and political movements. Benjamin Disraeli wrote in his 1844 novel *Coningsby*: 'Manchester is as great a human exploit as Athens … It is the philosopher alone who can conceive the grandeur of Manchester and the immensity of its future.'[2]

Its population had increased sixfold in as many decades, creating both unprecedented opportunities and dire social conditions. Ultimately, the Industrial Revolution would allow living standards to rise, though in the short term it also created filthy slum terraces and cellars, ill health and pollution. French writer Alexis de Tocqueville, who visited in 1835, called it 'this new Hades' and added: 'From this foul drain the greatest stream of human industry flows out to fertilise the whole world. From this filthy sewer pure gold flows. Here humanity attains its most complete development and its most brutish, here civilisation works its miracles and civilised man is turned back almost into a savage.'[3]

Manchester was at the centre of the world's largest cotton industry, yet also continued to diversify as a commercial, financial and engineering centre. While activity was growing strongly in surrounding towns, cotton employed only 18 per cent of Manchester's labour force by 1841, compared with 50 per cent in Ashton-under-Lyne and 40 per cent in Oldham. Oldham, a cotton-spinning centre, saw perhaps the most dramatic transformation of any place in northern England. Its population rose from 12,000 in 1801 to 137,000 in 1901. At its peak in 1918, Oldham had 320 mills. A big factor behind Oldham's growth was the presence of Platt Brothers, the world's largest textile machinery manufacturer. Stockport, another textiles town – woollen and linen cloth from the Middle Ages, then cotton – was also a centre of hat-making from the seventeenth century and later the silk industry, along with Macclesfield. Stockport's last hat-making factory, Christy's, closed in 1997.[4]

The nineteenth century saw a growing separation of classes. While workers remained close to their workplaces, the growth of public transport from the 1820s enabled a rising middle class to move to new suburbs. Industrialisation saw the emergence of 'Manchester Man', a new order of merchants and manufacturers who symbolised the changing society and economy. Stereotypically, these were portrayed as vulgar, self-made philistines, epitomised by Josiah Bounderby of Coketown in Charles Dickens's *Hard Times* (1854): 'He was a rich man: banker, merchant, manufacturer, and what not. A big loud man, with a stare, and a metallic laugh … A man who could never sufficiently vaunt himself a self-made man. A man who was always proclaiming … his old ignorance and his old poverty. A man who was the Bully of humility.'[5]

It was a caricature. In reality, there were few rags-to-riches stories: most early factory masters began with some capital of their own or borrowed from relatives. The humblest came from lower-middle-class occupations such as shopkeepers, skilled craftsmen and yeomen farmers. While undoubtedly there were brutal and exploitative employers, several were at pains to show themselves public-spirited.

They founded voluntary societies, libraries and museums, institutes and clubs. Manchester Literary and Philosophical Society, one of the oldest surviving learned societies devoted to science, first met in 1781. The Royal Manchester Institution was founded in 1823 to promote fine arts, housed in what is now the Manchester Art Gallery building on Mosley Street, a neoclassical edifice designed by Charles Barry, who later rebuilt the Houses of Parliament. Manchester Statistical Society, the first in the country and a pioneer of social science, was founded in 1833. The Athenaeum Club on Princess Street, completed in 1839, aimed to provide 'rational recreations' for sons of the middle classes. It was also designed by Barry.[6]

No doubt self-interest lay behind many initiatives. Some business people were motivated by religious zeal, others by desire for social recognition. At the same time, many Manchester inhabitants lacked basic amenities for civilised life. Richard Parkinson, canon of the Collegiate Church, wrote: 'There is no town in the world where the distance between the rich and poor is so great, or the barrier between them so difficult to be crossed ... There is far less personal communication between the master cotton spinner and his workmen, between the calico printer and his blue-handed boys, between the master tailor and his apprentices, than there is between the Duke of Wellington and the humblest labourer on his estate.'[7] The cottonocracy's most visible national impact was the success of the Anti-Corn Law League. A principal spokesman was Richard Cobden (1804–65), who had already been the driving force behind the campaign for local government reform. One of eleven children of a Sussex yeoman farmer, he was a commercial traveller who became co-owner of a calico printing factory in Sabden, Lancashire. He settled in Manchester only in 1832, but fitted into the town's line of middle-class liberals, favouring free trade and opposing the interests of the landed aristocracy. Politics appeared to suit his enquiring mind better than business. Corn laws, introduced in 1815 to maintain farm prices by imposing a duty on corn imports, symbolised the landowning class's dominance. Manufacturers objected that high food prices forced up wages, reduced profits and undermined the nation's wealth. Cobden argued that free trade between nations would generate international understanding and peace.

The Manchester Anti-Corn Law Association was formed in 1838. The next year, delegates in London changed its name to the Anti-Corn Law League, though its headquarters remained at Newall's Buildings, Manchester. 'The League is Manchester,' Cobden wrote. The first Free Trade Hall to house League gatherings, a timber pavilion, was built in 1840 on the site of the Peterloo Massacre, on land owned by Cobden. It was replaced two years later by a brick structure and finally, in 1856, by a magnificent stone edifice. The hall was destroyed by German bombs in 1940, restored and reopened in 1951 and later converted into a hotel after Bridgewater Hall opened in the 1990s.[8]

Cobden became MP for Stockport in 1841. Fellow spokesman John Bright, a Quaker from a Rochdale mill-owning family and a talented orator, became MP for Durham in 1843, switching to Manchester in 1847. The campaign, modelled on the anti-slavery movement, became an effective pressure group through pamphleteering, petitioning and public meetings. Accurate leafleting was made possible by the penny post introduced in 1840. Although the League's cause appeared aligned in its key aim with working-class radicals, who had demanded abolition of the corn laws at the time of Peterloo, there was tension with Chartists, who suspected that employers wanted abolition in order to cut wages. Radicals also felt betrayed by the Reform Act 1832: they had fought for male enfranchisement alongside liberals, but only the middle class got the vote. Cobden and Bright opposed factory reforms, seeing regulation as interference with the free market.

It took a national crisis for the League to achieve its aim. Food shortages resulting from the Great Famine in Ireland prompted Sir Robert Peel, the Bury-born Conservative prime minister, to repeal the corn laws in 1846 with Whig and Radical support, splitting his own party. Peel, son of a wealthy textile manufacturer and MP, was

Britain's first prime minister from an industrial background. As prime minister, he cut tariffs to stimulate trade, replacing the lost revenue with a 3 per cent income tax. Major legislation included laws to regulate coalmines, factories and railways. Historian A.J.P. Taylor wrote: 'Peel was in the first rank of nineteenth-century statesmen. He carried Catholic emancipation; he repealed the corn laws; he created the modern Conservative Party on the ruins of the old Toryism.'[9]

Free trade became Britain's orthodoxy until the 1930s and still has a strong influence today. Benjamin Disraeli coined the term 'Manchester School' to describe Cobden and Bright's free-market economics, based on the assumption that free exchange of goods and labour would ultimately benefit everyone. German critics called it *das Manchestertum* ('Manchesterism') to symbolise selfish economic behaviour.

Manchester, however, was half-hearted about the Manchester School. Many businessmen supported free trade for self-interested reasons, but had little interest in the wider philosophy. Bright's effigy was burned in Manchester for his unpopular stance against the Crimean war and he was defeated at the 1857 general election. A few months later he became MP for Birmingham, a position he held for more than thirty years. Cobden switched seats from Stockport to the West Riding of Yorkshire and moved his family to London. He too was defeated in 1857 after opposing the Crimean war and Second Opium War with China, though two years later he returned as MP for Rochdale.[10]

The League's campaign had coincided with economic depression in the early 1840s, caused by a slump in trade and a bad harvest, which deepened the misery of Manchester's poor. Elizabeth Gaskell wrote of the suffering she saw in her first novel, *Mary Barton*. Gaskell visited the home of a local labourer; after she comforted the family, the head of the household 'took hold of her arm and grasping it tightly, said, with tears in his eyes: "Aye, ma'am, but have ye ever seen a child clemmed [starved] to death?"'[11] This question is repeated in the mouth of John Barton, Mary's father, in Chapter Six: 'Han they ever have seen a child o' their'n die for want o' food?'

Living conditions in parts of Manchester were appalling. A special Board of Health was created in 1831 in anticipation of a cholera epidemic that hit Manchester and other towns the following year. The board had limited powers and resources, but the choice of Rochdale-born Dr James Phillips Kay, twenty-seven-year-old medical officer at Ardwick and Ancoats Dispensary, as secretary proved inspired. Kay, a member of Cross Street Chapel, had studied infectious diseases at Edinburgh University. He commissioned a survey of social conditions that resulted in a pamphlet called *The Moral and Physical Condition of the Working Classes of Manchester*.[12] It observed: 'Near the centre of the town, a mass of buildings, inhabited by prostitutes and thieves, is intersected by narrow and loathsome streets, and close courts, defiled with refuse … In Parliament Street, there is only one privy for 380 inhabitants, which is placed in a narrow passage, whence its effluvia infest the adjacent houses, and must prove a fertile source of disease.'

The pamphlet described the Little Ireland area, around where Oxford Road Station now stands: 'The privies are in a most disgraceful state, inaccessible from filth, and too few for the accommodation of the number of people – the average number being two to two hundred and fifty people. The upper rooms are, with a few exceptions, very dirty and the cellars much worse; all damp and some occasionally overflowed.'[13]

Some fifteen thousand people lived in low-lying cellars. The Board of Health tried to protect people from cholera by draining some streets, clearing rubbish, whitewashing the worst houses and setting up patrols to look for suspected carriers entering the town, but the epidemic killed 674. At one point rumours spread that patients in cholera hospitals were being murdered by doctors; a mob stormed a hospital in Swan Street and carried patients back to their homes. Kay personally visited at least two hundred victims. Case notes recorded the fate of one mother who died shortly after her child:

Elizabeth Cavanagh, aged 36 – Residence, 5, Wakefield-street, Little Ireland, ground floor. Employment, mother of preceding. Constitution, healthy looking hearty woman. Natural susceptibility, had often had severe diarrhoea, esp. when suckling her children. Predisposing cause, half starved; got nothing but potatoes and tea when she had her meals at home, was brutally treated by the man with whom she co-habited. Exciting cause, fatigue from attending and grief for the loss of her child No. 3. Locality crowding filth, etc … Cavanagh's house … fronted an open area but an impure stream whose channel does the function of a sewer, passes by the door to an adjoining field where it collects and stagnates; house and inhabitants very filthy; three children and two adults sleeping in a straw bed … Communication or non-communication; as she was getting out of bed on Monday night to reach the basin for her child No. 3, he vomited upon her and part of the vomit entered her mouth. Soon after her seizure she mentioned the circumstance to her neighbour Mrs Featherstone, adding she was taken exactly as her child had been.[14]

Kay's report inspired another Manchester resident, Longsight-born Edwin Chadwick (1800–90), who became active in public health nationally and published a *Report on the Sanitary Condition of the Labouring Population of Great Britain* (1842). This made famous the fact (originally reported by Manchester Statistical Society) that the average age at death of 'professional persons and gentry, and their families' was no better in Manchester at thirty-eight years than the life expectancy of 'mechanics and labourers' in rural Rutland.[15] Chadwick's report led to the Public Health Act 1848, the first step on a long road to improving public health. John Fielden, mill owner and radical MP for Oldham, piloted through the Commons an act limiting daily working hours for women and children in textile mills to ten in 1847.

Horror of industrial cities caused a moral panic among intellectuals. Thomas Carlyle, who coined the expression the 'Condition of England' in 1839, thought that the 'working body of this rich

English Nation has sunk or is fast sinking into a state, to which, all sides of it considered, there was literally never any parallel'.[16] The backlash prompted a yearning for the supposed simplicity of medieval times, an infeasibly idyllic 'merrie England', and spawned a revival of medieval Gothic architecture. Not everyone was impressed. The *Manchester Guardian* highlighted the 'grinding merciless oppression' of the Middle Ages and urged enthusiasts for the barbaric past to feel profoundly thankful their lot 'had been cast in the nineteenth century, rather than in the twelfth'.[17]

Manchester's most notable foreign visitor was Friedrich Engels (1820–95), son of a textile factory owner from near Elberfeld, a town known as 'the Manchester of Germany'.[18] His father sent him in 1842 to work at the family cotton firm of Ermen & Engels in Weaste, Salford, in the vain hope that this would rid him of radical views. On the way, he met Karl Marx, many of whose views he shared. Engels arrived in Manchester just after the North's Plug Plot riots, which sparked fears of insurrection. He stayed for twenty-one months, gathering material for *The Condition of the Working Class in England*, published in German in 1845. By night he toured Manchester's slum districts, including Angel Meadow, which he called 'hell on earth'. He wrote: 'We must admit that 350,000 working-people of Manchester and its environs live, almost all of them, in wretched, damp, filthy cottages, that the streets which surround them are usually in the most miserable and filthy condition, laid out without the slightest reference to ventilation, with reference solely to the profit secured by the contractor.'[19]

Engels was to stay in Manchester on and off for almost thirty years. His book had no immediate impact in Britain because an English translation was not published there until 1892. His strongest influence was on Marx, providing factual underpinning to *Das Kapital*. Engels predicted in 1845 that social conditions seen in Manchester would lead to 'a revolution in comparison with which the French Revolution ... will prove to have been child's play'.[20] It was an unsurprising forecast in view of uprisings elsewhere in Europe

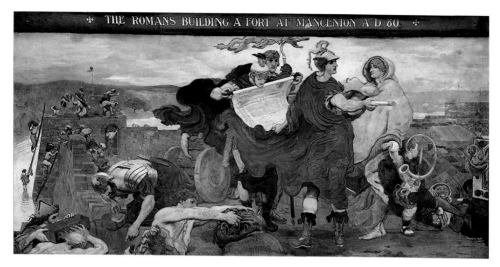

1. *The Romans building a fort at Mancenion AD 80*, by Ford Madox Brown.
Artepics / Alamy Stock Photo

2. Reconstruction of the north gate of the Roman fort, Castlefield.
Martin Beddall / Alamy Stock Photo

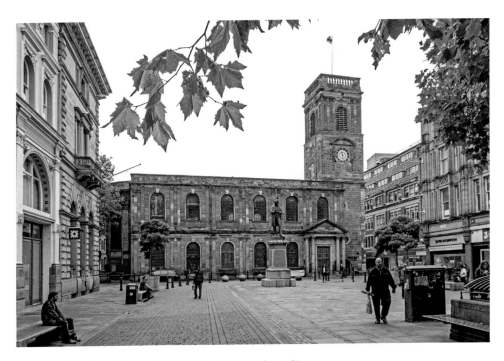

3. St Ann's Church and Square. Kevin Britland / Alamy Stock Photo

ELIZABETH RAFFALD.

4. Elizabeth Raffald from the 1782 edition of her book *The Experienced English Housekeeper*. Wikimedia Commons

5. Bridgewater Canal, Castlefield Basin. David Dixon / Wikimedia Commons CC BY-SA 2.0

6. John Dalton, 1766-1844, pioneer of modern atomic theory. Frontispiece of *John Dalton and the Rise of Modern Chemistry* by Henry Roscoe. Wikimedia Commons

7. Peterloo Massacre 1819, engraving by Richard Carlile.
GL Archive / Alamy Stock Photo

8. McConnel & Company mills, Ancoats, about 1820. Wikimedia Commons

9. Elizabeth Gaskell. The History Collection / Alamy Stock Photo

10. Soviet statue of Friedrich Engels, First Street, Manchester. Mark Waugh / Alamy Stock Photo

11. *Manchester Exhibition of Art Treasures*, wood engraving by W.E. Hodgkin, 1856 (Wellcome Library, London). Wikimedia Commons

12. *Manchester and Salford Children*, 1861, by Thomas Armstrong (Manchester Art Gallery). Artepics / Alamy Stock Photo

PROVISION-SHOP WHERE GOODS ARE OBTAINED FOR TICKETS ISSUED BY THE MANCHESTER AND SALFORD PROVIDENT SOCIETY.

13. Provision shop during the cotton famine, Manchester and Salford Provident Society, 1862.
The Granger Collection / Alamy Stock Photo

14. Manchester Town Hall. Michael D
Beckwith / Wikimedia Commons CC0

15. Lydia Becker, the suffragist movement's
leading strategist. Wikimedia Commons

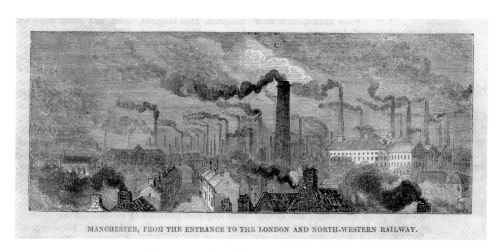

16. A view of the factories of Manchester, circa 1870. Chronicle / Alamy Stock Photo

in 1830 and 1848, but Engels underestimated the potential for reform. Despite his revolutionary convictions, Engels drank wine and smoked cigars with other German business émigrés and even joined them in foxhunting in Cheshire. He grudgingly accepted in 1885 that a revolution had not happened because the working class shared in the benefits of 'England's industrial monopoly', but continued to predict that when the monopoly broke down, 'there will be socialism again in England'.[21]

The liberals who took control of Manchester's first borough council in 1838 were to dominate much of the century. Their reformist intentions were good. Key figures including the mayor, Thomas Potter, and town clerk, Joseph Heron, had served on the special Board of Health in 1831–2. Social problems were deep, however, and progress was mixed. On the plus side, in 1844 the council required all houses to have a privy with doors and coverings and an ashpit, which in effect outlawed new back-to-back housing more than eighty years ahead of national legislation. Prior to that, developers had saved on land costs by building back-to-backs, which meant privies were located in the street, where they were overused and overflowed. In the first six years, more than a third of homes were brought up to a standard of at least one privy per three dwellings.[22]

Cellar dwellings, however, were not effectively tackled until a medical officer of health was appointed in 1868. It took until 1874 to appoint factory chimney inspectors to tackle air pollution. Commercial development destroyed many notorious slums, but private-sector house-building did not keep pace, so people moved to new slums in even more overcrowded conditions. It took Manchester sixty years to sort out sanitation problems. The council defended the privy midden system and resisted water closets, fearing these would use too much water and that effluent would flow into watercourses. Proper sewerage was not in place until the 1890s and a sewage treatment works not until 1904. Water supply was a constant problem. Supplies were obtained from Derbyshire's Longdendale Valley from 1851 and from Thirlmere in the Lake District in 1894.[23]

Health improved slowly. Real wages for the majority rose in the second half of the century, bringing a general improvement in living standards. Leisure time for textile workers increased after 1850, when new legislation closed mills from 2pm on Saturdays; in Manchester, this soon spread to other occupations. Three public parks opened in 1846: Queen's Park in Harpurhey, Philips Park in Bradford (east Manchester) and Peel Park in Salford (supported by £1,000 from Sir Robert Peel and subsequently sold to Salford Corporation). Salford opened England's first free public lending library, the Royal Museum and Library in Peel Park, in 1850 under the Museums of Art Act 1845. In 1852 Manchester followed in becoming the first large town to open a public library under the Free Libraries Act 1850, which allowed authorities to impose a local tax of one penny to pay for the service. Initially this was at the Hall of Science building at Campfield near the city centre. It was a star-studded opening attended by authors Charles Dickens, Sir Edward Bulwer-Lytton and William Thackeray, along with the Earl of Shaftesbury and John Bright (who had opposed the bill through which the library was established). Thackeray, tired after a speaking tour and feeling financial pressure, got stage fright three minutes into his remarks and simply sat down.[24]

Education began to spread with Sunday schools from 1784. In the early 1800s, the town had some charitable schools run on the Bluecoat and Lancasterian models, the former Anglican in emphasis, the latter favoured by dissenters. Manchester Mechanics' Institute, aimed at educating workers, founded in 1824, was one of England's first. A survey in 1834 by Manchester Statistical Society revealed, however, that only 28 per cent of school-age children attended a day school; even when Sunday schools were added, only 56 per cent received any education. There were many 'dame schools', generally 'in very dirty, unwholesome rooms', where teachers were usually women or old men 'whose only qualification for this employment seems to be their unfitness for every other'. Compulsory education had to wait until the 1870 Education Act.[25]

Higher education free from sectarianism began when John Owens, a cotton merchant, died in 1845 leaving £100,000 in his will to establish a college. Owens College began in Richard Cobden's old house in Quay Street in 1851, with three full-time professors and five part-time staff. Attendance was restricted to males. Its first principal was A.J. Scott, an influential figure in the Christian Socialist movement. Its early years were difficult, but in 1873 it moved to a new building on Oxford Road, in Chorlton-on-Medlock, designed by Alfred Waterhouse. When it sought university status and the right to confer degrees, it faced opposition arising from snobbery and vested interests. The *Saturday Review* said that 'anyone educated in Manchester would certainly be dull and probably vicious'. In 1884 the government compromised by creating a Victoria University with limited degree-awarding powers, comprising Owens and the universities of Leeds and Liverpool. Manchester Victoria University began to admit women in 1883. It finally became a university in its own right in 1903.[26]

Queen Victoria's visit in 1851, the year when the adjective 'Victorian' was first coined, symbolised mid-century Manchester's ability to excite emotions. Though the queen noted 'a painfully unhealthy-looking population', she said streets were 'immensely full and the cheering and enthusiasm most gratifying'.[27] The Exchange became the Royal Exchange. Writer Samuel Sidney reckoned Manchester was 'the second city in the empire, and perhaps, considered in relation to the commercial influence of Great Britain, scarcely second'.[28] Sayings such as 'What Manchester thinks today, England will think tomorrow' (or its variant 'What Lancashire thinks today ...') would soon be common.

Not everyone agreed. To Carlyle, Manchester was 'quite puffed up, and fancies *it* can rule the world, ever since that Anti-Corn Law achievement. One of the most palpable mistakes on the part of Manchester; which is, and will for a long time remain, a very dark, greasy-minded, and quite *limited* place, in spite of its skill in calicoes!'[29]

After achieving city status in 1853, Manchester's quest for recognition and respectability reached its height in the 1857 Art Treasures Exhibition, one of the most ambitious collections of art works ever assembled. The driving force was cotton manufacturer J.C. Deane. Under one glass roof at Old Trafford were 1,800 paintings, including ones by Michelangelo, Raphael, Van Dyke, Turner, Constable, Holbein, Titian and Giotto, along with 16,000 objects such as glass, porcelain and fine furniture. A site in the city's south-west was chosen because prevailing winds blew the smoke to the north-east; it was one of the few places where flowers would grow. More than 1.3 million visitors attended.

The *Illustrated London News* said Manchester now 'hurls back on her detractors the charge that she is too deeply absorbed in the pursuit of material wealth to devote her energies to the finer arts'. Music was provided by Charles Hallé (born Carl Halle), a German who had fled the 1848 Paris revolution. He created a new orchestra and gave daily concerts. After the exhibition, weekly concerts were inaugurated in 1858 and the orchestra that took Hallé's name became one of the finest in Europe.[30]

Manchester's spell as the world's 'shock city' was coming to an end, however. There were further achievements but, as the city became established, it became taken for granted. Many Manchester capitalists, having achieved free trade and a wider electoral franchise, were content to leave governing to the country's imperial elite. The spotlight on municipal reform shifted to Birmingham in the 1870s where Joseph Chamberlain, as mayor, achieved rapid strides in gas and water supply, slum clearance, and facilities such as libraries, swimming pools and schools. As Briggs put it: 'Manchester's story lacked the excitement and public appeal of the story of Chamberlain's Birmingham.'[31]

6

MIGRANT TALES

Two millennia after soldiers arrived from parts of the Roman Empire, Manchester is a multi-ethnic, polyglot city. The Industrial Revolution and its aftermath drew migrants from elsewhere in the British Isles, the rest of Europe and other parts of the world, including Asia. Manchester likes to think itself open-minded, liberal and tolerant; many from migrant groups have gone on to play prominent roles. Yet at times there has been prejudice and hostility. The city played an equivocal part too in the slave trade: it was a leading centre of the campaign for abolition, but merchants and manufacturers made fortunes directly or indirectly from slavery. Fine buildings were erected using proceeds of slave-grown cotton.

In the early nineteenth century, internal migrants arrived from Scotland, Wales, other parts of England and especially Ireland to work in Manchester's rapidly expanding industries, led by cotton. The city's global trade drew in merchants, agents and their families, notably Germans, most of whom were Jewish. There were also French, Russians, Italians, Greeks, Dutch, Spaniards, Armenians, Danes, Swiss, Turks, Portuguese, Swedes, Syrians, Lebanese and Moroccans. The Germans' cultural contribution included bankrolling the Hallé Orchestra in its early years.

Later in the century there was a wave of working-class immigration from overseas, notably Jewish east Europeans escaping discrimination and pogroms, and Italians escaping rural poverty. After the Second World War, Poles and Ukrainians arrived, fleeing the Soviets. From the 1950s, large numbers came from ex-colonies of the British Empire, notably Afro-Caribbeans, Pakistanis and, later, Bangladeshis. Minorities such as the Chinese expanded. Recent decades have brought a wide range of migrants, including Afghans, Nigerians and Somalians. A new wave from central and eastern Europe arrived after the European Union expanded in 2004.

Today, out of the city of Manchester's roughly 550,000 population, 32 per cent were born outside the UK, according to the 2021 census. A majority of residents identify ethnically as white (57 per cent), 21 per cent as Asian and 12 per cent as black. After English, the most common language spoken is Urdu, followed by Arabic, Polish, Punjabi, Spanish, Bengali, Portuguese, Italian, Romanian and Persian or Farsi. Christians account for about 37 per cent of residents, those of no religion 33 per cent and Muslims 23 per cent. (The ethnic composition of Greater Manchester is slightly different, with a higher proportion identifying as white.)[1]

Occasionally, political or religious violence from conflicts originating elsewhere has erupted on Manchester's streets, including the Provisional IRA's 1996 bombing, in which more than two hundred were injured though mercifully no one died. In May 2017, twenty-three people were killed, including the attacker, and 1,017 injured when an Islamist suicide bomber of Libyan descent, Salman Ramadan Abedi, detonated a home-made bomb as people were leaving a concert at the Manchester Arena.

The Irish were a large migrant group and many experienced dire poverty. Numbers rose sharply during the Great Famine of 1845–52. By 1851 the Irish-born accounted for 13 per cent of Manchester and Salford's population compared with 22 per cent in Liverpool, 18 per cent in Glasgow and almost 5 per cent in London.[2] Little Ireland on the town's south-west fringe, viewed as notoriously squalid, was a small area with a brief life; the city's main Irish neigh-bourhoods were Angel Meadow and Ancoats, just north of the centre. Men often found work as day labourers in the building trade and women as domestic servants.

There was an anti-Irish backlash, fuelled by insecurity in a coun-try unnerved by urbanisation and unrest. The Irish were portrayed as stupid, drunk, violent and happy to live in squalor. James Kay said in his 1832 essay on social conditions: 'The Irish have taught the labouring classes of this country a pernicious lesson ... Debased alike by ignorance and pauperism, they have discovered, with the savage, what is the minimum of the means of life, upon which exist-ence may be prolonged ... and this secret has been taught the labourers of this country by the Irish.'[3]

Not everyone shared that view. A registrar in Angel Meadow blamed poverty and overcrowding, not habits of the Irish, for deaths from disease.[4] Even Engels, however, claimed the Irish had lowered working-class morals, living standards and wages, asserting in *The Condition of the Working Class in England* that they were at home with filth and drunkenness, lacked furniture and shared their domes-tic space with pigs. That view was despite Engels having set up home with his lover Mary Burns, a second-generation Irish mill worker, and her sister Lizzie. Engels later modified his opinion after visiting Ireland with them.[5]

Manchester experienced Britain's first riot between Irish Catholics and Irish Protestants in July 1807.[6] There were anti-Irish distur-bances in England, including a riot in Stockport in 1852 in which two Catholic churches were wrecked.[7] In 1867, the Irish Republican Brotherhood (known as Fenians, from *Fianna*, mythological warri-ors) boldly attacked a police van in Manchester and rescued two prominent prisoners, IRB chief executive Thomas J. Kelly and his aide Timothy Deasy. Shots were fired and a police officer, Sergeant Charles Brett, was killed. The prisoners escaped: Kelly hid in a water cistern and swapped clothes with a priest. Eventually they reached New York. After a trial in Manchester, three men involved – William

Allen, Michael Larkin and Michael O'Brien – were hanged. They shouted 'God save Ireland' in the dock and were commemorated by Irish nationalists for decades as the 'Manchester Martyrs'.[8]

A constitutional home rule movement emerged in the 1870s and Manchester's Irish community developed a working relationship enabling councillors to be elected on the Liberal ticket. Daniel McCabe, a second-generation Irish, devout Catholic and keen supporter of home rule, was the first Catholic to become lord mayor, serving two terms from 1913 to 15, and was knighted by both King George V and the Vatican.[9] Revolutionary Irish nationalism revived in the twentieth century. Éamon de Valera, president of Sinn Féin, which won three-quarters of Irish seats in the 1918 election, was sprung from Lincoln Jail and hid in Manchester before returning to Ireland. The Irish Republican Army, the army of the newly declared Irish Republic, as part of its guerrilla war in 1919–21 tried largely without success to set fire to hotels, cafés and business premises in Manchester. There was a gun battle in Hulme in which three police were injured and one IRA suspect killed. In 1939, three bombs placed by IRA militants exploded in the city centre, one of which killed a fish porter.[10]

After Northern Ireland's Troubles re-emerged in 1968, many Irish Mancunians cautiously distanced themselves. Two bombs exploded in the city centre in December 1992, injuring sixty-four. The IRA detonated two bombs in Warrington town centre in 1993, killing two children. In an attack on 15 June 1996, it detonated in Manchester the biggest bomb in Britain since the Second World War. Four coded warnings saved lives; deaths would have been especially sensitive in a society with a rich Irish heritage. The IRA said it 'sincerely regretted' causing injury to civilians. A scheme to rebuild the city centre proved successful, linking St Ann's Square and the cathedral through pedestrian spaces.[11]

Manchester's Irish have for the most part integrated while maintaining a distinctive culture. Rose Hyndland in 1899 was the first woman elected to the Manchester Board of Poor Law Guardians.[12]

Not all fully embraced their background: writer and composer Anthony Burgess, whose paternal grandmother was from Tipperary, was a lapsed Catholic who distanced himself from nationalism. Mancunians with Irish roots have been influential in the music industry, including all four members of The Smiths, and Liam and Noel Gallagher of Oasis. Comedians include Caroline Aherne (London-born but raised in Wythenshawe), Steve Coogan, Les Dawson and Peter Kay, while actors include Rochdale-born Anna Friel. Manchester United, with a tradition of Irish players, was almost named Manchester Celtic in 1902.

A Welsh community has existed since the sixteenth century. In 1906 there were seventeen Welsh chapels in the Manchester and Salford region, though by 2015 there was just one in Manchester and another in Altrincham. Notable residents of Welsh heritage included cotton merchant Absalom Watkin; Edward Edwards, appointed public librarian in 1851, the first such post in the UK; John Owens, founder of Owens College; industrialist Robert Owen; and poet and socialist Robert Jones Derfel. David Lloyd George, Liberal prime minister, was born in Chorlton-on-Medlock.[13]

Scottish migrants were often professionals such as engineers and surgeons or skilled craftsmen, particularly from south-west Scotland, attributed to the high level of technical education in Scottish colleges and universities. Cotton spinners Adam and George Murray, James McConnel and John Kennedy came from Kirkcudbrightshire. James 'Paraffin' Young, a chemist from Glasgow, became known for his method of distilling paraffin from coal and oil shales, developed while working in Manchester.[14]

Other Europeans came to do business or in a few cases to acquire industrial expertise. One Frenchman, F.C.L. Albert, served four years in prison at Lancaster Castle for industrial spying and attempting to induce Manchester operatives to emigrate to France.[15] German merchant Charles Frederick Brandt was a juror and member of Manchester Literary and Philosophical Society before becoming boroughreeve in 1799. When he died in 1814, obituary notices said he was 'as loyal and excellent a subject as his Majesty could boast of'.[16] Nathan Mayer Rothschild, who arrived from Frankfurt with £20,000 capital in 1799, bought a large warehouse to store goods to export to north Germany's trade fairs. He had trebled his capital by the time he left for London in 1810 to found a banking dynasty.[17]

Germans participated enthusiastically in local society while maintaining their own organisations such as the Albert and Schiller clubs. Philip Goldschmidt, a non-practising Jew from Oldenburg, became the first foreign-born mayor in 1883 and won a second term in 1885–6. The Germans' most enduring contribution was the Hallé Orchestra. Charles Hallé (born Carl Halle) came to Manchester in 1853 to direct the Gentleman's Concerts. He created a small orchestra to give daily performances during Manchester's Art Treasures exhibition in 1857, after which he began his own weekly concerts. He also helped found the Royal Manchester College of Music. After his death, Hans Richter became the Hallé's musical director.[18]

The German Empire became more militaristic after 1870, making liberal German Mancunians uneasy. Public opinion turned against Germans when the First World War broke out. There were riots across the country, including in Manchester, after the *Lusitania* was sunk in 1915; homes and businesses were attacked. Local institutions banned or sacked Germans and eventually German males aged seventeen to fifty-five were interned, many on the Isle of Man, and females repatriated. Manchester's German community was destroyed.[19]

Among early signs of a Jewish community establishing itself, fourteen families founded a synagogue in a rented room in Long Millgate in 1786. By 1851 there were about one and a half thousand Jews in Liverpool and one thousand one hundred in Manchester, with smaller communities in Sheffield, Leeds and Hull. Manchester was to become the largest community outside London.[20] Cotton manufacturer Salis Schwabe, who converted to Unitarianism, and his wife Julie campaigned with Richard Cobden for free trade and brought

Frédéric Chopin to play in Manchester. Their philanthropic projects included an asylum offering humane treatment for the mentally ill.[21]

Later came poorer Jews from eastern Europe, notably Russian Poland, driven by persecution and economic discrimination. They clustered in Red Bank, between Cheetham Hill Road and the River Irk, and worked long hours in clothing and footwear workshops. A campaign against the 'alien flood' led to the Aliens Act 1905, Britain's first immigration controls, which aimed to deny entry to paupers and criminals.[22] The First World War, however, boosted the cause of Zionists, who wanted a Jewish homeland in Israel. Chaim Weizmann, later Israel's first president, lectured in chemistry at the University of Manchester from 1905 to 1918. He also invented a process to produce acetone in large quantities, which helped the war effort by removing a bottleneck in producing explosives. Weizmann and allies argued that a British-sponsored Jewish homeland would protect the Suez Canal, the lifeline to India. Their reward was the 1917 Balfour Declaration.[23]

After 1918, Jewish immigrants started to move up the economic ladder, though the process had begun before the war. Michael Marks, for example, had progressed from pedlar to market trader in Leeds and then, in Manchester, to shopkeeper and eventually co-founder of Marks and Spencer. Antisemitism grew in the 1930s, however. The British Union of Fascists led by Oswald Mosley – descendant of the former lords of the manor – held meetings in the city, sometimes in the heart of Jewish neighbourhoods. Communist Benny Rothman was prominent in opposing the BUF and also played a leading role in the mass trespass on Kinder Scout in 1932. Later in the decade, about eight thousand German, Austrian and Czech refugees from Nazism made their way to Manchester. The Second World War brought a clamour to intern enemy aliens, with many refugees held in detention camps, the largest of which was in the Isle of Man. The government started deporting them to Australia and Canada, fearing implausibly that they might aid a German invasion. After a German submarine sank the Canada-bound *Arandora Star* with many deaths, public opinion turned against deportation and mass internment.[24]

After the war Jewish Mancunians were prominent in national Labour politics. Leslie Lever and his younger brother Harold became Manchester MPs in 1945. Harold served in Harold Wilson's governments. Both became life peers and Leslie was the first Manchester Jew to enter the Lords. He was succeeded in his Ardwick seat by Gerald Kaufman. Robert Sheldon, Paul Rose and Joel Barnett also became MPs; Barnett and Sheldon became Treasury ministers. In the arts, Maisie Mosco (1924–2011), born as Maisie Gottlieb in Oldham, published sixteen novels and wrote multiple stage and radio plays. She was also the editor of the *Jewish Gazette*, making her a chronicler of the Manchester Jewish community. Theatre director Sir Nicholas Hytner (born in Didsbury, 1956), a barrister's son, became artistic director of London's National Theatre.

In recent decades the Jewish community's move to the suburbs has accelerated. The 2011 census found that Greater Manchester's Jewish population had risen by more than 15 per cent since 2001 to 25,000; the largest number was in the Bury district with 10,300, followed by Salford with 7,700 and Manchester with 2,600. The ultra-Orthodox Haredi grew strongly and in 2014 created an Eruv in north Manchester, with a symbolic thirteen-mile boundary within which the faithful could move and carry out certain tasks on the Sabbath.[25]

From Italy, craftsmen, pedlars, street musicians and cotton merchants were arriving from the late eighteenth century, but the biggest influx was between 1881 and 1901, largely consisting of peasant farmers or landless labourers from the southern province of Campania. They clustered in streets in Ancoats known locally as 'Little Italy' and became best known for families making and selling ice cream. Among Italian Mancunians was Jerome Caminada, a policeman sometimes known as Manchester's Sherlock Holmes, whose methods included dressing in disguise to gather evidence; his mother was Irish and his father Italian. The Second World War was a disaster for the Italian community, with all men aged seventeen to sixty interned on the Isle of Man, children evacuated to Lytham St Annes and a curfew imposed on Little Italy. Many died when the *Arandora Star* was torpedoed. After the war the community fragmented as people married out and moved to the suburbs, but there has been a revival of awareness. A plaque recognising Little Italy's role in the War effort was erected in Ancoats in 2021.[26]

There have been Chinese people living in Manchester since the 1850s. In the early twentieth century many worked in laundries, most of them from the southern province of Guangxi. Numbers grew after the Second World War, notably from Hong Kong. The growth of home washing and laundrettes forced them to look for alternative employment, so many moved into takeaways and restaurants. Manchester's first Chinese restaurant, Ping Hong, opened in 1948. Chinese banks opened branches and the Chinese government opened a consulate in the early 1980s. In 1986 Manchester was twinned with the city of Wuhan and in 1987 a Chinese arch was erected in what became known as Chinatown, a concentration of restaurants, takeaways and supermarkets. Increasing numbers of Chinese students came to study. The growing sensitivity of UK–China relations was highlighted, however, in December 2022 when Chinese officials were reported to have assaulted a protester taking part in a pro-democracy demonstration outside the consulate.[27]

There is evidence of a black presence in Greater Manchester from the eighteenth century, notably as servants. Juba Thomas Royton was a 'negro' 'belonging to' Oldham linen manufacturer Thomas Percival, probably acquired in an exchange of goods for slaves. His name is recorded in the baptism register of St Paul's Church, Royton, on 2 June 1760. A later parish record, from St Mary's Oldham, confirms that Juba – by then a 'waitingman' – was married to Betty Mellor in March 1765. Their three boys – Thomas, John and Robert – were baptised at St Paul's.[28]

Manchester had close links with the slave trade. In 1788 it was estimated that the town sold £500,000 of cloth to be traded for slaves in West Africa or as clothing for slaves in the Caribbean. Wealthy families benefited. The Hibberts sold cloth to slave-ship captains and were slave traders and plantation owners in Jamaica. Samuel Greg, who built a model village for workers at his Quarry Bank Mill in Styal, also owned a slave plantation in Dominica. All manufacturers and merchants benefited from cheap, slave-grown cotton, without which Manchester might not have grown so fast. In 2023 the Scott Trust, owner of the *Guardian*, apologised for the role its founders played in slavery and announced a £10 million programme of restorative justice, including millions for descendant communities. Research found that John Edward Taylor, the journalist and cotton merchant who founded the newspaper in 1821, and nine other Manchester businessmen who helped to fund it, had slave links, mainly through importing cotton.[2]

When abolitionist Thomas Clarkson visited Liverpool in 1787 to collect evidence, he narrowly escaped assassination as a gang of sailors tried to push him off a pier. Clarkson went on to Manchester, which he found more welcoming. Giving an address in the Collegiate Church, he noted: 'I was surprised also to find a great crowd of black people standing round the pulpit. There might be forty or fifty of them.' Manchester campaigners collected a petition with more than ten thousand names, one out of every five people in the city. Industrial workers may have seen parallels between their own conditions and the system of slavery. Britain abolished its slave trade in 1807 and slavery across most of the empire in 1833. With slavery continuing in the US, African American abolitionist campaigners such as freed slave Frederick Douglass visited Manchester. Sarah Parker Remond, the first African American woman to embark on a lecture tour in the UK, came to Manchester in 1859 to appeal to mill owners and cotton workers to support the anti-slavery movement.[30]

The American Civil War of 1861–5 divided opinion in Manchester. A US government blockade of southern cotton helped to cause a cotton famine in the North West of England, bringing much suffering. For the first couple of years the tendency in Britain, including in mill towns, was to support the south. In April 1862 in Ashton-under-Lyne, 6,000 unemployed mill workers gathered to condemn the northern blockade. The next year 8,000 met in Oldham to support the south. Rochdale was a rare example of a town where support for the North was strong.

British opinion shifted against the Confederacy in late 1862 when President Abraham Lincoln issued the Emancipation Proclamation, which promised to free southern slaves. Previously Lincoln had said the war was waged to preserve the Union; now it was seen as a struggle against slavery. That resonated in Britain, which had already abolished it. Late in 1862, pro-North meetings were held across the country. The most dramatic was at Manchester's Free Trade Hall on 31 December, which drafted an address to Lincoln saying: 'Heartily do we congratulate you and your country on this your humane and righteous cause.' Lincoln replied in his address 'To the Working-men of Manchester': 'Under the circumstances I cannot but regard your decisive utterances on the question as an instance of sublime Christian heroism which has not been surpassed in any age or in any country.'[31]

Manchester's black population grew slowly. Circus owner Pablo Fanque spent much of his life in what is now Greater Manchester. The Beatles' *Being for the Benefit of Mr Kite* was based on one of his posters from Rochdale. Arthur Wharton, regarded as the first black professional footballer – born in Africa's Gold Coast – played for clubs including Stalybridge Rovers, Ashton North End and Stockport County. In the late 1890s a number of black workers settled in Salford's Greengate district, mostly former labourers on the Ship Canal and discharged seamen. In 1919 there were race riots in Britain's ports as returning servicemen alleged that newcomers had taken their jobs. Manchester saw an increase in fights and racial abuse.[32]

The Second World War brought more black seamen and workers. In 1945, the Fifth Pan-African Congress was held in the city, with delegates including Jomo Kenyatta, a Manchester resident who later became Kenya's president. A notable local delegate was Len Johnson, former middleweight professional boxer who had been banned from competing for British titles because of a colour bar. Johnson joined the Communist Party and co-founded the New International Club, which provided a vehicle for black political and social activism, including organising a concert and rally featuring his hero Paul Robeson. In the 1950s and 1960s, growing numbers arrived from the West Indies. Many clustered in Moss Side, which already had a small black population, and worked in poorly paid jobs in catering and cleaning. Arthur Lewis, an economist from St Lucia, became Britain's first black professor at the University of Manchester in 1948. He stayed in Manchester until 1957 and established social and educational centres in Moss Side and Hulme. One of these survives as the West Indian Sports and Social Club. He was knighted in 1963 and won the Nobel Prize for Economics in 1979.[33]

By the late 1970s, alienation among the black community had grown amid youth unemployment, racial prejudice and insensitive policing, leading to forty-eight hours of rioting in Moss Side in July 1981 after similar outbreaks in London's Brixton and Liverpool's Toxteth. An inquiry chaired by Benet Hytner QC for Greater Manchester Council could not pinpoint a single cause. It generally supported the police's actions, but questioned some tactics. The riot made civic leaders more aware of the need for policies acknowledging distinctive traditions. A Moss Side carnival evolved into a city-wide event. Oral history projects were organised. Sierra Leone-born Yomi Mambu became lord mayor in 1989–90, as did Jamaica-born Roy Walters in 2002–3.[34]

Prominent black figures included Jamaica-born Louise Da-Cocodia (1934–2008), Manchester's first black senior nursing officer and later an anti-racism campaigner. She dedicated her time to improving race relations after coming to the UK in 1955 to train as a nurse and experiencing openly racist attitudes. Erinma Bell, a Rusholme-born peace activist of Nigerian heritage, set up a charity to give young people in Moss Side and Longsight alternatives to street and gun crime. Ruth Ibegbuna, originally from West Yorkshire, left teaching to found Manchester-based Reclaim, a charity that promotes leadership and achievement among young people in inner cities. Poet Lemn Sissay, of Ethiopian heritage, grew up in care in Wigan. He was chancellor of the University of Manchester for seven years, succeeded in 2022 by Nazir Afzal, former chief crown prosecutor for the North West of England.

There is evidence of South Asians in Manchester since the mid-nineteenth century, but significant numbers arrived in the second half of the twentieth century. By 2011 there were more than 60,000 Manchester residents born in the Indian subcontinent, of whom 70 per cent were from Pakistan, almost 19 per cent from India and 11 per cent from Bangladesh. Many worked in remnants of the cotton industry or in transport, cleaning and catering. There were clusters in Moss Side, Cheetham Hill, Whalley Range, Longsight and Levenshulme. Muslim students in the late 1940s joined local families in buying a house in Victoria Park for use as a mosque, after which a group of mosques evolved. The first Hindu temple opened in 1969. In 1953, Sikhs dedicated a house in Moss Side as a gurdwara, or place of worship, the first of several. In the early 1970s Sikhs expelled from Uganda settled in the city.[35]

Some migrants experienced racism and discrimination. Anjum Malik, who arrived from Pakistan as a young girl in 1968, said: 'I was picked on ... My headteacher's favourite saying to Asian kids was, "Go back to where you came from, stop wasting my time." When he said that to me, I told him he couldn't do that, and that would cause tremendous problems for me because I would get chucked out of school all the time.'[36] In 1959, Gyani Sundar Singh Sagar, a Sikh, won a legal battle against Manchester Corporation for barring him from becoming a bus conductor because he wore a turban.[37] In 1981, Oldham experienced a brief period of violent rioting after a build-up of ethnic tensions.

The popularity of Indian food led to the creation from the 1960s of what later became known as Curry Mile, a collection of restaurants on Wilmslow Road. Since then the number of Indian restaurants has declined, but Middle Eastern restaurants moved in. In recent decades South Asians have become prominent in the professions, notably law and accountancy, and in politics. Mohammed Afzal Khan in 2005 became the city's youngest lord mayor and the first Pakistan-born person and first Muslim to hold the post. He served as a Labour member of the European Parliament for the North West from 2014 to 2017, and has been MP for Gorton since 2017.[38] Sajid Javid, former Conservative home secretary and chancellor of the exchequer, was born in Rochdale to a British Pakistani family.

Manchester's journey to become one of Europe's most diverse cities has been at times difficult. Its contemporary culture would be unthinkable without the varied history and traditions of its many ethnic groups. Like migrants everywhere, these have had to contend with how to blend cultural distinctiveness with participation in the city's civic and social life. Some still struggle with economic disadvantage. Historic prejudices periodically resurface. To succeed in the future, Manchester will need to ensure all its citizens feel valued.

7

SCIENCE AND TECHNOLOGY

John Dalton, a weaver's son from the village of Eaglesfield in Cumberland, was by all accounts gruff and unpolished, a Quaker who led a frugal bachelor life in Manchester. When presented to William IV, the king nervously asked him how people in Manchester were getting on (alluding to the recent Peterloo Massacre). Dalton replied: 'Well, I don't know, just middlin', I think.' On his return, a companion accused him of not showing courtly manners, to which he answered in broad Cumbrian: 'Mebby sae, but what can yan say to sic like fowk?'[1]

Dalton (1766–1844) was also one of Britain's greatest scientists, best known for formulating a new atomic theory to explain chemical reactions, on which much of modern chemistry and physics is based. He researched colour blindness from which he suffered, which became known for a time as Daltonism. He was also a noted meteorologist.

As Manchester's population and industry grew, the city became a centre for scientific breakthroughs and technological developments. Salford-born James Prescott Joule (1818–89), who managed a family brewery, was a physicist who established that the various forms of energy – mechanical, electrical and heat – can be changed for one another, forming the basis of the first law of thermodynamics.

Scottish chemist Robert Angus Smith discovered the existence of acid rain, a by-product of the Industrial Revolution, while in Manchester. Catherine Chisholm, the University of Manchester's first female medical student in 1899, became an influential paediatrician.

New Zealander Ernest Rutherford achieved the first ever artificially induced nuclear reaction while chair of physics at the university from 1907 to 1919. Manchester at that time became a world centre for nuclear physics, attracting scientists including J.J. Thomson, Niels Bohr, Hans Geiger, Ernest Marsden, John Cockcroft and James Chadwick. Marie Stopes, later famed for activities in birth control and sex education, was a palaeobotanist from Edinburgh who became the University of Manchester's first female lecturer in 1904. She worked on coal deposits and seed ferns. Later she founded (in London) Britain's first birth control clinic with her second husband, Patricroft-born Humphrey Verdon Roe, who manufactured aircraft in Manchester alongside his elder brother Alliott.

A team at the university created 'Baby', the world's first computer to run a programme electronically stored in its memory, in 1948. Mathematician Alan Turing, who worked on the next version, Mark I, took his own life after being convicted of 'gross indecency' and subjected to hormone injections intended to curb his homosexuality, which he accepted as an alternative to prison. Mary Lee Berners-Lee – mother of Tim Berners-Lee, inventor of the World Wide Web – worked on the first commercially available computer, the Ferranti Mark 1.

Radio astronomer Bernard Lovell created Jodrell Bank Observatory in Cheshire, away from Manchester in part because electric tramcars on Oxford Road had interfered with cosmic ray detection experiments. Louise Brown, the world's first test-tube baby, was born at Oldham General Hospital in 1978 after pioneering work by Robert Edwards and Patrick Steptoe. In 2010, Andre Geim and Konstantin Novoselov, physicists at the University of Manchester, won the Nobel Prize in Physics for their work on graphene, the so-called 'miracle material'.

Manchester's scientific culture was shaped by its relationship to industry and by the social conditions that manufacturing created, though activity began earlier. William Crabtree of Broughton, a merchant who practised astronomy, in 1639 made the first recorded observation (along with his friend Jeremiah Horrocks of Much Hoole, Lancashire) of the transit of Venus, a breakthrough depicted in Ford Madox Brown's mural sequence in Manchester Town Hall. Crabtree and Horrocks were at the heart of a correspondence network of amateur astronomers in northern England who did much to establish research astronomy in Britain.[2]

A crucial early development was the founding in 1781 of the Manchester Literary and Philosophical Society. Prime mover Thomas Percival was a physician and more than half the founders were medical men. Among them Charles White, a surgeon obstetrician (or 'man-midwife'), pioneered hygienic childbirth and also co-founded Manchester Royal Infirmary, which treated poor patients through donations from wealthy citizens. Another Lit and Phil co-founder, Wrexham-born Thomas Henry, was an apothecary who became rich as a manufacturing chemist, making products including 'Henry's Magnesia', an indigestion remedy; he was one of the first to manufacture and sell mineral and soda waters, initially for medicinal purposes. There were some setbacks. Lit and Phil leaders set up a College of Arts and Sciences in 1783, which closed within five years.[3]

Percival, Henry and several Lit and Phil organisers were Unitarians. In 1786 Percival and colleagues created Manchester Academy, a theological college to train nonconformist ministers, which also taught maths and technical subjects. The Lit and Phil required members to leave religion and politics at the door, but Manchester Infirmary became a political battleground between reformers and Tory Anglicans. Another Unitarian physician, John Ferriar, believed that social conditions and overcrowding were the cause of fever. He called for space, light and more treatment at the Infirmary, which would lift the limits on the size of its staff. Reformers prevailed after a stormy controversy during a typhus outbreak in 1790. Charles White and other Tories resigned and created a new 'Lying-in Hospital', which became St Mary's. At the Infirmary, Percival drew up a code of conduct that he expanded into an influential treatise, *Medical Ethics* (1803), coining the name for a significant branch of study.[4]

Dalton, who at age twelve had taught younger boys in a Cumbrian village school, took up a job teaching maths and natural philosophy at the Academy in 1793 and was quickly elected to the Lit and Phil, his main base for the rest of his life. In his first paper to the society, he diagnosed his own colour blindness. Though sometimes criticised for the quality of his experiments, he was a dedicated researcher who often worked late into the evening. He read more than a hundred papers to the society and became secretary, vice-president and eventually president.

The central part of Dalton's atomic theory was a method of calculating relative atomic weights for chemical elements, which enabled molecular formulas to be assigned for all chemical substances. He established that all matter is made up of atoms – tiny, unbreakable particles. All the atoms of each element weigh the same, but differ from atoms of other elements. Atoms of different elements combine with each other to make what we would call molecules. Dalton assigned weights to atoms of the twenty elements he knew at the time, a novel concept that would later contribute to development of the periodic table.

Dalton's theory overcame scepticism among some chemists to become the accepted basis for explaining chemical composition. After the Academy moved to York in 1803, he made his living from freelance tutoring. The Lit and Phil gave him a room that served as office and laboratory. For twenty-six years until his death, he lived in a room in the home of a botanist and his wife. Dalton had the rare honour of a statue erected in his lifetime. When he died in 1844, 40,000 people filed past his coffin. German incendiary bombs burned out the Lit and Phil's premises in George Street in the 1940 Christmas Blitz, destroying Dalton's laboratory and most of his papers. His eyes were preserved after his death because of curiosity about his colour blindness and they are now in Manchester's Science and Industry Museum.[5]

By the time of Dalton's death, Manchester had developed an unrivalled engineering culture. The textile industry spurred production of alkalis and other chemicals for dyeing, bleaching and printing; metalworking and mechanical engineering were needed to supply looms, spindles, engines and mills' load-bearing structures. Roots of the city's expertise have been traced to an eighteenth-century skill base of clockmaking, tool production and foundries.[6] Welsh engineer Richard Roberts, who arrived in 1816, built a range of machine tools. Edinburgh-born James Nasmyth built awesome steam hammers, which could forge huge iron pieces, in the 1840s. Joseph Whitworth's breakthroughs, in addition to his standard system for screw threads, included a measuring machine that could detect differences of less than one millionth of an inch; he also designed rifles and cannon.[7]

James Prescott Joule, who had been a pupil of Dalton, became manager of his family's brewery on New Bailey Street, on the Salford side of the River Irwell, in 1837.[8] He fitted his early scientific experiments around a nine-hour working day and formulated what became known as Joule's First Law, which defined the relationship between the amount of heat produced and the current flowing through a conductor. He ran into stiff opposition, however, when he looked at the nature of heat and matter. Work and heat, he reckoned, were two forms of the same phenomenon, later called energy. Energy could not be created or destroyed, but could be converted from work to heat and back again. In 1843 he was met by stony silence when he presented these results to a meeting of the British Association for the Advancement of Science. His first paper on the conservation-of-energy theory was rejected by the *Philosophical Transactions of the Royal Society*.

He was challenging the accepted wisdom, calorific theory, which considered heat to be a material – a type of fluid that flowed from warmer to cooler bodies – whereas Joule asserted that heat was a form of molecular motion. The existence of atoms and molecules was not widely accepted until later in the century, despite Dalton's work. Joule later commented that it was hard to convince the scientific elite that a new fundamental theory had again come from 'a town where they dine in the middle of the day'. Some questioned the accuracy of his calculations, but Joule had the advantage of being a brewer, reliant on finely tuned temperature measurement. He was supplied with precision equipment by John Benjamin Dancer, a talented instrument maker with a shop on Cross Street (who also achieved the first successful microphotographs, paving the way to microfilm and microfiche).[9] Joule presented his ideas again to the British Association in 1847 and won support from a young Glasgow professor called William Thomson, the future Lord Kelvin.

Joule's fortunes began to turn. In 1850 he was made a fellow of the Royal Society, in 1852 he was awarded the Royal Medal and in 1872 he was named president of the British Association, which had earlier given him such a cool reception. He is commemorated in the joule, the standard name for a unit of energy. His statue faces Dalton's across the entranceway to Manchester Town Hall.

A Natural History Society was formed in 1821, initially to preserve collections left by John Leigh Philips, manufacturer and antiquarian. It created an impressive museum on Peter Street. Manchester Geological Society followed in 1838, led by lawyer and geologist Edward Binney. In the early 1850s, the societies pooled their collections at Peter Street. Problems soon arose: the Natural History Society charged a penny for admission, while the Geological Society wanted its collections available for free. A compromise was reached whereby visitors could go to the geological rooms without paying. However, the Natural History Society introduced an umbrella stand; any visitor with a stick or umbrella had to leave it for a charge of one penny. The geologists saw this as an underhand way to make their visitors pay. Eventually they acquired their own umbrella stand in their part of the museum. In 1868 the specimens came under control of Owens College and are today part of Manchester Museum.[10]

A Mechanics' Institute was founded in 1824 by leading engineers to provide a basic education for working men, though it did not quite live up to its aim; it found a niche catering for skilled tradesmen, shopkeepers and clerks. A Hall of Science, opened on Byrom Street in 1840 by followers of Robert Owen, incorporated teaching in physical sciences. The Royal Manchester Institution, founded in 1823, focused on arts but also held lectures in chemistry, physiology and natural history. Robert Angus Smith, who arrived in Manchester in 1843, studied the effects of pollution on the atmosphere, which resulted in the formation of carbonic acid, or 'acid rain', a term he coined. He became the first chief inspector of the Alkali Inspectorate, the world's first national pollution control agency, and advocated use of smokeless fuels. A century later, Manchester and Salford became the first cities in Britain to have 'smokeless zones' in 1952.[11]

Aside from science, the region had a role in the history of vegetarianism. William Cowherd, a Salford minister who founded the Bible Christian Church, demanded in 1809 that his congregation eat a meat-free diet. 'If God had meant us to eat meat, then it would have come to us in edible form as is the ripened fruit,' he reputedly said. His followers helped to form the Vegetarian Society in 1847, today located in Altrincham.[12]

James Braid, a Scottish surgeon and pioneer investigator of hypnosis, worked in Manchester from 1828 until his death in 1860. In 1841, he watched Swiss 'animal magnetiser' Charles Lafontaine induce trances in animals and humans at Manchester Athenaeum. The theory of 'animal magnetism' had been propounded by Franz Anton Mesmer, a Viennese physician, who believed that some illnesses were caused by depleted levels of magnetism in the body and that a physician could transmit his own magnetic force by touch to a patient in a trance. Braid, sceptical but seeing that Lafontaine's subjects were indeed in an altered state, sought an alternative explanation by experimenting on himself, his wife, friends and servants.

He proved that physical contact was unnecessary and believed his patients were in a kind of sleep, so he named the phenomenon after Hypnos, the Greek god of sleep. Later, he moved away from thinking that trances were sleep-induced and concluded that they could be induced by concentrating the patient's attention on a single object or idea.[13]

The Reverend George William Garrett, brought up in Moss Side and educated at Manchester Grammar School and Owens College, was an unlikely pioneer of submarine design. In 1879 he produced the *Resurgam* (Latin for 'I shall rise again'), a forty-five-foot-long steam-powered submarine that could reach a depth of 150 feet; it was built in Birkenhead. Trials were apparently successful, but it sank off the coast of Wales while being towed in a storm. Garrett later made submarines for Greece and Turkey and emigrated to America, but he died penniless after losing his savings on a failed farm.[14]

The opening of Owens College in 1851 created roles for scientific professionals. Its first chemistry professor was Edward Frankland, pioneer of the concept of valency, or an element's combining power. His successor Henry Roscoe (uncle of Beatrix Potter) established Manchester as a leading chemical research centre. He is also credited, with his friend Robert Bunsen (of Bunsen burner fame), with taking the first flashlight photograph, using magnesium as a source of light.

As fears grew about Germany overtaking Britain in technical education, the Mechanics' Institute was revived by John Henry Reynolds, a self-educated working man originally trained as a bootmaker, who became superintendent in 1879. He rebuilt the curriculum around industrial priorities, with classes from bleaching and printing to the principles of workplace management. The Institute was renamed Manchester Technical School in 1883, known as 'the Tech'. Joseph Whitworth died in 1887 leaving money to be used partly for an institute incorporating the Tech on the site of his former engineering works in Sackville Street. The Technical Instruction Act 1889 also provided funding from local government taxation and the building opened as the Manchester School of Technology under municipal control in 1902.[15]

Manchester Royal Infirmary had initially been in a house in Garden Street, off Withy Grove, before moving in 1755 to a new building in what became Piccadilly Gardens. In 1903 the Infirmary reluctantly decided to leave Piccadilly and join a growing cluster of hospitals on Oxford Road, tied to the University Medical School. Catherine Chisholm (1878–1952), from Radcliffe, became a general practitioner near the university and a campaigner for infant welfare provision and for women in medicine. She was instrumental in founding Manchester Babies Hospital in 1914, initially in Levenshulme (later it became the Duchess of York Hospital for Babies in Burnage).

Australian researcher Grafton Elliot Smith, professor of anatomy at the university, developed the controversial theory that Egypt was a central origin point for the spread of all human culture. As Egyptology boomed, extensions to Manchester Museum, which had opened on Oxford Road in 1888, pushed its focus beyond natural history into ancient human cultures.[16] Archaeologist Margaret Murray, who worked at the museum, in 1908 'unwrapped' the mummified priest Khnum-Nakht in a public demonstration. Later, distinguished Egyptologist Rosalie David spent several decades as professor at the university, where she established the Manchester Egyptian Mummy Project in 1973; she was keeper of Egyptology at the museum.

In physics, Cheetham Hill-born Joseph John Thomson (1856–1940) was admitted to Owens College aged fourteen. He became a professor at Cambridge, where he identified the electron, the first subatomic particle to be discovered. He won the Nobel Prize in Physics in 1906.[17] Among his pupils had been Rutherford, who assembled a 'nuclear family' of scientists in Manchester. He and Geiger developed the first radiation counter. Geiger and Marsden carried out an experiment that demonstrated the nuclear nature of atoms by deflecting alpha particles passing through a thin gold foil. Rutherford's interpretation of this led him in 1911 to formulate the Rutherford model – that atoms are composed mostly of empty space, with most of their mass packed into a tiny nucleus, orbited by electrons.

In 1917, Rutherford achieved the first ever artificially induced nuclear reaction by firing particles from a radioactive source that disintegrated the nuclei of nitrogen atoms, resulting in the release of subatomic particles that he afterwards named protons. This is sometimes described as 'splitting the atom', a term that some prefer to apply to later experiments. His work in Manchester ultimately led to nuclear energy and the atomic bombs that devastated Hiroshima and Nagasaki in 1945. Rutherford's ideas were developed by Bohr and Chadwick; the latter later discovered the neutron.[18]

Also in Manchester, Ludwig Wittgenstein, later a leading philosopher, studied aeronautical engineering in 1908–11, testing box kites at an atmospheric research station in the hills above Glossop. He became frustrated at his failure to turn his design for a jet-powered propeller into a machine and instead turned to maths and logic. Albert Einstein, already famous as the pioneer of relativity theory, gave his first British lecture at the University of Manchester in 1921 – a symbolic step in restoring international scientific relations after the First World War. Kathleen Drew-Baker, a star botany student, made breakthroughs in the cultivation of seaweed, used as food in Japan, for which grateful farmers commemorate her as 'Mother of the Sea'.[19]

Manchester became renowned for cancer therapy. In 1921 a Radium Institute was opened with support from brewer Edward Holt, merging in 1932 with Christie cancer hospital on a new site in Withington. Ralston Paterson from Scotland, who became the institute's director in 1931, commissioned studies to determine optimum doses of radiation for particular tumours, creating a standard that spread worldwide as the 'Manchester system'. His wife Edith Paterson, initially working without salary, became one of the founders of radiobiology, exploring radiation's influence on human tissues.[20]

Commercial technology continued to develop. Engineer Henry Royce (1863–1933) was introduced to London-based dealer Charles

Rolls at a Manchester hotel on 4 May 1904, creating the luxury car marque and later aero-engine manufacturing business. Royce, originally from near Peterborough, had first set up in business in Manchester making domestic electrical fittings, but his fascination with all things mechanical led him to start building cars at his factory at Cooke Street, Hulme. Rolls was impressed by his two-cylinder Royce 10 and agreed to take all the cars Royce could make, which would be badged Rolls-Royce. They formalised their partnership by creating Rolls-Royce Limited, with Royce as chief engineer and works director. It moved to a new factory in Derby in 1908.

Manchester also became notable for aviation. Stretford-born John Alcock (1892–1919), with navigator Arthur Whitten Brown, piloted the first non-stop transatlantic flight from St John's, Newfoundland, to Clifden, Connemara, Ireland, in June 1919. Later that year Alcock died when the plane he was flying crashed in fog near Rouen in Normandy. Alliott Verdon Roe (1877–1958), born in Patricroft, Eccles, founded manufacturer Avro at Brownsfield Mill on Great Ancoats Street in 1910. Avro, through the work of Farnworth-born designer Roy Chadwick, went on to design some of the most recognisable British aircraft, including the Lancaster bomber. Beatrice Shilling, a former Manchester University engineering student, combined a career in aeronautics with a love of fast motorbikes, lapping Brooklands at 106 miles per hour in 1934. During the Second World War she modified the Rolls-Royce Merlin carburettor, making British aircraft more manoeuvrable.[21]

Chemist Sir Harry Kroto was born in Wisbech, Cambridgeshire, after his Berlin-born Jewish parents fled Nazi Germany. Kroto was raised in Bolton while his father was interned on the Isle of Man as an enemy alien during the war; he went to Bolton School, where he was a contemporary of actor Sir Ian McKellen, and the University of Sheffield. He went on to share the 1996 Nobel Prize in Chemistry for the discovery of fullerenes, or molecules that have hollow structures.[22]

After the war, Manchester emerged in the forefront of electronic computing. Mathematician Max Newman had developed codebreaking machines at Bletchley Park; electrical engineers Freddie Williams (born in Romiley, Stockport) and Tom Kilburn had worked together on radar, giving them the idea of adapting cathode-ray tubes into a data store. Chadderton-born engineer Geoff Tootill also joined the team. By mid-1948 the prototype 'Baby' was built. The team worked with Ferranti – based in Hollinwood, Oldham – whose Mark I brought short-lived hopes that Britain might dominate the new industry.

Turing, another Bletchley hero, tackled philosophical questions raised by computers and forecast the arrival of artificial intelligence. In a 1950 article for psychology journal *Mind*, he proposed an experiment that became known as the Turing test, an attempt to define a standard for a machine to be called 'intelligent'. He suggested that a computer could be said to 'think' if a human questioner could not tell it apart, through conversation, from a human being. He prophesied in a 1951 lecture in Manchester: 'It seems probable that once the machine thinking method had started, it would not take long to outstrip our feeble powers … At some stage therefore we should have to expect the machines to take control.' In 2013 Turing – who died by cyanide poisoning at his Wilmslow home in 1954 – was granted a belated royal pardon for his homosexuality conviction.[23]

Bristol-born Bernard Lovell (1913–2012) was another wartime radar researcher who had previously worked on cosmic rays at the university under the direction of Patrick Blackett, professor of physics and later Nobel Prize winner. Lovell created Jodrell Bank Observatory on land near Holmes Chapel owned by the university's botany department, initially using equipment left over from the war. His Mark I, towering over the plain, was built in 1957 – the world's largest steerable dish radio telescope at the time (now the third largest). Costs overran, but it was built in time to be the only radar device that could track the carrier rocket of the Soviet Union's Sputnik I, the first artificial satellite. In 1959 it received the first pictures transmitted from the far side of the moon. The telescope has played an important role in research of quasars and pulsars. In 1963, Lovell became mysteriously ill after a visit to a Soviet Union astronomy centre in Crimea. British intelligence feared the Soviets had poisoned him with radiation to try to remove memories of the trip.[24]

ICI's pharmaceutical division, based at Alderley Park in Cheshire after initially being at Blackley, north Manchester, became noted for drug development. James Black produced the first effective beta blockers there and Dora Richardson synthesised tamoxifen, originally proposed as a morning-after contraceptive, but now the most widely used drug for treating breast cancer. At Wrightington, near Wigan, John Charnley (1911–82, son of a Bury pharmacist) pioneered hip replacement operations. The birth of Louise Brown in 1978 brought accolades for the work of Steptoe and Edwards at Oldham's Centre for Human Reproduction.[25]

The Tech became the University of Manchester Institute of Technology (UMIST) in 1966. Academics there, notably science historian Donald Cardwell, were the driving force in creating the North Western Museum of Science and Industry – now the Science and Industry Museum – in 1969. A key priority was to rescue plant and tools as factories closed. UMIST merged with the University of Manchester in 2004. In that year, Russian-born Geim and Novoselov isolated graphene – a one-atom-thick layer of carbon that is lighter and stronger than steel and a good conductor. A National Graphene Institute opened in Manchester in 2015 and a Graphene Engineering Innovation Centre in 2018. Commercialisation has been slow, despite predictions that it would revolutionise electronics, computers, energy, biotechnology and transport. Technological revolutions can, however, take decades to get going.[26]

The University of Manchester can boast of having produced twenty-five Nobel laureates, one of the highest figures in British universities outside Oxbridge.[27] Notable scientists today include Chadderton-born Brian Cox, physicist and broadcaster, a notable populariser of science. While matching the city's illustrious past will not be easy, Manchester's innovation story is far from over.

8

WORDS AND PICTURES

Margaret Hale, a young gentlewoman from Hampshire and the main character in Elizabeth Gaskell's novel *North and South* (1854), feels disconcerted on arriving in Milton, a fictionalised Manchester: 'Long, straight, hopeless streets of regularly built houses, all small and of brick. Here and there a great oblong many-windowed factory stood up, like a hen among her chickens.'[1]

Manchester not only gave the world its first experience of the industrial city, but also played a big part in efforts to describe and depict it. Gaskell, brought up by an aunt in Knutsford, Cheshire, lived most of her life in Manchester and became one of the city's subtlest portrayers. Almost a century later, L.S. Lowry, who lived in Salford, created the abiding visual impression of England's industrial North. 'My ambition was to put the industrial scene on the map because nobody had seriously done it,' he said.[2] Not everyone may have felt pleased with the image of the North that Lowry fashioned, but it has proved powerfully influential.

For two centuries Manchester has been a significant cultural centre, with varying strengths in literature, theatre, art and music (see also chapters 11 on popular culture and 15 on music). The city has been shaped by hardships that industrialisation entailed and generally open to new cultural influences. It has a reputation for singing its own praises, sometimes with exaggeration. Anthony Burgess, brought up in Moss Side, wrote of his 1930s youth: 'In those days, for a Mancunian to visit the capital was an exercise in condescension. London was a day behind Manchester in the arts, in commercial cunning, in economic philosophy … London had something of the air of Chorlton-cum-Hardy.'[3]

Author Jeanette Winterson, born in Manchester and raised in Accrington, describes a city both provincial and cosmopolitan: 'Manchester is in the south of the north of England. Its spirit has a contrariness in it – a south and north bound up together – at once untamed and unmetropolitan; at the same time, connected and worldly.'[4] Manchester became a UNESCO City of Literature in 2017, committed to inspiring readers and writers.

Manchester writers before Gaskell were a mixed bag. John Byrom (1692–1763), born into a family of merchants and linen drapers, is best known for a poem written as a Christmas present for his daughter Dolly, which became the lyric for the hymn 'Christians Awake'. He also invented a system of shorthand. He is credited with early use of the phrase 'Tweedledum and Tweedledee', later employed by Lewis Carroll in *Through the Looking Glass*. It came in an epigram describing disputes between composers Handel and Bononcini:[5]

Some say, compar'd to Bononcini
That Mynheer Handel's but a Ninny
Others aver, that he to Handel
Is scarcely fit to hold a Candle
Strange all this Difference should be
'Twixt Tweedle-dum and Tweedle-dee!

Thomas De Quincey (1785–1859), son of a Manchester merchant, is known for his autobiographical *Confessions of an English Opium-Eater* (1821), which sparked off a global tradition of addiction literature. The family name was Quincey: after Thomas's father died, his mother added the 'De' and moved to Bath with her son, before sending him to Manchester Grammar School as a boarder with the aim of getting a place at Oxford. Thomas was miserable and ran away to Wales at seventeen, then lived penniless in London before reconciling with his family. He did eventually go to Worcester College, Oxford, and began taking opium, initially to relieve the pain of facial neuralgia, but it led to a lifelong addiction. He became an admirer and associate of William Wordsworth and Samuel Taylor Coleridge, and rented Wordsworth's former home, Dove Cottage, at Grasmere. De Quincey married, had eight children and turned to journalism. *Confessions* was first published in *London Magazine*, making him famous. He describes the 'pleasures' of his early drug-taking and the 'pains' it brought him, including insomnia, nightmares and frightening visions. There were accusations that he was encouraging others to take opium. His language sometimes conveys a compelling experience, amplifying his sense of space and time. Thomas's account contributed to bohemianism and modern drug counter-culture. Even today, writers remain divided over whether to praise or blame him.[6]

Rapid industrial growth led to a spate of social novels in the 1830s to 1850s. Several were written by outsiders, fascinated and alarmed, including Harriet Martineau's *Manchester Strike*, Charles Dickens's *Hard Times* (written after visiting Preston) and Benjamin Disraeli's *Coningsby* and *Sybil*. Novelist Frances Trollope visited Manchester in 1832. Her *Michael Armstrong: Factory Boy* (1840) tells of a boy rescued by a wealthy benefactor but who later returns to the mills. She aimed to expose the misery of factory life and suggest that private philanthropy alone could not solve the problem.

Essayist Thomas Carlyle, who first visited in 1838, wrote that 'Sooty Manchester' was built 'on the infinite Abysses'. He called for it to have 100 acres of green fields and trees 'for its little children to disport in; for its all-conquering workers to take a breath of twilight air in'.[7] Disraeli came often. His speeches acknowledged Manchester's greatness, but his novels also explored its darker side. In *Sybil: or the Two Nations* (1845) he drew attention to the gulf between England's rich and poor, focusing on a town called Mowbray, inspired by Manchester.

Elizabeth Gaskell (1810–65) arrived when she married William Gaskell, assistant minister at Cross Street Unitarian Chapel (born in Latchford, a suburb of Warrington), in 1832. She helped with his work, offering support to the poor and teaching in the Sunday school. They had three daughters before their only son, William, died of scarlet fever aged nine months. She had already had a few short stories published and her husband suggested she write a novel to distract her from grief. Her first novel, *Mary Barton: A Tale of Manchester Life* (1848), tells of a young woman who attracts the romantic attentions of Jem Wilson, a hard-working engineer, and Harry Carson, son of a wealthy mill owner. The mill owner is murdered by Mary's father, a Chartist, but Jem is wrongly accused. The plot was based partly on the assassination of manufacturer Thomas Ashton. In the preface, Gaskell says she had 'always felt a deep sympathy with the careworn men, who looked as if doomed to struggle through their lives in strange alternations between work and want'.[8]

The novel was initially published anonymously, though that did not last long. There was angry criticism from manufacturers in the Cross Street congregation, including Unitarian mill owner and friend William Rathbone Greg, who felt that Gaskell disregarded employers' efforts to respond to workers' suffering and improve living conditions. Much of Gaskell's writing was innovatory or controversial. There was a national moral storm over *Ruth* (1853), a compassionate portrait of an unmarried orphan girl made pregnant by her aristocratic lover and her efforts to gain a respectable position in society. In 1850 the Gaskells moved from Dover Street, off Oxford Road, to a grand villa on Plymouth Grove (recently handsomely restored).

Mary Barton attracted the attention of Dickens, who published many of Gaskell's stories in periodicals he edited. He was often in Manchester, where his sister Fanny lived in Ardwick. The Cheeryble brothers in *Nicholas Nickleby* are reputedly based on William and

Daniel Grant, calico printers and cotton spinners. Dickens's relationship with Gaskell soured, however, notably when he serialised *North and South* in his weekly magazine *Household Words*. They tussled over style and length and the ending had to be compressed. Sales dropped, probably because it followed quickly after Dickens's *Hard Times*, though he blamed it on Gaskell's 'wearisome' novel.[9]

North and South is a romantic novel, but more than an industrial *Pride and Prejudice*. It is kinder to the business class than *Mary Barton*. Its theme is the need to pull down barriers between self and others – not only barriers between sexes and classes but between cultures and faiths, town and country, North and South. Margaret Hale is forced to leave the rural South and settle in Milton when her vicar father turns dissenter. She sympathises with the poor and clashes with cotton manufacturer John Thornton, a product of the Manchester school of self-help. She is also attracted to him. After a bitter strike, they come to a better understanding of each other and of the complexity of labour relations. She finally accepts his marriage offer.

Gaskell was friend and biographer of Charlotte Brontë, who came to Manchester in 1846 with her father Patrick for him to have cataracts removed. They stayed in the town for a month while Patrick convalesced. During that time Charlotte learned that her first book *The Professor* had been rejected. Undaunted, she began writing *Jane Eyre*.

Other writers of the time included Ancoats-born poet Charles Swain (1801–74), friend of Robert Southey, poet laureate. Geraldine Endsor Jewsbury (1812–80) lived in the town for many years from age six. She was known for novels such as *Zoe: The History of Two Lives*, about a girl who falls in love with a Catholic priest, causing his faith to lapse. Much of her work questioned the role of wife and mother as a woman's only option.

Dialect writers included Urmston-born John Collier (1708–86), a schoolmaster at Milnrow, Lancashire, who wrote as 'Tim Bobbin', and Rochdale-born poet Edwin Waugh (1817–90), whose most famous poem was 'Come whoam to thi childer an' me'. Middleton-born

Samuel Bamford (1788–1872), weaver and radical, wrote personal memoirs and poems in standard English as well as dialect poetry. He witnessed the Peterloo Massacre and was jailed for a year for inciting a riot despite evidence that his conduct was peaceful. Later he became disillusioned by the increasingly violent rhetoric of 'physical-force' Chartism, though he continued to support legal and political reforms. His writings have been of great use to social historians. Other dialect writers included poet Ammon Wrigley (1861–1946) from Saddleworth.

William Harrison Ainsworth (1805–92), born in King Street and educated at Manchester Grammar School, moved to London and wrote forty historical novels, of which the best known is *The Lancashire Witches*, about the witches of Pendle. Isabella Banks (1821–97) is best remembered for *The Manchester Man* (1876), the rags-to-riches story of Jabez Clegg, whose crib is snatched from the River Irk. It encompasses the Peterloo Massacre and corn law riots. Frances Hodgson Burnett (1849–1924) was born in Cheetham Hill, daughter of an ironmonger on Deansgate. After her father died of a stroke, her mother took over the business, but the family struggled and eventually moved to America. Her novel *Little Lord Fauntleroy* (1886) made her reputation as a children's author; she also wrote *A Little Princess* (1905). She divided her time between the US and England and had the idea for the children's classic *The Secret Garden* (1911) while living at Great Maytham Hall, Kent, though much of it is said to have been written in Buile Hill Park, Salford, during visits.[10]

In the twentieth century, Louis Golding (1895–1958) came from a Ukrainian-Jewish family in deprived Hightown. His novel *Magnolia Street* (1932), set in the fictional city of Doomington (Manchester), was a bestseller. Partly autobiographical, it tells of a street divided between Gentiles on one side and Jews on the other. Howard Spring (1889–1965), from a poor background in Cardiff, worked for the *Manchester Guardian* for sixteen years before moving to London. His first novel *Shabby Tiger* and sequel *Rachel Rosing* were fairly successful, while *My Son, My Son!* (1938) – about two friends' sons who become tragically estranged over Irish independence – was a critical and financial hit. All were set in Manchester.

Richmal Crompton (1890–1969), author of the *Just William* children's books, was born in Bury. Dodie Smith (1896–1990), author of *I Capture the Castle* and *The Hundred and One Dalmatians*, was also born in Bury, specifically Whitefield. After her father died when she was two, she and her mother went to live at her maternal grandparents' house on Stretford Road, Old Trafford, until 1910, when her mother remarried and they moved to London. The first part of her autobiography, *Look Back With Love: A Manchester Childhood*, was published in 1974.

Jack Hilton (1900–83), a Rochdale plasterer, wrote experimental, semi-autobiographical fiction about working-class life that won praise from George Orwell and W.H. Auden, but went out of fashion and out of print after the Second World War. His debut novel *Caliban Shrieks* (1935) has been republished after Jack Chadwick, a bartender, chanced on an old copy at Salford's Working Class Movement Library in 2021 and tracked down the copyright holder, the widow of one of Hilton's friends.

John Burgess Wilson (1917–93) was born in Harpurhey to Catholic shopkeeper parents. His mother and only sister died in the 1918 influenza pandemic. His father married a publican and the family lived in Miles Platting and later Moss Side. Educated at Xaverian College and the University of Manchester, he left Manchester at twenty-three and returned only occasionally, yet the city's accents and landmarks pervade his work. He also composed more than two hundred musical works. Wilson served in the Royal Army Medical Corps and Army Educational Corps during the Second World War, and following its conclusion he taught in Wolverhampton, Banbury, and then Malaya. His first published novel, *Time for a Tiger*, appeared under the name 'Anthony Burgess'. Teaching in Brunei, he collapsed in the classroom and was flown back to England with a mysterious illness, wrongly thought to be a brain tumour.

Visiting Leningrad in 1961, Burgess recognised pungent tannery smells that he recalled from his youth. He drew on both Leningrad and Manchester to create the future urban dystopia in *A Clockwork Orange*. Adapted into a controversial film by Stanley Kubrick, this work was initially inspired by an incident during the London Blitz in which Burgess's pregnant wife was raped and assaulted by four American deserters; perhaps as a result, she lost the child. In his memoir *Little Wilson and Big God*, Manchester is 'an ugly world with ramshackle houses and foul back alleys', yet in his novel *The Pianoplayers*, Manchester and Blackpool in the 1920s and 1930s are portrayed as places of excitement and adventure. In 1989 Burgess wrote 'The Manchester Overture', performed there for the first time in 2013. His most substantial novel, *Earthly Powers*, was published to international acclaim in 1980. He once told an interviewer: 'I've always regretted that while Dublin produced a great novel, *Ulysses*, I feel that Manchester should have had a novel like that but never did, and I don't think I'm qualified to write it.'[11]

Cheshire's Alan Garner (born in Congleton in 1934, raised in Alderley Edge), writer of children's fantasy novels, went to Manchester Grammar School, as did Sale-born playwright Robert Bolt (1924–95), best known for screenplays for *Lawrence of Arabia*, *Doctor Zhivago* and *A Man for All Seasons*, the latter two of which won him Oscars. Howard Jacobson, born in Manchester in 1942 and raised in Prestwich, is known for comic novels involving Jewish characters. *The Mighty Walzer* (1999) is about a teenage table-tennis champion resembling a youthful Jacobson. He won the Man Booker Prize in 2010 for *The Finkler Question*, which explores Jewishness while following the lives of three friends. Jacobson described himself as a 'Jewish Jane Austen', but only because he was sick of others calling him the 'English Philip Roth'.[12] German writer W.G Sebald (1944–2001), who taught at the University of Manchester from 1966 to 1969, paints a bleak picture of Manchester's industrial decline in his novel *The Emigrants* (1992), exploring exile and loss. Ex-policeman turned writer Maurice Procter (1906–73) set crime novels in a fictional 1950s Manchester, notably *Hell is a City*, made into a 1959 film that has become a cult *film noir*.

Modern poets include 'punk poet' and 'bard of Salford' John Cooper Clarke (born in the city in 1949), who gave rapid-fire renditions of poems, performing alongside bands such as the Sex Pistols, The Fall and New Order. His poem 'I Wanna Be Yours' has been wildly popular on social media, making it arguably the world's favourite British poem. Carol Ann Duffy (born Glasgow 1955), professor of contemporary poetry at Manchester Metropolitan University, was poet laureate from 2009 to 2019. Her former partner Jackie Kay (born Edinburgh 1961) was chancellor of the University of Salford from 2014 to 2021. She returned in 2023 as a professor of Creative Writing. Performance poet Tony Walsh (born Denton 1965), known as Longfella, came to wider attention in 2017 for reading his poem 'This is the Place' to crowds in Albert Square after the Manchester Arena bombing. Lemn Sissay, born in Wigan in 1967, had a terrible experience growing up in foster and care homes. At seventeen he used his unemployment benefit to self-publish his first poetry pamphlet, which he sold to striking miners.[13] He has been a full-time writer, performing internationally, since age twenty-four.

Among novelists, Hilary Mantel (1952–2022), who won the Booker Prize twice, for *Wolf Hall* and *Bring Up the Bodies*, was born in Glossop and raised in Hadfield, a Peak District mill village. She described it as occupying 'some no-man's land, some place not well-defined in any book. There were very few streets, but very few trees.'[14] Novels by Rosie Garland (born London 1960) include *The Night Brother*, set in dark nineteenth-century Manchester. Emma Jane Unsworth (born Bury 1979), author of novels including *Animals*, grew up in Prestwich. Gwendoline Riley (born London 1979) studied English at Manchester Metropolitan University: her first two novels, *Cold Water* and *Sick Notes*, have protagonists in their early twenties in Manchester. Crime writer Joseph Knox is creator of a maverick Manchester detective, Aidan Waits.

Early development of theatre was held back by religious and moral objections, though these were increasingly overcome by the later nineteenth century. Actor-manager Charles Calvert's Shakespearean revivals at the Prince's Theatre, starting with *The Tempest* in 1864, drew large audiences. An even greater landmark was when Annie Horniman established Britain's first permanent provincial repertory company at Manchester's Gaiety Theatre in 1907.[15] The daughter of a London tea merchant, she had already co-founded Dublin's Abbey Theatre with poet W.B. Yeats. For the Gaiety venture she assembled a talented group of young directors and actors who went on to stage some two hundred plays in Manchester, London and North America.

The Gaiety spawned the Manchester School of playwrights, including Harold Brighouse, Stanley Houghton and Allan Monkhouse. In Houghton's *Hindle Wakes*, which opened at London's Aldwych in 1912, mill girl Fanny Hawthorn has a fling with the boss's son but refuses to marry him, confident in her ability to support herself. Houghton died in 1913, aged thirty-two. Brighouse's *Hobson's Choice* is a comedy about the battle of wills between a hard-headed cobbler and his daughter Maggie, who defies him by marrying his downtrodden worker, Will. It was first performed in New York in 1915 and Brighouse moved permanently to London.

Because of her tea connection, Horniman was known as 'Hornibags'. She held court at the Midland Hotel wearing exotic clothing, smoked Turkish cigarettes in a long holder and was a firm believer in equality of the sexes. She lived modestly in rooms in Oxford Road, surrounded by cats and books on astrology, feminism, travel and politics. Horniman's venture was successful artistically but less so commercially and it was starved of capital in the First World War. She disbanded the company in 1917 and sold the theatre to a cinema company in 1920.

Serious drama subsequently entered the doldrums for decades with little beyond touring productions of musicals and revues. The postwar growth of public subsidy, including of the Library Theatre Company in the Central Library's basement, started a revival, though there were hiccups: Wythenshawe's Forum Theatre, opened in 1971, closed in 1999. The biggest breakthrough was conversion of the redundant Royal Exchange in St Ann's Square into a theatre, temporarily housing the 69 Theatre Company in 1973 until a permanent structure opened in 1976.

Manchester's businessmen were keen art collectors. The Royal Manchester Institution from 1823 stimulated the local art market, bringing dealers and artists to the city. By 1861 Manchester had 181 professional painters, more than any other provincial town.[16] They included forty women, but it was a largely male world. Although women could exhibit at the Royal Institution, they were denied entry to the Manchester Academy of Fine Arts, founded in 1857, for almost thirty years. The 1857 Art Treasures exhibition boosted Manchester's art-loving credentials, though not everyone was persuaded: the *Art Journal*, critical of what it saw as curatorial flaws, opined that 'the great lesson which Manchester has taught, is the total unfitness of Manchester for such an exhibition, and of such an exhibition for Manchester'.

Philanthropist Thomas Coglan Horsfall, inspired by John Ruskin's educational art gallery in Sheffield, established the Manchester Art Museum for the poor in Ancoats in 1884 (taken over by the city in 1918, closed 1953). Manchester City Art Gallery opened in 1882 after financial problems saw the Royal Institution pass its Mosley Street building and collection to the corporation. Whitworth Art Gallery opened in 1890, funded by a bequest from Sir Joseph Whitworth; *Manchester Guardian* proprietor John Edward Taylor donated 150 watercolours.

The city commissioned Ford Madox Brown, painter of moral and historical subjects, to paint twelve murals depicting the city's history in the new town hall; they were begun in 1879 and completed in 1893, the year he died. A local antiquarian, W.E.A. Axon, complained that many of the historical episodes that Brown was asked to paint were fictional. Before Brown's death, Manchester Corporation met in private and resolved to whitewash his murals and replace them with advertisements for locally manufactured products. The resolution was never carried out, but the painter's son,

Ford Madox Ford, claimed that news of the resolution caused the apoplectic fit that led to his father's death.[17]

Annie Swynnerton (1844–1923), born as Annie Robinson in Hulme and trained at Manchester School of Art, became the first female associate member of the Royal Academy of Arts. Best known for portraits and symbolist works, she depicted women as independent, confident individuals. Subjects ranged beyond those deemed feminine, such as domestic scenes and flora, and incorporated aspects of Neoclassicism, Pre-Raphaelitism and Impressionism, but were not bound by them. She produced more than two hundred paintings over sixty years and set up the Manchester Society of Women Painters with eight other female artists. Swynnerton visited Italy with fellow Manchester artist Susan Isabel Dacre (1844–1933) and was captivated by the light and landscape. She married Manx sculptor Joseph Swynnerton and the couple spent much of their life alternating between homes in London and Rome.[18]

Dacre was a women's suffrage campaigner; among her best-known works is a portrait of fellow suffragist Lydia Becker. Manchester-born Louise Jopling (1843–1933) became a fashionable portraitist, with a studio in Chelsea and a social circle that included James McNeill Whistler, Oscar Wilde and Ellen Terry. Glasgow-born Gertrude Thomson (1850–1929) studied at Manchester School of Art and painted portraits, illustrated books and designed stained glass.

Among other notables, Irish sculptor John Cassidy (1860–1939) spent most of his career in Manchester, where his work includes a bronze bust of Charles Hallé in Bridgewater Hall, marble statues of John and Enriqueta Rylands in the John Rylands Library, and a bronze statue of Edward VII in Whitworth Park. His bronze statue *Adrift*, depicting a family clinging to a raft in a stormy sea, is beside the Central Library.[19]

One of Manchester's finest imports was Adolphe Valette (1876–1942), a French impressionist who taught at Manchester School of Art, where Lowry was among his pupils. Valette is acclaimed for his cityscapes, which captured Manchester's damp fogginess. Pupils also included Emmanuel Levy (1900–86), painter, teacher and art critic, and Denton-born Harry Rutherford (1903–85), one of the most prominent 'Northern School' painters. Manchester was the home of a distinctive school of industrial landscape painters. The focal point for local artists was the Manchester Academy of Arts' annual exhibition, at which Lowry's works were often the outstanding feature. It could justifiably claim to be the art centre of the North of England.

Lawrence Stephen Lowry (1887–1976), born in Old Trafford, part of Stretford, but living mostly in Salford, represented the industrial North so successfully that the world came to see it through the prism of his paintings. In his pictures, people move in crowds yet appear lonely. A solitary man, Lowry also painted haunting portraits and empty landscapes and seascapes. Although he exhibited from the 1920s and had a London exhibition in 1939, he worked as a rent collector until retiring on his sixty-fifth birthday in 1952. His motifs – chimney, mill, warehouse, terraced row – reflected the repetitive narrowness of factory and slum life. He used only five colours: flake white, ivory black, vermilion, Prussian blue and yellow ochre. His use of a white background to lighten the pictures was suggested early on by D.B. Taylor of the *Manchester Guardian*. After the Second World War, Lowry's painting became more upbeat, including pictures of people at play as well as at work. Lowry is said to hold the record for rejecting British honours (five), including a knighthood (1968).

Other notables included Lees-born Helen Bradley (1900–79), who began to paint seriously only in her sixties; Lowry encouraged her in creating a style based on her childhood memories. Sylvia Melland (1906–93), from Altrincham, studied at Manchester School of Art, started as a painter and later moved to printmaking. Harry Kingsley (1914–98), also from the School of Art, taught in a Manchester secondary school and painted townscapes. William Ralph Turner (1920–2013), of Chorlton-on-Medlock, was largely self-taught and influenced by Lowry. Tyldesley's Roger Hampson (1925–96) became head of Bolton College of Art and took inspiration from his local area. Arthur Delaney (1927–87), another Lowry-influenced painter, is known for tramcars in most of his pictures.

Harold Riley (1934–2023) spent most of his life documenting his native Salford. Rusholme's Geoffrey Key (born 1941) is known for a vibrant palette and dreamlike compositions. Linder Sterling, born in Liverpool in 1954 and raised near Wigan, became known in Manchester's punk and post-punk era for photography, radical feminist collages and confrontational performance art. Manchester-born Chris Ofili (born 1968) is a Turner Prize winner renowned for paintings incorporating elephant dung.

Manchester's achievements in words and pictures are among the most wide-ranging and substantial of any non-capital city in the world. Culture today continues to form a big part of its hopes for the future.

9

VICTORIAN, EDWARDIAN EXPANSION

After Manchester officially became a city in 1853, the world's 'shock city' no longer seemed so shocking. It grew prosperous and respectable, albeit still with daunting social problems. Attention shifted first to Joseph Chamberlain's Birmingham and by the end of the century to London, which swelled dramatically through internal and international migration.

Manchester had less political impact – and became more Conservative with a big 'C' – but it had set the template for the industrial city. The first Trades Union Congress was held in the city in 1868. Manchester was instrumental in the creation of the Labour Party. It created one of the nineteenth century's most massive engineering projects, the Manchester Ship Canal, along with Trafford Park, the world's first planned industrial estate. And it became central to the campaign for women's suffrage, most visibly through Emmeline Pankhurst's militant suffragettes before the First World War (see Chapter 10).

'Our age is pre-eminently the age of great cities', wrote Robert Vaughan, president of Lancashire Independent College, Manchester, in 1843.[1] In 1800, there were no cities or towns in England and Wales outside London with a population of 100,000 or more; by 1891 there were twenty-three.[2] As pioneers, Manchester's cotton merchants were mindful of their place in history. By the 1840s they were building great warehouses modelled on *palazzi* of Renaissance Italy, merchant princes presenting themselves as Europe's modern Medici. Salford-born Thomas Worthington, one of the most successful architects, described Manchester as 'the Florence of the nineteenth century'.[3] This pretension did not protect the cottonocracy from charges of philistinism – hence the 1857 Art Treasures exhibition as a riposte – but these warehouses remain one of the glories of the city's architectural heritage, even though German bombs destroyed several in 1940.

The elegant showrooms were built with rows of tall front windows on four storeys or more. Customers reached sample rooms on the upper floors via a central staircase. Offices were on the ground floor and the packing room in the basement, leading to a loading bay at the side or rear. Iron kerbs were a feature of surrounding streets because heavy carts cracked stone kerbs. These were 'structures fit for kings … which many a monarch might well envy', said *Bradshaw's Guide to Manchester*. These palaces of commerce flanked the main thoroughfares, notably Portland, Princess and Mosley Streets. Perhaps the most spectacular was that of S. & J. Watts on Portland Street (now the Britannia Hotel), opened in 1858. The Watts brothers ran the city's largest wholesale drapery business. Sir James Watts, twice mayor of Manchester, was knighted when Queen Victoria visited the Art Treasures exhibition. He entertained aristocrats and royalty at his country house, Abney Hall in Cheadle.[4]

Manchester's business district was dominated not just by warehouses but also by banks, hotels, railway stations, shops and markets. The Royal Exchange, enlarged several times, was at the heart of Lancashire's cotton trade. While Liverpool traded raw cotton, Manchester traded cotton textiles for global export. Visitors to the third building (completed 1874) at 2pm each Tuesday and Friday would see 6,000 men engaged in discussions and deals. The last extension was commissioned in 1913 to house 10,000 subscribers. It finally closed for business in 1968, by which time members had dwindled to 660. The last day's prices can still be seen on the display board in what now houses the Royal Exchange Theatre.

Manchester was the North's financial centre, second only to London, and its private banks were gradually absorbed by joint-stock ventures. Heywood's, the most prominent name for more than a century, was absorbed in 1874 by Manchester and Salford Bank, which became Williams Deacon's Bank, now part of NatWest. The insurance sector grew to encompass most industrial and personal risks. Refuge Assurance opened its massive Oxford Street premises in 1895, designed by Alfred Waterhouse, architect of the town hall. Various elements of co-operative insurance gathered under the umbrella of the Co-operative Insurance Society in Corporation Street.[5]

While remaining cotton's commercial centre, Manchester's economy diversified to include not just metals and engineering, but also areas such as the production and sale of food and drink, road and rail transport, and clothing. Tailoring sweatshops grew in areas such as Strangeways and Cheetham as rising real wages and the Saturday half-day holiday fuelled demand for fashion among the lower-middle classes and young working women. Manchester and Salford had also become the centre of UK rubberised rainwear production after Charles Macintosh, who experimented with waterproof fabric in Glasgow, and partner H.H. Birley, opened a factory in Chorlton-on-Medlock in 1825. Early coats had problems with smell, stiffness and a tendency to melt in hot weather, but another associate, Thomas Hancock, patented a method for vulcanising rubber.

William Marsden, son of a Manchester cotton manufacturer, and Robert Lowes, a Salford warehouse clerk – and great-great grandfather of actor Sir Ian McKellen – played a central role in the campaign for the half-day holiday and thus the invention of the modern weekend as a leisure time. They met at the Athenaeum and formed a committee to press for change. In 1843, more than 400 Manchester employers agreed to grant the half-day holiday. The idea spread to other towns and cities and in 1850 became law in textile mills as part of the Factory Act.[6]

Cotton suffered from periodic booms and slumps. The 1860s cotton famine hit towns such as Ashton-under-Lyne and Stockport more severely than Manchester. There was also a depression in the cotton trade from the late 1870s through the 1880s, which was widely felt. On the whole, however, setbacks created no lasting check to Manchester's economic vitality. From the late eighteenth century, residential suburbs grew around the urban core, at first nearby but later more distant as railways developed.

Expansion of omnibus and later tram routes helped inner suburbs to grow. Ardwick Green, Manchester's first suburb, and the Crescent in Salford were a short walk or carriage ride from the centre. Ardwick residents included cotton spinners John Kennedy and James McConnel and, later, engineer William Fairbairn and the city's foremost cotton merchant, John Rylands. Plymouth Grove, where Elizabeth Gaskell lived from 1850, was an exclusive suburb of detached and semi-detached villas. Victoria Park, Rusholme, begun in 1837, was a walled estate containing some of Manchester's grandest mansions. Banker Samuel Brooks, aiming to attract rich merchants, built a suburb two miles south that he named Whalley Range, after Whalley in his native north Lancashire; subsequently, he also created Brooklands, near Sale. An 1833 poem, 'Suburban Sortie' by John Stanley Gregson, satirised the suburban merchant who, seeking the landed life, 'talks of his *estate*' and 'Thinks … 'tis time to *rusticate*'.[7]

As the city expanded and the middle and working classes encroached on suburbs, the wealthy moved further out. Mill owners Wilson and Joseph Crewdson, for example, moved from Ardwick Green to Plymouth Grove and then to Alderley Edge in Cheshire, made possible by the railway. Some settled on the Lancashire coast, especially Southport or Lytham, or the Lake District. By the 1890s there were enough business commuters for the Lancashire and Yorkshire Railway to run a 'Blackpool Club Train' offering a saloon with light refreshments for first-class season ticket holders.

Alderley Edge and Altrincham marked the limits of suburban expansion into Cheshire. A turn-of-the-century memoir by

Katherine Chorley described first-class commuting from Alderley Edge as an exclusively male preserve, while during the day the Edge became a genteel female world of golf, charities and card games. Clusters grew around stations on the London line at Wilmslow, Cheadle Hulme, Bramhall and Heaton Moor. Sale, Stretford and Timperley grew along the Altrincham line. Withington and Didsbury initially opened up as a horse omnibus route, later reinforced by the Midland railway line. To the north, there were suburbs at Prestwich and Crumpsall on the Bury line and to the west at Urmston and Flixton on the Warrington line.[8]

Reaching beyond Manchester, Bolton-born William Lever and his brother James, in their company Lever Brothers, in 1886 became one of the first to manufacture soap from vegetable oils. Their product, Sunlight Soap, was initially made at Warrington, after which they created a works and 'model' village at Port Sunlight in the Wirral.

Salford-born Sir Edward Watkin, Liberal MP and railway entrepreneur – son of a cotton merchant – was an ambitious visionary who became chairman of several railway companies. As a young man, while a director of Manchester Athenaeum, he was involved in the Saturday half-day holiday movement, campaigned for parks and co-founded the *Manchester Examiner* newspaper. He built the Great Central Main Line (an extension of the Manchester, Sheffield and Lincolnshire Railway) between Sheffield and London's Marylebone, along with a new railway between Manchester and Liverpool. He made a failed attempt to dig a tunnel under the English Channel to connect his rail empire to the French rail network. Watkin hoped that his railway would carry passengers from Manchester to Paris, but there were fears that the tunnel might enable a French invasion; more than a mile of tunnel was dug at Shakespeare Cliff between Folkestone and Dover before Watkin gave up trying to win support in parliament. Watkin also developed Grimsby into the world's largest fishing port and created the holiday resort of Cleethorpes. For a period he ran eastern Canada's Grand Trunk Railway and advised on railways in countries such as India. He half built a tower at London's

Wembley Park, intended to rival the Eiffel Tower in Paris, which later became known as 'Watkin's Folly'.[9]

By the mid-century, Manchester seemed established as a Liberal stronghold. That was to change radically, however, as the city turned increasingly Conservative. Even the Chartist Ernest Jones, whom Engels and Marx hoped might be a revolutionary leader, became ever more moderate. Liberals won all Manchester's parliamentary contests from 1832 to 1867. After that, Manchester, which was divided into three constituencies by the 1867 Reform Act and six in 1884, returned more Conservatives, many of them local business-men, than Liberals until 1906, when there was a brief Liberal revival because free traders distrusted Tory tariff reform policies. The first Tory to win was Hugh Birley, who topped the poll in 1868; he was a nephew of the Hugh Birley who led the fatal charge at Peterloo.

Conservatives won a remarkable twenty-one of the thirty seats available between 1885 and 1900. Scots-born Arthur Balfour, MP for Manchester East from 1885 to 1906, was Conservative prime minister between 1902 and 1905. (Winston Churchill was Conservative MP for Oldham from 1900, but crossed the floor to the Liberals in 1904 after opposing the Tories over trade protection-ism; he was Liberal MP for Manchester North West from 1906 to 1908, where he lost a by-election before becoming MP for Dundee.) Much of the Conservatives' success was down to male workers enfranchised in the 1867 and 1884 reform acts. A strain of militant Protestantism and hostility to Irish Catholic immigration ran through much of Lancashire's working class and Manchester was an Orange Order stronghold. Many of the city's businessmen, too, tended to be of a deferential and conservative mentality once free trade had been achieved.[10]

Trade unionism as it developed in Manchester was generally moderate, aside from a violent dispute in the brick trade in the 1860s in which workers fought, ultimately unsuccessfully, to resist mechanisation. Manchester and Salford Trades Council, formed in 1866, was neither radical nor revolutionary: William Wood and

Samuel Nicholson, its first secretary and president, were enthusiastic Conservatives, though most union leaders were Liberal. The trades council convened the first ever Trades Union Congress at the Mechanics' Institute on Princess Street in June 1868. New legislation in the 1870s ensured the legal position of unions, recognising them as corporations and entitling them to protection under the law. During the century's last quarter, unionisation spread to less skilled workers. Jewish workers in Manchester's tailoring sweatshops were among the first wave of 'new unionists'. Groups such as dockers, tram guards and drivers, shop assistants and railway workers also became unionised.[11]

Other forms of mutual self-help included friendly societies and the co-operative movement, boosted by the Rochdale Pioneers in 1844, a group of twenty-eight weavers and other tradesmen who banded together to open a shop selling food items they could not otherwise afford. Other towns followed suit. In 1863 the Co-operative Wholesale Society opened in Balloon Street, Manchester, providing goods bought in bulk to retail store members. Its buildings came to dominate the area around Victoria Station. The Manchester Unity of Oddfellows, a friendly society founded in 1810, became the largest organisation of its type in the country, with lodges throughout the empire.[12]

Despite its Conservative tendencies, Manchester was also important in the Labour Party's emergence. The Independent Labour Party was born at a meeting in St James Hall, Manchester, in May 1892 and formally became a national party a year later in Bradford. Manchester's first Independent Labour councillors were elected in 1894. An estimated 40,000 people gathered at Boggart Hole Clough, Blackley, in July 1896 to hear Keir Hardie, the ILP's first MP. Left-wing organisations came together nationally in 1900 to form the Labour Representation Committee to sponsor parliamentary candidates; it was renamed the Labour Party in 1906. In that year's general election, trade unionist G.D. Kelly overturned a large Conservative majority to take South-West Manchester, while future ministers J.R. Clynes and John Hodge won Manchester North-East and Gorton respectively. The more militant Social Democratic Federation engaged in direct action, including a 1905 demonstration against the Tory government's unemployment policy, in Albert Square, that led to police baton charges and arrests. There were similar disturbances in 1908.[13]

The most widely read socialist newspaper was the weekly *Clarion*, launched in Manchester in 1891 by Robert Blatchford, an ex-army sergeant turned journalist. It inspired the Clarion movement of social, recreational and political groups such as choirs and rambling and cycling clubs. The Clarion Café in Market Street held weekly debates. Stella Davies, a switchboard telephonist, described life in the Clarion Cycle Club: 'The Clarionets, as we called ourselves, met at appointed places on the outskirts of Manchester ... furnished with stacks of leaflets, pamphlets and the *Clarion* ... Arriving at some village in Derbyshire or Cheshire we held an open air meeting trying to catch the people as they came out of church or chapel. We were young and given to buffoonery ... we scrawled slogans in chalk on barns and farmhouse walls ... We sang "England arise, the long, long night is over" outside pubs and on village greens.'

The *Clarion* preached equality of the sexes: columnists included Eleanor Keeling and Julia Dawson. Dawson launched a 'Clarion Van' that toured towns and villages with three female speakers. *Clarion* supporters were divided in 1914, however, when Blatchford supported the First World War at a time when many readers vehemently opposed it. The paper survived until 1931 but was never the same.[14]

Manchester developed into a significant newspaper centre. The *Manchester Guardian*, founded in 1821, was for decades supportive of cotton manufacturers' interests, but under Charles Prestwich Scott, editor from 1872 to 1929 and owner from 1907 until his death in 1932, it became more radical, supporting Irish Home Rule, opposing the Boer War and becoming seen as the voice of progressive Liberalism, with a national and international reputation. Scott was born in Bath, but was the nephew of John Edward Taylor, the paper's founder. He cycled three miles to work each day from his villa in Fallowfield into his eighties. He never installed a telephone in his office and never used a typewriter, preferring to write leading articles in pen and ink. He was a Unitarian who ensured there was no coverage of horse-racing in his paper since he saw it as encouraging gambling. The Scott Trust was set up by his son and still owns Guardian Media Group.[15]

There were two other morning papers: the *Manchester Examiner* (seen as more radical than the *Guardian*), which suffered from an equivocal stance on Irish Home Rule in 1886 and folded ten years later; and the Tory *Manchester Courier*, which survived until 1916. In the evenings there was the *Manchester Evening News* (1868–), *Manchester Evening Mail* (1874–1902) and *Manchester Evening Chronicle* (1897–1963).

Edward Hulton, journeyman printer and horse-racing enthusiast, built a publishing empire at Withy Grove on the growing world of commercial sport, starting with a racing tip-sheet, the *Prophetic Bell*, which became the *Sporting Chronicle*. It was followed by *Athletic News* and the *Sunday Chronicle*. His son, also called Edward, founded the *Evening Chronicle, Daily Dispatch* and *Daily Sketch*. The *Daily Mail* began a northern edition in Manchester in 1900. By 1940, when the *Daily Telegraph* and *Sunday Times* began publishing in the city, seven dailies and four Sundays were printing locally and Withy Grove, with 3,000 staff, was probably Europe's biggest print hub. Since the 1950s, however, the 'second Fleet Street' has been wrecked by closures, technological changes and relocations, including that of the *Guardian*, which dropped 'Manchester' from its masthead in 1959 and moved editorial headquarters to London in 1964.[16]

Mancunians on average shared in better living standards as real wages rose, leading to improved nutrition and personal hygiene, but the city remained an unhealthy place. Irregular employment and economic insecurity did not help. Manchester's wide pool of casual workers in sectors such as transport and storage, construction, shops and pubs made it more like ports such as Liverpool and Hull than other inland cities such as Birmingham and Leeds.

Crude annual mortality rates did not improve until the 1880s despite efforts by Manchester and Salford Sanitary Association, formed in 1852 to promote health education and sanitary reform. Its ladies' branch can claim to have invented health visiting by deciding in 1862 to employ a respectable working woman to visit the homes of the poor and 'assist in promoting comfort, urging the importance of cleanliness, thrift and temperance on all occasions'. Isolation hospitals built from the 1870s helped to reduce infectious diseases.

Sewage disposal remained a problem, though this improved in the early twentieth century. The city needed even more water despite completion of Longdendale reservoir in 1851 and Thirlmere in 1894 (opposed among others by John Ruskin, who accused Manchester of 'plotting at last to steal for a profit the waters of Thirlmere and the clouds of Helvellyn'). It took the construction of a third reservoir, Haweswater, in the 1930s to meet the city's demands.

There were some improvements in housing, but the council, rather than building new homes itself, passed bye-laws for private construction. This led to 'bye-law streets' with small walled back-yards and alleyways, fashioning the 'Coronation Street' image of the North. The council created a small housing estate at Blackley in 1901 and stepped up the rate at which substandard homes were improved or 'reconditioned'.[17]

Manchester reformers played a leading part in campaigning for a rate-supported system of public elementary education culminating in the Education Act 1870, which created a national network by adding locally financed 'board schools' to existing voluntary provision. By 1899 free and compulsory attendance until age twelve was enforced by truant officers. The Education Act 1902 introduced state secondary schools and created local education authorities to administer both levels.

Lobbying had begun in 1847 by the Lancashire (later National) Public Schools Association, whose members included Richard Cobden,

Jacob Bright and Samuel Lucas (John Bright's younger brother and brother-in-law respectively). It campaigned for a non-sectarian system. Its secular approach was opposed by a committee formed by Anglican and Methodist ministers. The Manchester Education Aid Society, a charity, was formed in 1864 in response to articles in the *Manchester Guardian* by businessman Edward Brotherton. He described at first hand children's impoverished lives, but died two years later from an infection contracted on one of his slum visits. The society's chief work was to pay poor children's school fees, but it acknowledged that a voluntary approach was inadequate. Manchester's first board school opened in Vine Street, Hulme, in 1874.[18]

It was a struggle to get poor children to attend school instead of engaging in street trading or begging. In 1881, the school board asked the city council to stop using salt to thaw snow in the street since 'many thousands of young children, a large proportion of whom are poorly shod and some actually bare foot, are compelled to traverse the streets four times a day to and from school … [in] an intensely freezing mixture'.[19]

One problem for Manchester was the emergence of 'scuttlers', or territorial fighting gangs – typically lads aged fourteen to eighteen – in the slums of central Manchester as well as Bradford, Gorton, Openshaw and Salford. These began in the early 1870s and continued sporadically for thirty years. They went by names such as the Bengal Tigers from the cluster of streets and courts off Bengal Street in Ancoats and the Meadow Lads from Angel Meadow. Sometimes viewed as the first modern youth cult, they wore distinctive clothes: tilted caps peaking down over one eye, a silk scarf tied around their necks, fringed hair, ornate belt buckles and bell-bottom trousers. Their reign of terror peaked in the 1890s and then declined, aided by factors such as slum clearances and the growth of lads' clubs.[20]

A hero of the age was Salford's Mark Addy (1838–90), who over his lifetime saved more than fifty people from drowning in the River Irwell and was awarded the Albert Medal by Queen Victoria for his 'gallantry and daring'. He lived in a house on the riverbank and made his first rescue at age thirteen, before he had learned to swim, by wading in and pulling out a friend who had fallen in. On a later occasion he left his Christmas dinner and jumped into icy water to rescue a woman who was trying to drown herself. In his final rescue, he saved a little boy who had fallen into a stretch of water heavily polluted with sewage, after which Addy contracted tuberculosis and died.[21]

Literacy appears to have declined in Lancashire's cotton district during the Industrial Revolution since factory owners had little use for it. It has been estimated that in the 1830s only 36 per cent of Manchester's population was literate, giving impetus to the need for wider education and public libraries. The free library founded at Campfield in 1852 moved to the old town hall building on King Street in 1877. Branch libraries opened in residential districts such as Hulme, Ancoats and Ardwick. By 1895, the city had eleven branch libraries. The system was so popular that Sunday opening was controversially adopted in 1878. There were separate reading rooms for boys (but none for girls). Reading rooms were popular as warm places in winter.[22]

Public libraries were part of a broader expansion of municipal services and enterprise. Manchester had had a municipal gas supply since 1823. The corporation developed markets and abattoirs; the principal markets at Smithfield, east of Shudehill, became the largest outside London. In 1864 the council decided to build a new town hall on a grand scale, a gesture of faith in the future despite the cotton famine. It took almost ten years to erect the building in Albert Square at a cost approaching £1 million, described at its opening as 'unequalled for size, completeness and adaptability for its purpose among the municipal buildings of Europe'. It was designed by Alfred Waterhouse, a Liverpool-born Quaker, and mixes elements of English medieval and Venetian Gothic styles. It was controversial: many prominent citizens wanted a more Gothic design, with more turrets and pitched roofs. Waterhouse also designed Manchester Assize Courts, Strangeways Prison and the University of Manchester, along with London's Natural History Museum and Liverpool

University's Victoria building. His love of red brick and terracotta led to him being nicknamed 'Slaughterhouse Waterhouse'. One of his brothers, Edwin, was an accountant who was the Waterhouse in what is now PricewaterhouseCoopers.

Construction of the town hall took almost ten years, with errors and cost overruns. Queen Victoria declined to attend the opening, supposedly because she was in mourning for Prince Albert, although Tories had managed to keep Peterloo out of Ford Madox Brown's murals, for fear of offending her. It was opened in 1877 by Abel Heywood, the mayor who had championed the project.[23] Some suspected the queen had refused because of Heywood's radical past or the fact that a statue of Oliver Cromwell had been erected in the city.

Heywood (1810–93), the son of a poor family from Prestwich, began work for a manufacturer aged nine and later became a successful newsagent, bookseller and publisher. A radical who fought for cheap newspapers for the working class, he refused to pay stamp duty intended to suppress mass publishing and spent four months in Salford New Bailey prison after refusing to pay a £54 fine. Heywood was elected a police commissioner in 1836 and a councillor in 1843. For forty-seven years he chaired the paving, sewering and highways committee; he was a motive force in Manchester's waterworks and sewerage building programme and later in the development of its tramway system. His Oldham Street business became the country's largest wholesale news agency as well as a bookshop and publishing house, with a subsidiary interest in paper-making. He pioneered mass distribution of books, from 'penny dreadfuls' to Dickens novels. He also had a 'penny reading room' open from 6am to 10pm. The town hall's clock bell, *Great Abel*, was named after him and he was given the freedom of the city in 1891.[24]

The corporation began supplying electricity in the 1890s, the largest municipal undertaking in England. It bought out the private tramway company and replaced horse trams with electric trams. By the start of the twentieth century, council trading committees covered water, gas, electricity, transport and markets. Even if not as pioneering as Birmingham, it was one of the most extensive civic authorities ever known.

The council bought Heaton Park from the Earl of Wilton in 1902 and acquired Platt Fields in 1907. The borough's boundaries widened as neighbouring authorities struggled to make needed investments in sewerage, which was welcomed by the council because its population was declining from 1871. As well as Manchester, the original borough in 1838 comprised Chorlton-on-Medlock, Hulme, Ardwick, Beswick and Cheetham. In 1885 Harpurhey, Bradford and Rusholme were added, followed by Blackley, Moston, Crumpsall, Newton Heath, Openshaw, Kirkmanshulme and West Gorton in 1890. In 1904 Withington, Didsbury and Chorlton-cum-Hardy were absorbed, followed a little later by Moss Side and Burnage. Levenshulme and Gorton were added in 1909. The last phase of expansion came with the acquisition of Wythenshawe in 1931. Manchester was 'a great octopus stretching out its "fangs" [*sic*] in every direction to take in all the tit-bits around the city,' said some Gorton residents.[25]

Manchester Ship Canal was launched initially as a private venture and rescued by the council when it stood on the brink of failure. The opening of the Liverpool–Manchester railway in 1830 had brought the two towns within less than two hours' journey of each other but, as the century progressed, Manchester's merchants complained about excessive charges levied by Liverpool's docks. Grandiose ideas for linking Manchester directly to the sea had been mooted for a while and the 1870s slump gave new impetus. An engineer called Daniel Adamson drove the scheme forward, facing intense opposition from railway companies and Liverpool port interests. After an Act of Parliament was passed in 1885, he became chairman of the Manchester Ship Canal Company. Fund-raising was slow, however, and Adamson was replaced by Lord Egerton, a relative of the Bridgewater Canal's creator. Manchester City Council rescued the project with loans of £5 million in 1891–2, becoming the majority interest on the board.[26]

The thirty-six-mile waterway, wide enough for ocean-going vessels and linking Manchester to the Mersey estuary, was opened by Queen Victoria in 1894. Chief engineer was Edward Leader Williams and the canal was a technical marvel. It was as deep as the Suez Canal, five railway lines had to be raised above it, and the tidal River Gowy was carried underneath it in iron siphons. Joseph Brindley's Barton aqueduct was replaced by the Barton Swing Aqueduct, which rotated a huge trough of water. The main docks were on the Salford side, with others at Trafford Wharf and Pomona. The cost had soared from a projected £8.4 million to £14.4 million and some ordinary investors did not see a return until 1915. Trade was slow at first, though eventually it enabled the Port of Manchester to become Britain's third-busiest port. Tonnage on the canal peaked in 1958 and declined after containerisation made it more difficult to use.

Industry grew along its banks, notably Trafford Park (also Partington, which became a major coal-exporting port). A local baronet, Sir Humphrey de Trafford, sold his estate to Ernest Hooley, an opportunistic Nottingham company promoter (and later fraudster), while Manchester Corporation dithered over whether to buy it. Hooley planned to build grand villas and a racecourse, but changed his mind and opted for an industrial estate. It attracted engineering, chemicals and food-processing firms, including leading American businesses starting with Westinghouse, which built Europe's largest factory complex there. Henry Ford established his first European assembly plant at Trafford Park in 1911, making the Model T car initially from parts imported from the US. By 1903, Trafford Park employed 12,000 people. That reached 40,000 by the 1930s and at its peak in 1945 an estimated 75,000 worked there.[27]

Manchester looked in fair shape, at least outwardly, as it entered the twentieth century. Commerce, industry and transport communications were linchpins of its economy. While the central area's population was declining, that of the wider Manchester region had grown from an estimated 322,000 in 1801 to just over 1 million by

1851 and 2.1 million by 1901.[28] The quality of life was getting better, people were becoming healthier and the housing stock was starting to improve, though stark inequalities remained.

Cultural life was enhanced in 1899 when Enriqueta Rylands opened the neo-Gothic John Rylands Library on Deansgate in memory of her husband, who died in 1888. John Rylands, a devoutly Christian entrepreneur and philanthropist, was Manchester's greatest merchant-manufacturer during cotton's golden age; he became the industry's largest manufacturer as well as the city's first multi-millionaire. He was born near St Helens and worked alongside his father and two brothers in Rylands and Sons, established in 1819. Later, as sole proprietor, he was employing 12,000 people in seventeen mills by 1875. The firm would endure until 1989. A Congregationalist with Baptist leanings, Rylands sought to foster unity between Christian denominations. He built his Italianate home, Longford Hall in Stretford, now sadly demolished. Charitable activity included provision for orphans, widows and the aged poor.

Enriqueta, born in Havana, Cuba, had been a companion to his second wife and married John after she died. She aimed to commemorate John, particularly in his commitment to Bible study. The library took ten years to build and cost three times the original estimate. Innovative features included a ventilation system incorporated in internal columns, aimed at improving book preservation; it meant during the recent Covid pandemic that the old library was deemed a safer place to work than the modern extension attached to it. The library was not an instant success: there was a dearth of readers in the early months and Enriqueta fell out with the first librarian. Eventually, based on Enriqueta's purchase of Earl Spencer's library and an important collection of manuscripts, it became one of the world's great libraries. Built on the site of a slum, it stimulated local improvements and helped to make Deansgate a main civic thoroughfare. Enriqueta was awarded the freedom of Manchester, the first woman to be so honoured. The library became part of the University of Manchester in 1972.[29]

Manchester had become a major shopping centre. Entrepreneur David Lewis, who already ran a department store in Liverpool, opened a large new store in Manchester's Market Street in 1877 (other Lewis's branches later opened in Sheffield and Birmingham). His retail empire was built on low profit margins and high turnover, using aggressive advertising and bargain sales to capture the rising wages of the working and lower-middle classes. Lewis's boasted the biggest soda fountain in the empire and once, to replicate Venice, flooded the sub-basement and invited customers to sail on gondolas. Kendal Milne, a local firm, aimed at wealthier clientele. It began as Kendal, Milne and Faulkner when three men bought a shopping bazaar in Deansgate, originally opened in 1796, from S. & J. Watts. They ran a furniture and drapery business from two stores on opposite sides of Deansgate, catering for 'the elite of society in town and country'.[30]

Both Lewis's and Kendal Milne combined production with retail. Lewis's building included workshops employing 300 tailors and almost as many others making boots and shoes to sell to customers. Kendal Milne employed cabinet makers, upholsterers, general house furnishers and drapery warehousemen in a seven-storey building behind its furniture store. (In 1872 Ellen Edwards, a former assistant, horsewhipped her fiancé James Wishart in Kendal's, where both had worked in the dress department, after he accused her of cheating.[31]) Lewis's closed in 2001 and is now a Primark. Kendal's was renamed House of Fraser Manchester in 2005. The upmarket Affleck & Brown, founded by Robert Affleck and John Brown, opened in the 1860s in the elegant Smithfield building at the corner of Oldham Street and Church Street, advertising itself as a draper and house furnisher. It was taken over by Debenhams in 1950, became home to British Home Stores for a time from the 1960s and became one of the first city-centre buildings to be converted into flats in 1996 by Urban Splash.

Other fashionable retailers were located around St Ann's Square, Exchange Street and lower King Street. Barton Arcade, between

Deansgate and St Ann's Square, a cast-iron and glass shopping arcade inspired by London's Crystal Palace, opened in 1871 and is the only survivor of three such arcades built in Manchester. Ashton-born tea merchant Arthur Brooke opened his first shop in 1869 in a prime location at 29 Market Street, selling only tea, coffee and sugar. He added the name 'Bond' to his shop sign for alliterative effect even though no Bond existed, saying that it represented his bond of trust with customers. He later made a fortune selling packaged, blended tea wholesale to retail grocers and bought a country estate in Surrey.

William Timpson from Rothwell, West Yorkshire, in 1869 opened a boot and shoe shop at 97 Oldham Street, Manchester, which proved a great success. By the turn of the century there were fourteen Timpson shops and by 1939 the company owned 189 shoe shops around the country. In 1983 managing director John Timpson, great-grandson of William, bought back control of the family business from Hanson Trust for £42 million. Timpson Group acquired other brands such as Johnsons the Cleaners, and Snappy Snaps, and now has more than 2,000 stores. It is based in Wythenshawe and owned by Sir John, chairman, and his son James, chief executive. James pioneered recruitment of ex-offenders, who now number more than 600, over 10 per cent of the company's workforce.[32]

Britain was falling behind international rivals in industrial innovation, but Manchester could boast some achievements. Henry Royce had his famous meeting with Charles Rolls in 1904, leading to the creation of Rolls-Royce. In the 1910 London to Manchester air race, the £10,000 prize was won by Frenchman Louis Paulhan, but Stretford-born John Alcock and navigator Arthur Whitten Brown, from Glasgow, piloted the first non-stop transatlantic flight in 1919. Alliott Verdon Roe founded the Avro aircraft company in 1910. After experimenting with model aeroplanes, he had flown a full-size aeroplane at Brooklands in Surrey and became the first Englishman to fly an all-British machine, a triplane, on Walthamstow marshes. Avro's most popular model, the 504, became the backbone of allied flying training during the First World War. Thus he proved wrong the *Manchester Guardian*, which said in a leader dated 11 September 1908: 'We cannot understand to what practical use a flying machine that is heavier than air can be put.' Avro was bought by Crossley Motors in 1920 and by Armstrong Siddeley in 1928; it became a subsidiary of Hawker Siddeley in 1935. The Avro Lancaster became one of the Second World War's leading bombers and the delta-wing Avro Vulcan a stalwart of the Cold War.[33]

The Edwardian era saw peace and relative prosperity, but it also brought rapid, disconcerting changes in science, technology, society and politics. Robert Roberts, in *The Classic Slum* (1971), an account of his upbringing in Edwardian Salford, portrayed both the devastating effects of poverty and the complex status distinctions of working-class life. There was a dramatic increase in industrial conflict from 1908 as workers demanded their share of increased prosperity. A strike by dock workers and carters in Manchester in 1911 turned violent as police were stoned when they tried to escort lorries from a goods yard. A brick was hurled through the chief constable's carriage window as he drove down Deansgate.[34]

The years 1870 to 1914 were an Indian summer for Lancashire's cotton industry, which benefited from a large increase in global trade. Its efforts were aided by a worldwide network of telegraph cables created under the guidance of John Pender, a Scots-born Manchester textile merchant who presided over companies operating more than 73,000 nautical miles of cable, which later became Cable & Wireless. There were danger signs, however. India, Brazil and Japan started to build their own cotton textile industries and Britain was slow to adopt technological developments from America. In 1913 Lancashire supplied two-thirds of world trade in cotton cloth. People were aware of growing competition, though few imagined Britain's leading position to be precarious. Manchester had weathered economic downturns before. The 1920s and 1930s, however, were to prove a rude awakening.[35]

10

VOTES FOR WOMEN

On the evening of 13 October 1905, suffragettes Christabel Pankhurst and Annie Kenney attended a Liberal Party meeting at Manchester's Free Trade Hall. After Sir Edward Grey – soon to be foreign secretary – ended his speech with no mention of women's suffrage, Annie asked: 'Will the Liberal government give women the vote?' No answer was given, so Christabel unfurled a banner saying 'Votes for women' and enquired again, causing uproar. The chief constable asked them to put their question in writing to be handed to Sir Edward, but still no reply. Annie stood on her chair and asked again. The audience howled as stewards dragged the women outside, where Christabel deliberately committed the offence of spitting at a policeman in order to be arrested. Christabel and Annie refused to pay fines and were imprisoned respectively for one week and three days.[1]

'We shall sleep in prison tonight,' Christabel had earlier told her mother Emmeline, who had formed the Women's Social and Political Union (WSPU), an all-female organisation dedicated to 'deeds, not words', in 1903. Frustrated by lack of progress, Christabel embarked on a more confrontational course aimed at attracting publicity to their cause. On release, a packed welcome for the ex-prisoners was held at the Free Trade Hall, organised by the Manchester central branch of the Independent Labour Party. Songs of liberty were sung and Keir Hardie, soon to be the new Labour Party's first parliamentary leader, condemned the 'brutal and unjustifiable' treatment the two had received.

It was a seminal moment for Manchester's important role in the movement for women's rights, which can be traced back to Mary Fildes' beating by constables at Peterloo. Fildes, president of Manchester Female Reform Society, intended to hand Henry Hunt a banner and ask him to read out an address in which the female reformers 'as wives, mothers, daughters ... come forward in support of the sacred cause of liberty – a cause in which their husbands, their fathers, and their sons, have embarked the last hope of suffering humanity'.[2] She did not (at least publicly) advocate votes for women, which was not yet on the agenda, but like most female reformers of that time she supported a vote for all adult male householders, which could be exercised in the whole family's interest.

Charitable work was one of the few paths into public service for middle-class women in the nineteenth century. Wives and daughters of Manchester industrialists were prominent in campaigns against the slave trade and then slavery itself, acquiring experience in pamphlet writing, canvassing, fund-raising and petitioning that they later used in support of female suffrage. A Manchester Ladies Anti-Slavery Society was formed in 1847. One founder, Rebecca Moore, became the first female delegate to a British anti-slavery conference. She was also a member of the executive committee of the Manchester Society for Women's Suffrage, created in the 1860s.[3]

Its first secretary was Elizabeth Wolstenholme (1833–1913), daughter of a Methodist minister in Eccles. Whereas her older brother Joseph became a fellow in mathematics at Cambridge University, Elizabeth received only two years of formal education at the Moravian School, Fulneck, near Leeds. After further self-education, she became headmistress of a private girls' school at Boothstown, near Worsley. She began a lifetime career campaigning for women's rights. Sylvia Pankhurst, Christabel's sister, recalled her in later years as a 'tiny Jenny-wren of a woman, with bright, bird-like eyes, and a little face, child-like in its merriment and its pathos, which even in extreme old age retained the winning graces of youth'. Wolstenholme established the Manchester Board of Schoolmistresses to support women teachers and was active in the North of England Council for the Promotion of the Education of Women. She was among those who successfully pressed for lectures and higher exams for women that led to the foundation of Newnham College, Cambridge.[4]

Pressure for female emancipation grew. Philosopher John Stuart Mill, in campaigning successfully to be MP for Westminster in 1865, promised to pursue women's suffrage in a reform bill on condition that a petition was raised to support it. To that end, Wolstenholme established her women's suffrage committee in Manchester with support from local radical Liberals including Jacob Bright MP and his wife Ursula and a young lawyer, Richard Pankhurst. A national network of such societies was created.

The failure of the Reform Act 1867 to enfranchise women was a spur to further campaigning. In that year Wolstenholme moved to a new school at Moody Hall, Congleton, and handed secretaryship of the Manchester Society for Women's Suffrage to Lydia Becker. Wolstenholme later focused on issues such as campaigning to end coverture, whereby a woman's legal rights were subsumed by her husband's on marriage. She also joined her friend Josephine Butler in campaigning to repeal the Contagious Diseases Acts, legislation that attempted to control venereal diseases, particularly in the army and navy, through the forced medical examination of women judged to be prostitutes.

There was controversy over Wolstenholme's private life. A secular-ist and freethinker, after moving to London she entered a free union with a former Congleton neighbour, Ben Elmy, a teacher turned silk crape manufacturer and sometime vice-president of the National Secular Society. Though there appears to have been some kind of informal wedding ceremony, their marriage was not recognised under English law. When, some months later, her pregnancy became evident, the couple were urged in the interests of the women's movement to formalise their union. They did so a few months before their son's birth. When Wolstenholme sought to return to public life, she encountered opposition from moderate suffragists, notably Becker and Millicent Garrett Fawcett. However, campaigning by Wolstenholme and Ursula Bright helped to achieve the Married Women's Property Act 1882. It amended coverture and restored married women's legal identities, including the right to sue and be sued; they became liable for their own debts and able to hold stock in their own names.

Lydia Becker (1827–90) was to become the suffragist movement's leading strategist. She was born in Cooper Street, Manchester, the eldest of a chemical manufacturer's fifteen children. Her grandfather, who had arrived from Germany in the late 1790s, began the family business supplying dyes and other chemicals to the cotton industry. Like many girls, Becker was educated at home. She was a keen botanist and astronomer who won a gold medal from the Horticultural Society of South Kensington and corresponded with Charles Darwin. In Manchester she started a Ladies' Literary Society for the study of science, providing free lectures, which was only modestly successful.[5]

A National Society for Women's Suffrage was formed at Becker's instigation. In 1867 Becker heard that a widowed shop owner, Lilly Maxwell, had mistakenly appeared on the register of voters in Manchester. Spotting a chance for publicity, Becker escorted her to the polling station, where she cast her vote. Becker urged other female heads of households to apply to appear on electoral rolls, but the High Court closed the loophole in a test case.

Becker, who never married, undertook onerous lecture tours on women's votes, the position of wives, female education and rights at work at a time when it was thought unseemly for women to speak in public. Despite being lampooned in the popular press for her stout appearance, flat face and wire-rimmed spectacles, she gained recognition as the movement's driving force. One local periodical condescendingly dubbed her 'a public man of whom Manchester has reason to be proud'.[6]

An amendment by Jacob Bright to the Municipal Corporations Act in 1869 gave women ratepayers the vote in council elections on the same basis as men. The Education Act 1870 not only allowed women to vote in elections for new school boards; they were also able to stand as candidates. Becker was among those elected to Manchester's first school board in that year and retained her seat until she died in 1890. She worked particularly for provision of educational facilities for girls, for the welfare of children in ragged schools and to improve the position of women teachers. She demanded equality for girls and boys in the curriculum. 'Every boy in Manchester,' she insisted, 'should be taught to darn his own socks and cook his own chops.'[7]

Becker co-founded the influential *Women's Suffrage Journal* and served as its editor and chief contributor. There were divisions within the movement, however, notably over proposals to exclude married women from the franchise, an exclusion that Becker came to support on the grounds that this might be more acceptable to opponents. Many northern radical suffragists disagreed. Becker established a base in London, becoming secretary of the central committee of the National Society for Women's Suffrage in 1881 and subsequently its parliamentary agent. Failure to achieve women's suffrage in the Reform Act 1884 led to a period of retrenchment and reorganisation in the movement. Unremitting work eventually told on Becker's health and she died of diphtheria while 'taking the waters' at Geneva.

The suffrage movement was in the doldrums after the 1884 failure, but a younger generation came along in the 1890s. Esther Roper (1868–1938), one of the first female graduates of Manchester Victoria University, became secretary of the Manchester National Society for Women's Suffrage. She organised campaigns directed at working women, who were leafleted at factory gates and invited to suffrage meetings. Large numbers of women worked in Lancashire cotton mills and many were already involved in trade unions: the Women's Co-operative Guild, formed in 1883, held a grand festival in Manchester in 1892 and the Women's Trade Union League organised a thousand-strong meeting in the city in 1893.

Roper was aided by Eva Gore-Booth (1870–1926), younger sister of the Irish nationalist Constance, Countess Markievicz. The two met in Italy and became lifelong friends. Gore-Booth left Ireland and moved into Esther and Reginald Roper's Manchester home. She became co-secretary of the Manchester and Salford Women's Trade Union Council. After 1900 a growing number of working-class women linked the labour movement's campaigns, such as for equal pay and child benefit, with calls for electoral reform.[8]

Women who served on the school board after Becker included Rachel Scott, wife of the *Manchester Guardian* editor, and Mary Dendy, who persuaded the board to provide special schools for 'mentally defective' pupils. The Poor Law Union found itself in need of women's expertise to help its workhouses cope with a growing proportion of the chronically sick, mentally infirm, the aged and also orphan children. Florence Nightingale advised Chorlton (South Manchester) Board of Guardians on the design of its new workhouse at Withington (the building later became Withington Hospital and is now flats). A change in the franchise for election to boards of guardians in 1894 led women to seek office. Emmeline Pankhurst was elected to the Chorlton board and Hannah Mitchell (1872–1956), a working-class feminist, to the Ashton-under-Lyne board.[9]

In education, a Manchester Society for Promoting the Education of Women had been formed in 1867. In 1873 Manchester High School for Girls was established, a counterpart to Manchester Grammar School. Progress in admitting women to Manchester Victoria University was slow, but the first graduated in 1887. When the university became independent of its Leeds and Liverpool counterparts in 1903, two female graduates, Alice Crompton and Mary Tout, joined its governing body. Crompton, a niece of Lydia Becker, had in 1898 become joint warden of the Manchester University Settlement, housed in Ancoats Hall with Ancoats Art Museum. It ran talks, concerts and visits for residents of Ancoats, a populous industrial suburb. Active in the settlement were women who also became prominent in female suffrage campaigns, including Christabel Pankhurst, Roper, Gore-Booth and Teresa Billington. Christabel and Esther Roper started a drama club, the Elizabethan Society, which encouraged factory girls to read Shakespeare aloud and take part in productions of his plays.

Emmeline Goulden (later Pankhurst, 1858–1928) was born in Moss Side to a well-off manufacturing and Liberal family. Her paternal grandfather had been at Peterloo. Despite her parents' support for female suffrage, they expected their daughters to avoid paid work and become homemakers. One evening, feigning sleep, she heard her father say: 'What a pity she wasn't born a lad.' At age fourteen she became 'a conscious and confirmed suffragist' after hearing Lydia Becker speak. Later she began to work for the suffrage movement and married radical barrister Richard Pankhurst, twenty years her senior. Despite having five children in ten years, she remained politically active. After a spell in London they returned to Manchester. Both Richard and Emmeline were members of the newly formed Independent Labour Party.[11]

Richard's unexpected death in 1898 left the family in straitened circumstances. They had to move from their Victoria Park villa to a smaller house in Nelson Street, Rusholme (now a museum, the Pankhurst Centre). Emmeline took a paid job as a registrar. Five years after Richard's death, a hall was opened in his memory in Salford; his family were astonished to hear that women were not permitted to join the ILP branch that that would use it as its headquarters. Emmeline declared that her time in the socialist movement had been wasted and decided to form a new women's organisation. On 10 October 1903 she invited to her home some wives of ILP men and formed the WSPU to campaign for votes for women on the same terms as men.

At first, the WSPU engaged in peaceful activities such as campaigning at trade union meetings, street demonstrations and petitions to parliament. Christabel, a law student and her mother's eldest and favourite child, thought a more militant approach was needed – hence the heckling of Sir Edward Grey. Emmeline offered to pay the fines, which Christabel refused. Emmeline was impressed by extensive newspaper coverage that ensued, so heckling of politicians became a strategy in which innumerable suffragettes engaged. Her second child Sylvia, training as an artist, gave up her studies in 1906 to devote herself to the suffrage campaign. In that year Sylvia was jailed for the first time after protesting in court at a trial in which women had not been allowed to speak in their own defence. Youngest daughter Adela spent a month in Holloway jail following a riot at the House of Commons in 1906, after which she left teaching to work full-time for the WSPU. In that year the WSPU moved its headquarters to London, thinking that militant tactics there would get more newspaper coverage.[12]

In Manchester, Margaret Ashton (1856–1937) offered a more moderate tone as president of the North of England Society for Women's Suffrage, though she resigned from the Liberal Party because of the Liberal government's refusal to legislate on votes for women. Her father Thomas Ashton, a wealthy cotton manufacturer in Hyde, was a leading Liberal and Unitarian. In 1908 she became the first woman elected to Manchester Corporation, sitting for Withington. As councillor she campaigned to improve factory girls' wages and conditions and raise the age of employment of children. A fall in Manchester's notoriously high mortality rate is attributed in part to her health reforms, especially support for municipal mother and baby clinics and introduction of free milk for young children and nursing mothers. In 1914, she and paediatrician Catherine Chisholm founded Manchester Babies Hospital, staffed entirely by women. A constitutional suffragist, she did not approve of the WSPU's militant tactics. Politically, she gradually moved to the left, encouraged by her view that women would obtain the vote only with the support of the Labour Party, which she joined in 1913.[13]

Tensions within the Pankhurst family grew in 1907. Christabel, organising secretary and main policymaker, had declared that the WSPU would oppose not only all Liberal and Conservative parliamentary candidates, but also be independent of Labour men. While Emmeline agreed, Sylvia and Adela did not. Emmeline and Christabel resigned from the ILP, unhappy about socialists' lukewarm attitude towards women's suffrage: the Labour Party opposed extending the franchise to women if owning property remained a qualification for voting. Rumours of a WSPU coup emerged amid complaints about Emmeline and Christabel's autocratic leadership style. Emmeline rushed back to headquarters, abolished the democratic constitution, cancelled the annual conference and invited members to support her. The majority agreed, but dissenters, including Teresa Billington and Charlotte Despard, formed another militant organisation, later called the Women's Freedom League.

Emmeline was jailed for the first time in February 1908 when she tried to enter Parliament to deliver a protest resolution and was arrested for obstruction. She was sentenced to six weeks in prison. Between 1908 and 1914 she undertook twelve hunger strikes and went to prison fourteen times. WSPU members began hunger strikes in a bid to be granted political offender status. When the government responded with forcible feeding, Emmeline condemned it for violating and torturing women's exhausted and starved bodies.

Annie Kenney (1879–1953) was jailed thirteen times and repeatedly force-fed. Born in Springhead, Saddleworth, she was the fifth of twelve children and started working in cotton mills at age ten. She started as a 'half-timer' spending mornings in the mill and afternoons at school. As a weaver's assistant or 'tenter', she fitted bobbins and attended to strands of thread when they broke. One finger was ripped off by a spinning bobbin. She was attracted to the movement when she heard Teresa Billington and Christabel Pankhurst address

Oldham Trades Council. Christabel became her heroine. It was a close relationship, bringing comfort to Kenney after her mother had died a few months before; it is unclear whether she and Christabel were ever lovers.

To the Pankhursts she was particularly valuable as a symbol of working-class support for militancy, especially as many working-class women backed non-militant suffragists. She became the WSPU leadership's right-hand woman whenever action was required. She once said she had 'never known class distinction and class prejudice stand in the way of my advancement, whereas the sex barrier meets me at every turn'. When Christabel fled to Paris to avoid arrest in 1912, Kenney was put in charge of the WSPU in London. She had long-term health problems that may have been linked to hunger strikes. In 1999, Oldham Council erected a blue plaque in her honour at Lees Brook Mill near Oldham, where Kenney had started work. In 2018 a statue, funded by public subscription, was unveiled in front of Oldham's Old Town Hall.[14]

In 1910 the WSPU began smashing shop windows. Emmeline and two other women broke four of prime minister Herbert Asquith's windows, for which she was sentenced to two months in prison. By 1913 the WSPU was increasingly driven underground as it set fire to pillar boxes, attacked art treasures, cut telegraph and telephone wires and damaged golf courses. In Manchester, three members – Lillian Forrester, Annie Briggs and Evelyn Manesta – smashed the glass of several paintings in the City Art Gallery, using a hammer decorated with the WSPU's purple and green ribbons and leaving a card proclaiming 'No Forcible Feeding'. Suffragettes were blamed for burning down Rusholme Exhibition Hall and bombing the greenhouse in Alexandra Park.[15]

One curiosity is that Emmeline's penchant for wearing ostrich feathers in her hats arguably put her at variance with another female cause – the (Royal) Society for the Protection of Birds, co-founded in embryo in 1889 by Emily Williamson, a solicitor's wife, at her home in Didsbury, because she was angry about being barred from the all-male British Ornithologists' Union. This all-female group aimed to discourage women from wearing feathers on dresses and hats; they objected not only to destruction of bird populations that resulted from demand for feathers, but also to cruelty involved in the trade. In fact, ostriches were excepted because their feathers could be plucked painlessly. But Pankhurst, in encouraging suffragettes to dress elegantly to further their cause, boosted feather-wearing: suffrage rallies were a forest of feathers. Williamson's group combined with another from Croydon and the society was incorporated by royal charter in 1904.[16]

Moderate suffragists increasingly spoke out against the militants. Fawcett said hunger strikes were publicity stunts and that militant activists were 'the chief obstacles in the way of the success of the suffrage movement in the House of Commons'.[17] Several prominent members left the WSPU and Emmeline's relations with Sylvia and Adela, both socialists, became more strained. Sylvia had established a new organisation, the East London Federation of Suffragettes. Emmeline told her it must be separate from the WSPU, since it was allied with the Labour Party. Adela had left the WSPU in 1911. Emmeline paid her to move to Australia and they never saw one another again.[18]

When the First World War broke out, all imprisoned suffragettes were released unconditionally. Emmeline suspended militant action and asked followers to support the war effort, arguing that it would be pointless to fight for the vote without a country to vote in. Her rift with Sylvia and Adela, committed pacifists, deepened. Margaret Ashton and Hannah Mitchell were also both pacifists. Ashton's pacifism made her unpopular on the corporation and in her own family; she was branded 'pro-German' and ousted from the corporation in 1921. A portrait by Henry Lamb to commemorate her seventieth birthday was refused by Manchester City Art Gallery as a protest against her pacifist views.

In 1918, the Representation of the People Act removed property restrictions on men's suffrage and granted the vote to women over thirty who met minimum property qualifications. Emmeline and

Christabel reinvented the WSPU as the Women's Party, campaigning for equal marriage laws, equal pay for equal work and equal job opportunities. Christabel narrowly failed to get elected to Parliament, after which the Women's Party withered. Emmeline agreed in the 1920s to stand as a Conservative parliamentary candidate, impressed by the way prime minister Stanley Baldwin had handled the 1926 general strike. She said she wanted to 'strengthen the British Empire and draw closer together its lands and people'. She may also have seen the Conservatives as the best route to secure votes for more women. In 1928, the year she died, the Conservative government passed an act extending the franchise to all persons over twenty-one on equal terms.[19]

Christabel, for some years drawn to Christianity, became a Second Adventist and went to California, preaching the second coming. Sylvia Pankhurst caused a scandal by living openly with an Italian anarchist and having his son, whom she named Richard, out of wedlock, for which her mother refused to have anything more to do with her. In later life she became friend and adviser to Ethiopian Emperor, Haile Selassie. She and her son moved to Addis Ababa in 1956, where she died four years later. Adela was a founder of the Communist Party of Australia, but became disillusioned and founded an anti-communist organisation. In 1941 she was co-founder of the right-wing Australia First movement. In 1942 she was interned after advocating peace with Japan.

Historians differ about whether Emmeline's militancy helped or hurt the suffrage movement. Some believe extension of the franchise in 1918 became possible because public hostility to pre-war militant tactics had faded, while others think politicians made the concession to avoid any resurgence of militancy. There is general agreement, however, that her campaigns raised public awareness. In 2016, after a vote, Emmeline was chosen as the subject for the first female statue to be erected in Manchester city centre since Queen Victoria.

11

POPULAR CULTURE

Manchester is 'a city that thinks a table is for dancing on', goes the saying, sometimes attributed to Bolton-born broadcaster Mark Radcliffe.[1] The city that worked hard learned to play hard too. While life remained tough for many, disposable incomes rose in the later nineteenth century and people began to get some free time. That led to growth in popular entertainment and leisure, including music halls, variety theatres, pleasure gardens, shopping, excursions to the seaside or the Lake District. Some of this activity was raucous enough to provoke moral and religious panic, but there were also new parks, libraries and museums.

With due respect to the Hallé Orchestra, the serious theatre of Annie Horniman and others, and the present-day Manchester International Festival, the city has for most of its history been best known for popular culture – comedians, clubs, variety stars, pop musicians, footballers (see also Chapter 13 on sport and Chapter 15 on music). This is viewed as having been shaped by hardship and openness to new influences. 'Out of the trauma of the city comes energy,' wrote disc jockey and author Dave Haslam. 'Maybe if Manchester was less of a shit-hole then creativity in the city would die.'[2]

Rural dwellers brought traditional pastimes when they moved to the cities, notably fairs and wakes. The *Manchester Herald* reported in 1792 how thousands thronged the Easter Monday fair at Knott Mill to listen to the 'droll concert of whistles, halfpenny trumpets and threepenny drums'. Whit Week in May or June became the great Manchester holiday, with race meetings at Kersal Moor in Salford, a fair, Punch and Judy shows, music, dancing and drinking. 'Beside the fair and the races, plays, concerts, assemblies, and that cruel unmanly sport, cock fighting, make out the amusements of the week. Business is nearly at a stand; and Pleasure reigns with almost Parisian despotism,' wrote an observer.[3]

Churches sought to reclaim Whitsun from the hedonists by creating processions known as Whit Walks; the first in Britain are said to have been organised by Anglican Sunday schools in Manchester near the start of the nineteenth century. For decades, thousands took part in Whit Walks across the region. They provided a rare burst of brightness through drab industrial streets, with young girls resplendent in new white dresses, shoes and socks.

Angus Reach, investigator for the *Morning Chronicle*'s national survey of labour and the poor, portrayed a gaudy scene of cheap shops, pubs and pawnbrokers as he set out one Saturday night in 1849 to find the Apollo music saloon on Manchester's London Road: 'Itinerant bands blow and bang their loudest; organ boys grind monotonously; ballad singers or flying stationers make roaring proclamations of their wares. The street is one swarming mass of people. Boys and girls shout and laugh and disappear into the taverns, together ... Stalls, shops, cellars are clustered round with critics or purchasers – cabmen drive slowly through the throng, shouting and swearing to the people to get out of the horse's way; and occasionally ... the melodious burst of a roaring chorus, surging out of the open windows of the Apollo, resounds loudly above the whole conglomeration of street noises.'[4]

Beer shops proliferated, often in the front room of a terraced house, after the Beer Act 1830 allowed any ratepayer to obtain a licence to brew and sell beer on his premises. In 1843 the *Manchester Directory* recorded 930 beer shops, 624 taverns and pubs, and 31 inns and hotels; a total of 1,575 liquor establishments, or one for every 154 inhabitants.[5] Some were known for 'lower' forms of recreation such as gambling, dog fighting and prostitution. Traditional pub sing-songs morphed into the tavern concert or 'singing-saloon', a prototype of the music hall involving singers, dancers and jugglers. At the Apollo, Reach found a narrow, smoke-filled room where singers and dancers performed on a tiny stage, accompanied by three fiddles and a piano.

Not all activity in pubs was lowbrow. Newspapers were a common feature, where customers caught up with the latest news and read aloud to others who could not read. Poetry was a popular pastime: the Sun Inn in Long Millgate hosted a Poets' Corner where writers such as Samuel Bamford, John Critchley Prince, Isabella Varley (later Mrs G. Linnaeus Banks) and Robert Rose met. Friendly societies and even botanical societies met in pubs.[6]

Entrepreneurs were keen to exploit opportunities. Manchester became particularly known for pleasure gardens. The first was opened by coffee house owner Robert Tinker on a 32-acre site in the Irk Valley in Collyhurst. Initially called Elysian Fields, it offered a brass band, roundabouts, swings, balloon ascents and dancing on the lawns, plus a chance to 'partake of tea and other refreshments at small tables standing under overhanging trees or in alcoves covered with creepers'. Later known as Vauxhall Gardens after the famous counterpart in London, it attracted visitors for more than fifty years. Decline set in as the Irk became polluted and it closed in 1852.[7]

Belle Vue Zoological Gardens opened in Gorton in 1836 and Pomona Gardens on Old Trafford's border with Salford in 1845. In the 1850s both Belle Vue and Pomona had their own rival diorama of the siege of Sebastopol in the Crimean war, with nightly pyrotechnics restaging the onslaught. Pomona, originally called Cornbrook Strawberry Gardens, was renamed to reflect lush orchards around it (Pomona is the Roman goddess of fruit trees). James Reilly, who bought the gardens in 1868, built the Royal Pomona Palace, which had the largest ballroom in Britain, with capacity for 20,000. Uses also included political rallies, in which it hosted famous names such as Disraeli. By the 1880s the site was surrounded by factories. The gardens closed in 1888 after a chemicals factory exploded, severely damaging the palace, and the land was used to create Pomona Docks.[8] In the twenty-first century, the polluted site has waited years for regeneration.

Also in Old Trafford, the Royal Botanical Gardens opened in 1831, later used for the 1857 Art Treasures Exhibition and the 1887 Royal Jubilee Exhibition. The latter included a full-scale reconstruction of streets and buildings from Manchester and Salford's past. From 1907, part of the site became White City Amusement Park and later a sports stadium for athletics, speedway, greyhound and stock car racing. The gardens' grand gateway still stands incongruously at the edge of a retail park. Manchester Zoological Gardens opened in 1838 in Higher Broughton, Salford, intended not just as a visitor attraction but also for scientific study of animals and plants. Initially it was popular, as people came to see exotic animals such as polar bears, but the one shilling entrance fee excluded many. It became bankrupt and closed in 1842, with animals sold to Belle Vue.[9]

Belle Vue was created by entrepreneur and part-time gardener John Jennison, who had previously opened the grounds of his Stockport home to the public. It contained an Italian garden, lakes, mazes, hothouses and an aviary. Soon animals such as kangaroos, rhinos, lions, bears and gazelles were added, plus a racecourse. Manchester Museum possesses the skeleton of Maharaja, an Indian elephant that was a star attraction in the late nineteenth century. Bought at auction in Edinburgh, the creature destroyed the railway carriage in which he was due to travel and had to walk 220 miles to Manchester with his keeper. It was great publicity. In the twentieth century, Belle Vue also became an amusement park, with attractions such as the Bobs roller-coaster and a scenic railway. There was greyhound racing, speedway, boxing and wrestling. It had music and dancing in various ballrooms and the largest exhibition space outside

London. After a brief post-Second World War boom, visitors declined. The zoo closed in 1977 and amusement park in 1980.[10]

The advent of railways opened up the seaside to the working classes. Blackpool's first station opened in 1846 and Manchester was connected with Southport in 1855. Until then, Blackpool was a coastal hamlet that had become a sea-bathing spot for the wealthy, some of whom travelled from Manchester by horse-drawn coach. By the 1880s Blackpool had become a working-class pleasure ground with piers, fortune-tellers, pubs, trams, donkey rides, fish-and-chip shops and theatres.

Railway companies marketed cheap excursions to seaside resorts, sometimes for works outings, in which workers played beach games under the eye of a factory supervisor, who aimed to stop them sloping off to the pub. Successive factory acts helped to reduce working hours. American author Nathaniel Hawthorne, who lived briefly in Southport in the early 1850s, complained of itinerant nuisances such as organ-grinders, a man with a bassoon and monkey, guitarists, Punch and Judy, and a bagpiper 'squealing out a tangled skein of discord, together with a highland maid who dances a hornpipe'.[11] The Bank Holidays Act 1871 stipulated four paid public holidays, including Whit Monday and the first Monday in August, though it was not until 1938 that workers won the right to a week's paid holiday per year.

Among Britain's earliest music halls was the Star Inn at Bolton. Landlord Tom Sharples moved there in 1840, having previously created a singing-room at the Millstones Inn in 1832, and built the Star Theatre and Museum onto his hostelry. The museum contained wax figures, a menagerie, and an axe said to have been used to execute the Earl of Derby during the Civil Wars. At one point Barney the leopard killed his keeper. The theatre was reportedly capable of holding between a thousand and one and a half thousand people. Entertainments included: a 'Characteristic Yorkshire Dialect Singer'; a 'True Representative of Negro Character'; assorted acrobats and jugglers; ventriloquists and magicians; even readings from popular novels. According to the *Bolton Guardian*: 'Mr Geoghegan, the manager, acted as chairman, and he had a mallet and called out the names of the performers. Performances began at 7.30 each night, and the curtain was wound up by hand. A well-known character called "Museum Jack" lit the lamps and footlights with a taper, and also played the piano. If a "turn" failed to please, Mr Geoghegan said "You're no good" and ejected the hapless performer.'[12]

Several music halls opened in Manchester, such as the People's Music Hall (later known as the Casino) in 1853 on Lower Mosley Street; in 1897 it was demolished to make way for the Midland Hotel. Others included the Alexandra on Peter Street, originally a Methodist chapel, later known as the Folly and then the Tivoli from 1897; the London in Bridge Street, built in 1862 and later renamed the Queen's; and the Star in Pollard Street, Ancoats. Serious theatres also staged lighter entertainments such as operettas and, from the 1860s, pantomimes.

Among music hall stars, comedian Dan Leno, brought up in Liverpool, lived for a few years in Manchester. Charles William Murphy, a composer from Manchester, co-wrote two hugely popular songs – 'Oh, Oh, Antonio' and 'Has Anybody Here Seen Kelly?' – for Australian singer Florrie Forde. She performed every summer on the Isle of Man in the Edwardian era. Murphy also co-wrote 'She's a Lassie from Lancashire' and 'Hold Your Hand Out Naughty Boy' for Forde. From the 1860s, music halls were attracting lower-middle-class audiences as well as the working class. A journalist visited the Wolverhampton, one of the larger halls, in 1867 and found 'smart-looking mechanics', commercial travellers, clerks, warehousemen and shopworkers; 'steady, sober-looking men' had come with their wives and in some cases their children. Cheaper halls crammed in young people. In 1868, twenty-three were killed in a fire panic at the Victoria, popularly known as Ben Lang's, which created a crush on the stairs.[13]

The explosion of popular culture prompted alarm among moral campaigners, eager to rescue the working class from drunkenness and wasting their money on sin and frivolity. The temperance movement had working-class roots and grew strong in the North. Manchester's Palace Theatre of Varieties, promoted by a London syndicate and opened in 1891, was kept dry by the lobbying of local Methodists and fellow teetotallers. Although national levels of alcohol consumption were declining from the 1870s, Manchester still had Lancashire's highest density of licensed premises. There were several local breweries, including Boddington's at Strangeways and Joseph Holt's at Cheetham.

While temperance beverages generally offered little competition, Vimto was a Mancunian success. Blackburn-born John Noel Nichols first mixed his 'Vim tonic' concentrate in a backyard shed in Granby Row, in the city centre, in 1908 and sold it to temperance bars and herbalist shops. By the 1930s Vimto was so popular that Nichols' Britannic Works in Stretford was supplying twenty-seven countries.[14]

Music hall proprietors were themselves becoming less keen on alcohol as they strove for an industrious lower-middle-class audience. 'Variety theatre' or 'theatre of varieties' became the fashionable term. Content was similar, but new theatres were large, stand-alone venues, cutting the symbolic link with pubs. A new breed of entrepreneurs had begun to build national chains. Edward Moss, from Droylsden, joined forced with Richard Thornton, from South Shields, and later Edward Stoll to create Moss Empires, Britain's largest group. Architect Frank Matcham designed numerous theatres for Moss Empires, including Manchester's Ardwick Empire and the Hippodrome, both of which opened in 1904. The Empire on Ardwick Green could house 3,000. The Hippodrome on Oxford Street offered variety and circus acts, including horses, elephants, performing dogs and a trapeze artist.[15]

Music hall had a strand of Lancashire comedians, including Manchester-born Morny Cash (1872–1938), who billed himself 'The Lancashire Lad'. Among the best known was George Formby senior (1875–1921), born into poverty in Ashton-under-Lyne. He played characters including 'John Willie', an archetypical gormless

Lancashire lad, accident-prone but muddling through, whose cane twirl and duck-like walk allegedly inspired Charlie Chaplin (The Eight Lancashire Lads, a dancing troupe that gave young Chaplin his professional debut, was formed in Wigan). For years Formby battled against consumption, muttering asides such as 'coughing better tonight, coughing summat champion'. He was billed as the Wigan Nightingale, a reference to his croaky voice. Formby had a miserable childhood. His mother Sarah was a prostitute and a drunk. A music hall owner in Birkenhead, who booked him early in his career, thought that James Booth, his real name, was unsuitable for the stage and suggested 'George Formby' – George after comedian George Robey and Formby after the Merseyside town.[16]

Oldham-born Eric Sykes (1923–2012) said the North West was 'where all the good comics come from'. Sykes came to prominence writing radio scripts, notably collaborating with Spike Milligan on *The Goon Show*, and became a television star in the 1960s. Whence came this comic strain? Sykes said: 'My theory is that we are all idiots. The people who don't think they're idiots – they're the ones that are dangerous.'[17] A.J.P. Taylor, who had lectured in history at the University of Manchester in the 1930s, attributed Lancastrian whimsicality to the 'south-west wind, bringing an atmosphere that is always blurred and usually gentle'.[18] Salford's Walter Greenwood wrote even more fancifully of the 'wild, warm, amorous wind wenching with fat clouds and leaving them big with rain of which they deliver themselves on the Pennines' westerly slopes'.[19] It may, less fancifully, be simply the result of people thrown together by rapid industrialisation responding to their conditions.

Frank Randle (1901–57, born Arthur Hughes in Aspull, Wigan) was successful in the North but too subversive to make it nationally. His combative working-class persona embraced sex and drink, insubordination and violence, with catchphrases including 'I'll fight anyone', 'I'll spiflicate the lot of you' and 'bah, I've supped some ale toneet'. Defying propriety, he fought a running battle with Harry Barnes, Blackpool police chief, in the 1940s and 50s, and was regularly banned from the stage for using bad language and suggestive material.[20] Other comics included Ted Ray (1905–77, born Charles Olden in Wigan), whose BBC radio show *Ray's a Laugh* ran for twelve years. Al Read (1909–87, born in Broughton, Salford) had a successful career in his family's meat-processing business before his popularity as an after-dinner speaker led to a radio career; his humour reflected everyday life, situations and characters.

Tiny, fiery Hylda Baker (1905–86), from Farnworth near Bolton, was famous as Nellie Pledge in the 1970s ITV sitcom *Nearest and Dearest*. Increasingly, she is also recognised as a female comedy pioneer and producer. A comedian's daughter, she made her professional stage debut aged ten and toured for decades in variety and second-rank revues, several of which she produced herself – the first woman to do so. She wrote, directed and starred in shows, booked acts and venues, designed and transported sets and posters, liaised with theatres and even once conducted the orchestra when the conductor was ill. She had a reputation for being difficult to work with, probably because she was a perfectionist and had to fight for equal treatment in a male world. Her most popular act was malapropism-strewn gossip with a tall, mute stooge called Cynthia (usually played by a man in drag). Baker would utter her catchphrase 'She knows, you know' and lament the passing of time, saying: 'I must get another hand put on this watch.'

Baker became famous in 1955 after a guest appearance on BBC television's *The Good Old Days*. When success came, she lived a star's life to the full. She drove a car with 'She knows, you know' inscribed on the front; bought a big house at Cleveleys, near Blackpool, and put a flagpole at the front; dressed in furs; and bought two monkeys as pets. In *Nearest and Dearest* she played a prim northern spinster locking horns with dissolute brother Eli after they jointly inherit their father's pickle factory. Her brother was played by Jimmy Jewel. Off-screen the pair hated each other.[21]

Les Dawson (1931–93), a bricklayer's son from Collyhurst who grew up in poverty, became known for his curmudgeonly persona and jokes about his mother-in-law and wife. After appearing on the talent show *Opportunity Knocks* in 1967, he had several TV series. His most notable creation was (with Roy Barraclough) Cissie and Ada, a pair of stout Lancashire housewives who spend much time 'mimo-ing' to each other (the northern practice of mouthing vocabulary to communicate over noisy textile looms), especially when the words were about bodily functions or sex. Bernard Manning (1930–2007), born in Harpurhey, raised in Ancoats, achieved a high profile in the 1970s on TV shows such as *The Comedians* and *The Wheeltappers and Shunters Social Club*. As his humour began to be regarded as racist, TV appearances became rare, though he continued to perform live, including at his own Embassy Club. Syd Little (born 1942 in Blackpool, raised in Wythenshawe) was the straight man in double act Little and Large.

Caroline Aherne (1963–2016, born in London, raised in Wythenshawe) wrote and performed as acerbic chat-show host *Mrs Merton* and played Denise in *The Royle Family*, which she co-wrote. Actor, comedian, producer and screenwriter Steve Coogan (born 1965 in Middleton), is famed for characters such as Alan Partridge, a socially inept and politically incorrect media personality. John Thomson (born 1969 in Walkden) has played roles in TV shows such as *The Fast Show* and *Cold Feet*. Chris Addison (born 1971 in Cardiff, raised in Worsley) appeared in TV satire *The Thick of It* and was a regular panellist on *Mock the Week*. Peter Kay (born 1973 in Bolton) is celebrated for *Peter Kay's Phoenix Nights* and *Peter Kay's Car Share*. His 2010–11 stand-up tour sold more than 1.2 million tickets, hailed by Guinness World Records as a record. Comedian and singer Jason Manford (born 1981 in Salford) has presented TV shows and starred in stage musicals.

Victoria Wood (1953–2016, born in Prestwich, raised in Bury) was a stand-up comedian, singer and songwriter, TV dramatist and actor. Her observational comedy satirised neuroses about class and sex. As a middle-class woman in a traditionally male world, she was unlike typical northern comics. Her first inspiration was Joyce

Grenfell. 'Life's not fair, is it?' Wood once said. 'Some of us drink champagne in the fast lane, and some of us eat our sandwiches by the loose chippings on the A597.' As a northerner loosening Oxbridge's dominance of comedy, she was conscious of the cultural divide. 'We'd like to apologise to our viewers in the north,' she wrote for the snooty TV announcer played by Susie Blake. 'It must be awful for you.'

Her father was an insurance salesman who also wrote scripts for *Coronation Street*. Wood lost her way at grammar school: 'I'd look at other girls and wish I could be like them, interested in boys, meeting in the Wimpy bar on Saturday mornings and going to discos.' She learned piano and joined a youth theatre. After appearing on talent show *New Faces*, her first big break was on *That's Life!*, writing and performing satirical songs. She mounted stand-up tours and comedy shows such as *Victoria Wood: As Seen on TV*, including much-loved *Acorn Antiques*. There was the sitcom *Dinnerladies*. Later, she focused on drama such as the award-winning TV film *Housewife, 49*.[22]

Manchester's first recorded film shows were in 1896 at St James's Theatre, Oxford Street, and at the YMCA and Lesser Free Trade Hall, both on Peter Street.[23] The first true cinemas opened after the Cinematograph Act 1909, which required licences and strict fire regulations. Audiences were largely young, working class and increasingly dominated by women. The most prestigious was the Picture House, Oxford Street, opened in 1911 and used as a cinema until 1980. It now houses a twenty-four-hour branch of McDonald's.

Purchasing power grew between the world wars, despite two recessions; leisure became big business and cinema went through a golden age. Music hall's heyday was over, though some halls staggered on until after the Second World War. The first 'talkie' screened in Manchester was *Uncle Tom's Cabin* in 1928 at the former Picture House, renamed the New Oxford. While some large cinemas were grand, local houses could be more basic, as Anthony Burgess recalled in describing two cinemas in Miles Platting: 'The Rex was called a bughouse and the Electric was not. The Electric used a superior disinfectant like a grudging perfume; the Rex smelt of its patrons and its lavatories. With the Rex, it was said, you went in with a blouse and came out with a jumper.'[24]

There were few northern accents in films, whether American or British, but Gracie Fields (1898–1979, born as Gracie Stansfield in Rochdale above her grandmother's fish-and-chip shop) and George Formby junior (1904–61, born as George Hoy Booth in Wigan) were exceptions. Fields was a mill girl who became a global star. 'Our Gracie' made her professional debut at Rochdale Hippodrome in 1910. When she landed a Hollywood deal, she insisted that the four pictures be filmed in Britain. In her best-known film *Sing As We Go!* (1934, script by J.B. Priestley), she plays a high-spirited, resourceful heroine made redundant from her job in a Lancashire cotton mill, who is forced to seek work in Blackpool. She helps to reopen the factory, which is saved by adopting a new synthetic fibre. In the Second World War, Fields and her Italian husband went to America to avoid him being interned, but she entertained British troops all over the world.[25]

Formby was the ukulele- and banjolele-playing star of British comedy films. After an early career as a stable boy and jockey, Formby took to the stage when his father died in 1921. Early performances were taken exclusively from his father's act and he also took his stage name. In films Formby portrayed a gormless Lancashire innocent who wins through in an unfamiliar environment (in horse-racing, TT races, as a spy or policeman) and steals the heart of an attractive middle-class girl, usually from a caddish type with a moustache. The BBC banned his suggestive songs 'When I'm Cleaning Windows' and 'With My Little Stick of Blackpool Rock'. According to his producer Basil Dean, Formby 'didn't act gormless as many successful Lancashire comedians have done, he *was* gormless'. Whatever was thrown at him, he came through smiling and people loved him for it.[26]

Film Studios (Manchester), which operated from 1947 to 1954 and was founded by Ardwick-born John E. Blakeley, was the only feature film studio outside London. Based in a former Wesleyan chapel in Dickenson Road, Rusholme, it made northern comedies – attracting the nickname 'Jollywood' – using music hall stars such as Sandy Powell, Rochdale-born Norman Evans and Jimmy James, but chiefly Frank Randle, with titles such as *Holidays with Pay* and *School for Randle*. The films were box office hits in the North, but not the South. The BBC inherited the Dickenson Road studios, used for the first two years of *Top of the Pops* in the 1960s.[27]

Actors born or raised in Manchester include Robert Donat (1905–58) from Withington, best remembered for playing Richard Hannay in Alfred Hitchcock's film *The 39 Steps* and Mr Chips, the ageing schoolmaster in *Goodbye Mr Chips*; for the latter he won an Oscar. Dame Wendy Hiller (1912–2003), from Bramhall near Stockport, played stage roles and appeared in films including *A Man for All Seasons*. Brenda de Banzie (1909–81), raised in Salford, played Maggie Hobson in the film of *Hobson's Choice* and the hapless wife of comedian Archie Rice in that of John Osborne's *The Entertainer*. Beryl Reid (1919–96), born in Hereford and educated in Withington and Levenshulme, starred in stage and screen versions of *The Killing of Sister George*. Albert Finney (1936–2019), a bookmaker's son from Salford, starred in films including *Saturday Night and Sunday Morning*, *Tom Jones* and *The Dresser*. English-American actor John Mahoney (1940–2018), who played Martin Crane in the sitcom *Frasier*, was born in Blackpool and raised in Withington. He discovered acting at Stretford Children's Theatre. Actor and singer Bernard Cribbins (1928–2022), who played Albert Perks in the film of *The Railway Children*, came from Oldham. John Thaw (1942–2002), born in Gorton, starred in the TV series *Inspector Morse*.

Sir Ian McKellen, born in 1939 in Burnley, grew up in Wigan and Bolton. Over six decades, he has performed in genres from Shakespearean drama to science fiction. He came out as gay in 1988 and has championed lesbian, gay, bisexual and transgender social movements. Danny Boyle, from Radcliffe, Bury, directed films including *Trainspotting* and *Slumdog Millionaire* as well as the opening ceremony of the 2012 Summer Olympics. Maxine Peake, from

Westhoughton, Bolton, was rejected by every theatre education company in north-west England, but won a scholarship to London's Royal Academy of Dramatic Art. After roles in TV productions such as *Dinnerladies*, *Shameless* and *See No Evil: The Moors Murders*, she has starred in plays at Manchester's Royal Exchange. She also wrote, directed and starred in the play *Beryl*, about Leeds-born cyclist Beryl Burton, for radio and stage.

Other actors include Claire Foy (Stockport), Sir Ben Kingsley (born North Yorkshire, raised in Pendlebury), Suranne Jones (Chadderton), Christopher Eccleston (Salford), Sarah Lancashire (Oldham), Joanne Whalley (Salford, Levenshulme, Stockport), Robert Shaw (Westhoughton), Bernard Hill (Blackley), David Threlfall (Crumpsall, Blackley, Bradford, Burnage), Lesley Sharp (born Manchester, raised in Formby) and David Bamber (Walkden). Benedict Wong, from Eccles, is best known for Marvel films such as *Doctor Strange*, *Avengers: Infinity War* and *Spider-Man: No Way Home*.

Playwright Shelagh Delaney (1938–2011), raised in Broughton, Salford, failed her eleven-plus exam and left school at seventeen to do jobs including shop assistant, clerk and theatre usherette. Aged just nineteen when her debut work *A Taste of Honey* was produced by Joan Littlewood's Theatre Workshop in east London in 1958, she was nicknamed 'the Françoise Sagan of Salford' and 'an angry young woman', referring to the 'angry young man' genre exemplified by John Osborne's *Look Back in Anger*. Set in Salford, *A Taste of Honey* is about a teenage schoolgirl who has an affair with a black sailor, gets pregnant and then moves in with a gay male acquaintance. It also became a film. The work was controversial locally because it portrayed a side of Salford that people did not want the world to see; the *Salford City Reporter* letters page was filled with denunciations. Delaney said: 'I had strong ideas about what I wanted to see in the theatre. We used to object to plays where the factory workers came cap in hand and call the boss "sir". Usually North Country people are shown as gormless, whereas in actual fact, they are very alive and cynical.'[28]

Mike Leigh (born 1943), film and theatre director and play-wright, was also brought up in Broughton. His paternal grandparents were Russian-Jewish immigrants; the family name, originally Lieberman, was anglicised in 1939. His father, a general practitioner, regarded him as a problem child because of his creative interests.[29] Leigh uses lengthy improvisations developed over several weeks to build characters and storylines. He received Oscar nominations for his films *Secrets & Lies* (1996), *Topsy-Turvy* (1999), *Vera Drake* (2004) and *Another Year* (2010). TV productions include *Nuts in May* (1976) and *Abigail's Party* (1977, originally a stage play).

Ballroom dancing was also hugely popular in the 1920s and 30s. Manchester's top dance halls were the Ritz on Whitworth Street and the Plaza on Oxford Street. Those without a partner could hire one of the professional dancers by the dance. Dancing could be learned at local halls and one of several academies. Among larger local bands was Jack McCormack's, playing in the restaurant of Lewis's department store during the afternoon and in the top-floor ballroom in the evening. As cinemas closed in the 1950s and 60s, victims of television and wider choices of recreation, some were converted into ten-pin bowling alleys and bingo halls, while a few briefly became ballrooms run by commercial organisations such as the Locarno group. Others were replaced by garages, supermarkets and petrol stations.[30]

Working men's clubs had existed since the mid-nineteenth century, often initially conceived by wealthy philanthropists as a way to keep men out of the pub. From the late 1950s, liberalisation of licensing and gambling laws led to the growth of Manchester's 'club-land', including strip clubs, Afro-Caribbean shebeens, nightclubs and casinos. At the Garden of Eden casino in Whitworth Street, which had small alligators swimming in a channel around the dance floor, there was an all-night hairdressing salon and a shop where 'members can buy a shirt before going to the office after a night at the casino tables'.

Cabaret or theatre clubs attracted stars: Shirley Bassey played the Talk of the North, Pendleton, in 1965 and Eartha Kitt starred at the

Golden Garter, Wythenshawe, in 1970. At their peak in 1967, some twenty-five such clubs operated within a four-mile radius of the city centre compared with just four in Liverpool and three in Leeds. Clubland declined rapidly in the 1970s as new licensing regimes and introduction of the breathalyser undermined profits, but, as cultural historian Dave Russell puts it: 'In a period when the city is often cast as being in decline and backward-looking, it lent a veneer of glitzy modernity.' A *Manchester Evening News* headline in 1964 read: 'Manchester at Midnight. The verdict … it's SWINGING!'[31]

Broadcasting in Manchester began in May 1922 when Trafford Park-based Metropolitan-Vickers, seeking to advertise its manufacture of wireless receivers, made its first, short transmission. With other pioneers, it became part of the British Broadcasting Company in November 1922 (Corporation from 1927). Its 2ZY station was one of nine local providers that formed the initial core of BBC programming. In the early 1930s Manchester became headquarters of the BBC's North Region, stretching at one stage from the Scottish border to the Potteries. Despite the difficulty of encapsulating such a large region, it tried hard to reflect northern life and became noted for documentaries featuring 'ordinary' voices. Pioneer broadcaster Olive Shapley was born in Peckham but spent more than forty years of her career in Manchester, producing work about the North of England. She began as an organiser of *Children's Hour* in 1934 and later became presenter of *Woman's Hour*. Radio continued to hold a place in local culture into the television age, especially in the commercial sector, legalised in 1972. Piccadilly Radio (1974), originally located in Piccadilly Plaza, was the city's first commercial station. It now broadcasts as Bauer's Hits Radio Manchester. Radio DJ Chris Evans, born in Warrington, started his broadcasting career at Piccadilly as a teenager.[32]

Television became available to northern audiences only in 1951, with administration handled in Manchester. Notable national BBC broadcasters include Stockport-born Joan Bakewell, who presented the topical and arts show *Late Night Line-Up* from 1965 to 1972. In a crass example of 1960s sexism, she was dubbed 'the thinking man's crumpet' by comedy writer Frank Muir. Later she made documentaries and became a Labour peer in 2011.

Independent television was legalised in 1954. Granada, founded by Sidney Bernstein (an Essex-born owner of cinemas and theatres), was among the initial franchisees, covering the North West and Yorkshire on weekdays, while ABC provided the weekend service. Both began broadcasting in 1956. While ABC produced some significant programmes, including early productions of *Armchair Theatre*, Granada became Britain's most successful independent franchise. It settled on its Quay Street site after considering Leeds or Liverpool. Granada began a soap opera in 1960 created by a working-class writer, Tony Warren (1936–2016, born in Pendlebury as Anthony Simpson). He initially wanted to call it *Florizel Street*, which according to some accounts was dropped because a tea lady said it sounded like a toilet cleaner. Producers, torn between *Jubilee Street* and *Coronation Street*, opted for the latter. Initial reviews were not encouraging, but by October 1961 it was the country's most popular programme. Its success owned much to the quality of early scripts and performances and its portrayal of a fast-disappearing way of life. It was modelled on Archie Street, Ordsall, Salford, after Warren toured rows of terraced houses looking for the perfect prototype.[33]

Other popular Granada programmes included Jack Rosenthal's comedy *The Dustbinmen* and current affairs programme *World in Action*. An ITV restructuring led to Granada being absorbed into a single network in 2004. Production houses that became established in Manchester include Red Production Company, which created Channel 4's *Queer as Folk*. Cosgrove Hall Films, an animation house created by Brian Cosgrove and Mark Hall, was based in Chorlton-cum-Hardy. Its productions included *Danger Mouse*, *The Wind in the Willows* and *Count Duckula*. MediaCityUK, developed by Peel Media, opened in 2011 in Salford Quays with the BBC as its main tenant, marking a large-scale decentralisation from London. ITV Granada moved there in 2013.

Popular culture, even more than 'higher' art forms, has helped to define Manchester. Andy Burnham, Greater Manchester's mayor, aims to develop its night-time economy even further as a central strategy. A third of the city-region's workforce, or 464,000 people, are reckoned to work in jobs or businesses that are significantly active between 6pm and 6am.[34] That is in addition to those who are partying.

12

WORLD WARS AND DEPRESSION

When the First World War broke out in August 1914, not everyone was pleased by Britain's involvement. C.P. Scott, editor of the *Manchester Guardian*, wrote in an editorial: 'It will be a war in which we will risk everything of which we are proud, and in which we stand to gain nothing … Some day we will regret it.'[1] Mancunians, nonetheless, flocked to volunteer. The Earl of Derby came up with the idea of 'Pals' battalions, units based on community or occupational ties, and formed the first in Liverpool. Within days, Manchester's city leaders and businesses had raised funds to equip the first Manchester Pals battalion.

Manchester raised eight Pals battalions, part of the Manchester Regiment, with others formed in Salford and Oldham. Recruits included factory workers, clerks, warehouse staff, merchants and business owners. They trained at Heaton Park and fought in some of the Western Front's harshest conflicts, including the Battle of the Somme. Twenty-one Victoria Cross winners came from Greater Manchester and surrounding areas. One was Royton-born Sergeant John Hogan of the Manchester Regiment's 2nd Battalion, who, along with Second Lieutenant James Leach, retook a trench from the enemy in October 1914, killing eight, wounding two and taking sixteen prisoners. It is estimated that more than 22,000 soldiers from Manchester and Salford died in the war and 55,000 were wounded.[2]

On the home front, Manchester was beyond the reach of bombers, but could be attacked by Zeppelin. A night-time blackout was introduced, which led to fatal accidents. Away from the city, twenty-nine soldiers of the Manchester Regiment, billeted in a Baptist chapel at Cleethorpes, were killed when the chapel was destroyed by a Zeppelin attack. Zeppelin navigation was often inaccurate. One attacked Nottingham, which its captain thought was Manchester. Bolton suffered thirteen deaths in a Zeppelin raid. Its captain is said to have thought he was attacking Derby.

Manchester's industrial strength was redirected to the war effort. The Port of Manchester and Trafford Park came into full use for the first time, especially for making munitions, chemicals and aircraft. Avro, based at Brownsfield Mill, Great Ancoats Street, went from being a small-scale producer of largely one-off aircraft to mass production as its Avro 504 became the Royal Flying Corps' standard training plane. Women filled vacancies left by men at war.

There were industrial tensions. Engineering workers feared that employment of untrained women might lead to wage cuts and longer hours. Dublin-born Mary Quaile (1886–1958), organising secretary of the Manchester Women's Trades Council, campaigned to ensure women workers were not exploited by employers; later she was national women's organiser for the Dock, Wharf and Riverside Workers' Union, which became part of the Transport and General Workers' Union.

Strikes for higher pay in 1916 by dockers, engineers and railway workers were quickly settled. In 1917, the arrest of two Manchester engineering union leaders on a charge of 'impeding the supply of weapons' brought the threat of an all-out strike, averted only when shop stewards appealed for members to return to work pending settlement of the case. Charges were withdrawn after the men's union, the Amalgamated Society of Engineers, intervened. Tram workers won a bonus by working to rule and threatening to strike.

A doubling of food prices since 1914 and restrictions on alcohol consumption fuelled workers' complaints. In 1918, street cleaners, rubbish collectors, cotton spinners and railway workers threatened strikes. Even workers at CWS's Crumpsall biscuit factory walked out and joined a city-centre march.[3]

When the armistice took effect at 11am on 11 November 1918, there was silence – and some tears – in Albert Square as flags were raised at the town hall. Jubilation followed as workers joined processions. 'Crowds ... moved about as if they had no care and no thought beyond the burning joy of the moment,' reported the *Manchester Guardian*. 'The noise and shouting, the bugle bands and the processions went on in the main streets until far into the night.'[4]

There was more suffering the following year, however, with the global 'Spanish flu' pandemic. Prime minister David Lloyd George was taken ill on a visit to Manchester, where he was returning to his birthplace to receive the keys to the city. He spent a week confined to bed in isolation and needed a respirator. His valet later described his condition as 'touch and go'. Lloyd George had been born in Chorlton-on-Medlock to Welsh parents, though his family moved to Pembrokeshire when he was two months old.[5]

Lloyd George's coalition government, comprising mainly Conservatives and Liberals, won the 1918 general election by a landslide, promising to make Britain 'a fit country for heroes to live in'. Many wartime controls were lifted. Railways, shipping, even coalmines were returned to private hands. There was a vigorous, if short-lived, programme to extend health and educational services, raise pensions and spread universal unemployment insurance. A subsidised housing programme was launched by Liberal minister Christopher Addison.

There was a brief postwar boom, particularly in cotton, shipbuilding, shipping and engineering. Investors borrowed unwisely to finance mergers that created bloated companies. A total of 238 cotton mills, comprising 42 per cent of spinning capacity, changed hands. 'All over Lancashire there could be heard whispers of fortunes that left the riches of prewar days far behind,' wrote Benjamin Bowker in *Lancashire under the Hammer* (1928). Half the cotton-spinning industry, he said, was 'cast on to the gaming tables' as local syndicates traded in mill company shares at inflated prices.[6]

The boom ended abruptly when the government raised the key interest rate. Investment halted, prices began to fall and unemployment to rise. Cotton was particularly vulnerable: there had been little recent investment in new technology and 45 per cent of exports went to India. The war cut off supplies of UK-made cloth and left the Indian market to Japanese and Indian producers. In 1913 Lancashire supplied two-thirds of world trade in cotton cloth, but by 1938 that had shrunk to 25 per cent and output and employment had halved.[7] Oldham and Accrington were among places particularly hard-hit.

Cotton's crisis spread through the region's economy. Textile engineering companies suffered along with businesses that provided financial and legal services to the industry. Manchester banks had lent heavily in the postwar boom and were vulnerable. Williams Deacon's was in such a precarious state that the Bank of England had to step in and arrange a takeover by the Royal Bank of Scotland. In 1932 the government introduced import tariffs, creating the irony that Manchester, once a free trade champion, was looking to protectionism for salvation.

Manchester's diversified economy, notably the Ship Canal and Trafford Park, helped it to weather the downturn better than most. Trafford Park had no cotton mills; industries included the oil trade, engineering, chemicals and food. By 1933, more than two hundred American firms were based at Trafford Park. Westinghouse was reorganised as Metropolitan-Vickers in 1919. Trafford Park firms mostly survived the 1929–31 crash without bankruptcies, though Ford moved to Dagenham in 1931 to be nearer European markets.[8]

CWS and Hovis had opened flour mills at Trafford Wharf before 1914. Kellogg's established its European headquarters at Trafford Park towards the end of the 1930s. Brooke Bond imported tea at

Trafford Park and the CWS did so in Ordsall. Brooke Bond, founded by Arthur Brooke on Market Street in 1869, launched PG Tips in 1930. The name derived from 'Pre-Gestee' tea, a variant of 'Digestive Tea', which it was thought would aid digestion if drunk before eating. Only the tips, or best bits, of the tea plant were used. Salesmen thought the name long-winded and shortened it to PG Tips. The blend is still made at Trafford Park by Ekaterra, a former division of Unilever.[9]

Another famous product, Cussons Imperial Leather soap, known for its creamy lather and fragrance, was manufactured in Salford from the 1930s. Hull-born Thomas Cussons had opened a chemist's shop in Swinton in 1869, after which his son Alexander moved into manufacturing. Imperial Leather was based on a perfume called 'Eau de Cologne Imperiale Russe', while Russian leather carried a distinctive aroma from its birch-oil tanning process. The company was taken over by Paterson Zochonis in 1975, becoming PZ Cussons, but remains headquartered in Wythenshawe.[10]

Sir John Moores (1896–1993), founder of the Liverpool-based Littlewoods retail and football pools company, was born in Eccles, the son of a bricklayer and a millworker. After working as a telegraphist, he created Littlewoods Pools, in which punters could bet on the outcome of football matches, with two partners in 1923. It struggled at first but he turned it into a success after buying out his colleagues. In 1932 he started the Littlewoods Mail Order Store and in 1937 the first of many Littlewoods department stores opened in Blackpool. In the early 1960s he was chairman of Everton Football Club. By the 1980s, Littlewoods was said to be the largest private company in Europe, but it declined in the face of tough competition and the internet and was wound up in 2005.[11]

Manchester's clothing industry continued to expand, drawing on cheap labour, mainly women working at home or in workshops. A few clothing factories also opened, notably Montague Burton's Burtonville factory, created in the late 1930s in Swinton, beside that other symbol of progress the East Lancs Road: a straight highway between Manchester and Liverpool that opened in 1934. Clothing produced in Manchester included shirts, dresses, blouses and underwear.

Retailing remained vibrant. Manchester's wholesale markets supplied food and goods to shopkeepers and market traders across the North West and into the Midlands. Street sellers were less prominent than in the past, but Shudehill was a centre for bookstalls. Lewis's department store continued to invest in improving its premises. On Deansgate, Kendal Milne was bought by Harrods in 1919 and was called Harrods for a period in the 1920s, though the name reverted to Kendal Milne after protests from customers and staff. Manchester's first Woolworth's store had opened just before the war. National multiples strengthened their presence. Regional chains included the shops and restaurants of United Cattle Products (UCP), which sold tripe and other offal, reflecting Lancashire's working-class diet.

Michael Marks, a Jewish immigrant from the Russian Empire, came to Britain in 1884 and became a pedlar and market trader in Leeds, later joined by Tom Spencer. Ten years after Marks arrived, he and Spencer opened their first shop, at 20 Cheetham Hill Road in Manchester. They opened their first warehouse in Manchester in 1901, which became Marks & Spencer's headquarters until it relocated to London's Baker Street in the 1930s. After the founders died, Michael's son Simon joined forces with Israel Moses Sieff and they built the M&S empire. Both studied at Manchester Grammar School and Manchester University and later married each other's sister. In 1928 the 'St Michael' brand name was introduced as a tribute to Simon's father, which remained until 2000.[12]

Manchester's architecture went through a phase in which startlingly white neoclassical Portland stone buildings dominated everything around them until blackened by pollution. Examples include Ship Canal House, the headquarters of the Manchester Ship Canal Company, opened on King Street in 1927 and designed by Henry S. Fairhurst; Midland Bank's premises on King Street, designed by Sir Edwin Lutyens and built between 1933 and 1935; and Arkwright House in Parsonage Gardens, also designed by Fairhurst and completed in 1937 for the English Sewing Cotton Company.

In 1926 the city council held a competition to design an extension to the town hall and a new central library. The library was temporarily housed in Piccadilly, where Anthony Burgess claimed to have been helped to navigate the index by a 'charming' woman of about forty: 'running acceptably to fat, dressed in a green skirt and a blue sweater; her hair prettily mousy, before getting down to her study of Engels ... She put myself and herself in a tram and took me to Ardwick, where she had a small flat above a confectioner's shop. It was a bookish flat, warmed by a gas fire, with bright rugs and pictures on the walls ... I needed, she said, to be educated. She meant more than instruction in the visual arts.'[13]

Both new buildings were designed by E. Vincent Harris, whose circular design for the library, reminiscent of Rome's Pantheon, was based on libraries in America. The library, faced with Portland stone, was opened by George V in 1934, a startling expression of civic confidence during the Great Depression. It cost about £600,000, had one of the largest library reading rooms after the British Museum in London, accommodated 300 people and housed about a million books. Folk singer Ewan MacColl reminisced: 'The portico of the magnificent edifice quickly became a popular rendezvous and "Meet you at the Ref" became a familiar phrase on the lips of students, lovers and unemployed youths. I was there on the opening day and on many days thereafter; the Ref played an important part in my life for I made many friends there.'[14]

A rash of art deco buildings appeared in central Manchester, including Sunlight House on Quay Street, completed in 1932 by architect and developer Joseph Sunlight (1889–1978) as the headquarters of his property business, inspired by a visit to Chicago, with offices and shops to let and a basement swimming pool. Born to a Jewish family called Schimschlavitch in Belarus, then part of Russia, he and his parents emigrated to Manchester, where they changed their name to Sunlight, probably after Sunlight soap. He captured the public imagination as a racehorse owner and punter.[15]

The Rylands textile company bucked cotton's decline by opening one of Manchester's last grand warehouses in 1932 at the Piccadilly end of Market Street, designed by Fairhurst. It later became Pauldens department store and then Debenhams before closing in 2021. Kendal Milne opened a new store on Deansgate in 1939, designed by Harrods' in-house architect, Louis David Blanc, with input from a local architect, J.S. Beaumont. Also opened in 1939 was the futuristic Daily Express building on Great Ancoats Street, designed by engineer Sir Owen Williams, who was the engineer too for Express buildings in London and Glasgow. The Manchester building is considered by some the best of the three.

The coalition government collapsed in 1922 and the Conservatives won an election under Andrew Bonar Law. Labour more than doubled its seats and overtook the divided Liberals. Labour's breakthrough was achieved under the leadership of John Robert Clynes (1869–1949), a former Oldham cotton piecer who had begun working in a mill aged ten. Clynes was a self-taught man who loved to quote Shakespeare and Milton in parliamentary debates.[16] Less than a month after the election, Clynes was defeated in a leadership challenge by the more charismatic Ramsay MacDonald. Bonar Law stepped down after seven months because of a terminal illness and was replaced by Stanley Baldwin. Baldwin called an election in 1923, but the result was a hung parliament. MacDonald formed the first Labour government with tacit Liberal support, in which Clynes became leader of the Commons.

The Liberals' last great success in Manchester was in 1923 when they won five of the city's ten parliamentary seats (Blackley, Exchange, Moss Side, Rusholme and Withington), but these were all lost to the Conservatives less than a year later. The extension of the franchise to all adult males and women over thirty in 1918, and to women over twenty-one in 1928, not only aided Labour but also helped the Tories to gain working-class votes. The Liberals won Blackley and Withington once more in 1929, but no Liberal has represented a Manchester constituency since 1931. On the council, while individual Liberals such as Ernest Simon were influential, the party became marginalised and was virtually wiped out after 1945.[17]

Labour gained steadily, and would have much more success from 1945. But it was the Conservatives in Manchester who prospered in the interwar years. Between 1918 and 1937 Conservative and Unionist candidates won forty-three of the seventy-four parliamentary contests in Manchester constituencies compared with twenty-four for Labour and seven for the Liberals. Tory victories included several in working-class Hulme, represented by Lt Col Joseph Nall for most of the period. Salford meanwhile gained city status in 1926 despite a Home Office civil servant dismissing the borough as 'merely a scratch collection of 240,000 people cut off from Manchester by the river'.[18]

Industrial tensions rose as workers tried to hold on to wartime gains in the face of rising unemployment and employers' pressure for wage cuts. A lock-out in the engineering industry in 1922 resulted in defeat for the workers after a bitter thirteen-week dispute. Disputes occurred in cotton mills as employers introduced more machines per operative. The 1926 general strike in support of the miners' fight against a 20 per cent wage cut was called off after nine days by the Trades Union Congress, fearing a drift back to work. Manchester was virtually closed down by the dispute: trams stopped running and work ceased at the docks, though grain and other supplies were unloaded by strike-breakers after the arrival of the Royal Navy destroyer HMS *Wessex*. A Manchester edition of the TUC paper, the *British Worker*, was edited by Fenner Brockway and distributed by transport workers around the country.

The economic climate turned harsh again as the 1929 Wall Street crash led to the Great Depression, felt less severely in Britain than in countries such as the US, but concentrated in older industrial areas. MacDonald's second minority government in 1929 was engulfed by economic crisis. Clynes, home secretary, sided in 1931 with those opposing MacDonald's austerity measures and split with MacDonald when the prime minister left Labour in order to form a National Government. Clynes lost his Platting seat in the 1931 election, but regained it in 1935 and retained it until he retired as an MP in 1945. With little income, he died in relative poverty in 1949.

There were demonstrations in 1931 against the introduction of a means test to qualify for unemployment benefit, including one in Salford used as the basis for a fictional scene in Walter Greenwood's novel *Love on the Dole: A Tale of the Two Cities* (1933), which became a bestseller. Greenwood was a former textile clerk made unemployed at twenty-nine. The book centres on the Hardcastle family. Harry, the son, is sacked soon after he has made his girlfriend pregnant. Sally, the daughter, falls for a Labour activist, Larry, who dies after a police attack on protesting workers. Sally ends up selling her chastity to a businessman to get jobs for her father and brother. The book became a successful play, but efforts to turn it into a film were blocked in 1936 by the British Board of Film Censors, which disliked its radicalism and supposed sexual immorality. In 1940 a sanitised version was made as home-front propaganda. Greenwood, asked if fame had changed him, replied that he wanted only to get back to Salford rather than 'live soft' in London, though soon he ditched his Salford fiancée (who sued him successfully for breach of promise), relocated to the capital and married an American actress.[19]

The interwar years brought the most rapid physical expansion of the Manchester region's built-up area in its history. While overall population growth slowed dramatically – reaching just over 2.7 million by 1931 and remaining stable for the next four decades – the pattern was of suburban growth and inner-city decline.[20] The city of Manchester's population peaked at 766,300 in 1931 and fell to 392,800 by 2001 before rising again to 552,000 in 2021.[21] Salford's population also decreased, by 29 per cent, between 1921 and 1939.[22] Across the region, the number of homes grew strongly as smaller families occupied more space.

Manchester Corporation, which had previously relied on private construction, embraced government subsidies and built council estates, mainly on suburban sites. Progress was slow at first because of rising prices and shortages of labour and materials, but between 1920 and 1938 more than 27,000 council houses were built, plus a further 8,000 by private contractors with council financial assistance.[23] Private housing growth, meanwhile, filled in green spaces along commuter railway lines. The growth of Brooklands and Timperley physically joined the towns of Altrincham and Sale. Cheshire villages such as Gatley, Cheadle, Cheadle Hulme and Handforth were absorbed into a continuous south Manchester suburban belt. The north of the city was less affected by the building boom, except for the Prestwich–Whitefield–Bury corridor.

By the late 1920s council building was just about keeping up with housing demand. Manchester's overcrowding was below the national average and the city was ahead of Birmingham, Liverpool and London in slum clearance. However, surveys revealed squalid housing conditions in the inner city. The Greenwood Act of 1930 gave a central government subsidy to each council that had a scheme for demolition and rehousing. The city council launched a five-year programme in 1933 to clear 15,000 of the worst houses, starting in Hulme, Red Bank, Collyhurst, St Clement's and West Gorton, where most houses were verminous, had fundamental sanitary defects and no proper food storage or washing facilities. In 1942, however, the city's medical officer of health estimated that Manchester still had almost 69,000 unfit properties. Salford also began a slum clearance programme after a survey found some of the country's worst slums there.[24]

Manchester bought an estate at Wythenshawe, south Manchester, in 1926 and planned a garden city to house 100,000 people with jobs, schools, shops and leisure facilities. This was the vision of Didsbury-born Ernest Simon (1879–1970), who had been the city's youngest lord mayor. He and his wife Shena purchased Wythenshawe Hall and park, which had been under the control of the Tatton family for centuries, from Robert Tatton and donated them to the city. Manchester's boundary was extended in 1931 to include this, along with farmland and villages such as Northenden and Baguley. Barry Parker, planner of Letchworth Garden City, was hired to oversee the development.

Wythenshawe's population passed 35,000 in 1935 and eventually reached its target in 1964. Community facilities did not keep pace, however, and only about a fifth of new residents were former slum dwellers, who struggled to afford the higher rents. Wythenshawe's three industrial zones at Sharston, Roundthorn and Moss Nook did not take proper shape until the 1950s and the civic centre was completed in the 1960s. Simon, the son of a wealthy German-born industrialist, was Liberal MP for Withington in 1923–4 and 1929–31, and knighted in 1932. After the Second World War he joined the Labour Party and became Baron Simon of Wythenshawe and chairman of the BBC board of governors. Shena Simon, born in Croydon and Cambridge-educated, founded the Women's Citizens Association in Manchester and was a member of the city corporation from 1924 to 1933.[25]

Ernest Simon commented in the 1920s that Manchester Corporation's annual budget exceeded that of some smaller European states. Its trading activities included water, gas and electricity, transport, and markets, and its responsibilities included public assistance and relief works for the unemployed. About a tenth of the population lived in households of council employees. The corporation provided the city generously with further education facilities, but was slow to create secondary school places. By 1924 there were six candidates for every free place and the vast majority of pupils left elementary school at fourteen. A number of 'senior' schools opened during the 1930s, but for many students further education colleges remained their only option.[26]

Manchester began replacing trams with buses in 1929 and decided in 1937 to phase out the tram network. One problem was that people were being knocked down or killed by cars as they got on or off trams in the middle of the road. It gradually became clear that buses were quicker, cheaper and popular. The last trams were taken off the streets in January 1949, until a new light-rail network was introduced from 1992.

Civil aviation was important to Manchester's twentieth-century development, just as canals had been in the eighteenth and railways in the nineteenth centuries.[27] From May 1919, civilian flying was allowed from the wartime airfield at Alexandra Park (now Hough End Playing Fields). A converted Handley Page O/400 bomber made the first commercial flight to Manchester, carrying ten fare-paying passengers from London. Later that month, Britain's first scheduled domestic air service was launched between Alexandra Park, Southport and Blackpool. The corporation tried to buy the site from Lord Egerton of Tatton, but he refused to sell and flying ceased in 1924.

The corporation decided in 1928 on Barton, west of the city, as the site for a municipal aerodrome but, in its hurry to be the first city to have one, began flying from a temporary site on the Rackhouse estate at Wythenshawe. When Barton opened at the start of 1930, growth was slow and the site too small and boggy. After considering alternatives, including Audenshaw, Bury and Mobberley, the corporation decided by a single-vote majority to build an aerodrome at Ringway, beside the Wythenshawe estate. Ringway opened in 1938 to its first arrival, a KLM DC-2 from Amsterdam. KLM ran the airport's only international service before the Second World War and even offered passengers a 'request stop' at Doncaster.

Britain's economy began to recover after 1932. Manchester's engineering sector was boosted later in the decade by rearmament and the Second World War. The Royal Air Force pinned hopes on a new twin-engined bomber called the Manchester that Avro was developing at its new Chadderton factory, but test flights showed its Rolls-Royce Vulture engines were unreliable. Avro's designer, Roy Chadwick from Farnworth, Widnes, frantically redesigned the plane to take four of the proven Merlin engines. The result was the legendary

Lancaster bomber. Avro alone could not produce the numbers needed, so Metropolitan-Vickers at Trafford Park and other manufacturers co-manufactured the plane. More than 7,300 were made before production ended in 1946. Chadwick sadly died in 1947 when the prototype Avro Tudor crashed during take-off.[28]

Trafford Park increased its workforce from 50,000 pre-war to 75,000 by 1945, and Ford's former car factory there reopened to make Merlin engines. Metro-Vicks also manufactured specialised electrical and electronic equipment. W.T. Glover made subsea pipes for the Pluto (Pipe Line Under The Ocean) project to deliver fuel to allied forces in the Normandy landings, while the engines and pumps were made by Mather and Platt at Newton Heath. Imperial Chemical Industries made penicillin at Trafford Park. Dunlop's Manchester factory made barrage balloons.

Manchester, now within reach of enemy bombers, was more vulnerable than in the First World War. A total of 72,000 children and 23,000 adults were evacuated. L.S. Lowry served as a voluntary fire officer after the war's outbreak and became an official war artist in 1943. Manchester was not bombed as heavily as Liverpool, but it was a strategic target as a centre of engineering and military production. The first bombs fell in August 1940. On 22 and 23 December the city was hit by the ferocious two-night Christmas Blitz, in which thousands of incendiary bombs and hundreds of high-explosive devices were unleashed. Firefighters from London and all over Lancashire and Cheshire joined the fight against flames that threatened to engulf the city. Royal Engineers destroyed undamaged buildings in order to create a firebreak. This did its job, though the fires were not finally brought under control until the afternoon of Christmas Day.[29]

Within a three-mile radius of Albert Square, 31.3 acres had been laid waste. Landmarks lost included the Free Trade Hall, Cross Street Chapel, the Victoria Buildings at the junction of Deansgate and St Mary's Gate, and the headquarters of the Lit and Phil in George Street with its collection of scientific memorabilia. Others damaged included the Royal Exchange, Assize Courts, Corn Exchange, St Ann's Church, Chetham's Hospital and Smithfield Market. One side of Piccadilly was destroyed.

The death toll was estimated at almost a thousand, including fatalities in Salford and Stretford, and thousands more were homeless. Contemporary accounts reported a spirited response by citizens, perhaps with an eye to propaganda value, including the story of an eleven-year-old boy pulled from the rubble amid intense heat. One rescue worker said: 'By Jove, I could go for a pint!' The lad replied: 'And so could I!' Manchester Cathedral looked as if it might escape damage, but was hit by virtually the last bomb of the raid. Within twenty-four hours, a restoration fund had been launched and craftsmen were offering their skills. At Cross Street Chapel, worshippers held services in its roofless ruins and planned a new place of worship. The mayor issued a statement called *We Plan a Fairer City*, calling for eradication of slums.

The following March, Manchester United's ground was put out of action for the rest of the war. In a raid on 1–2 June 1941, the Assize Courts were among buildings destroyed. There were other, smaller raids, the last of which was in August 1942. It was a war-weary Manchester that celebrated Victory in Europe Day on 8 May 1945. Dancing broke out in Piccadilly Gardens and impromptu street parties were held across the region. Winston Churchill, prime minister, said: 'We may allow ourselves a brief period of rejoicing; but let us not forget for a moment the toil and efforts that lie ahead.'[30]

13

SPORTING PASSION

When a charter aircraft carrying the young Manchester United foot-ball team – the famous 'Busby Babes' – back to England from a European Cup tie in Belgrade on 6 February 1958 stopped at Munich to refuel, a blizzard swept in. Snow and slush covered the runway.

The British European Airways plane, an Elizabethan class Airspeed Ambassador, made two attempts to take off, both aborted because of engine problems. On the third attempt, at 3.04pm, the aircraft failed to get airborne, overshot the runway, crashed through a fence and crossed a road where one wing struck a house. Seven players were killed instantly along with the club secretary, first team trainer, first team coach, eight sportswriters, one of the aircrew and two other passengers. Two weeks later the co-pilot and Duncan Edwards, the brilliant young England half-back, also lost their lives, bringing the final death toll to twenty-three. Manager Matt Busby suffered multiple injuries and twice received the last rites, yet survived.

The tragedy stunned Manchester, including United and City fans and the uncommitted alike. Lanarkshire-born Busby had been a City player for eight years (including playing in their 1934 FA Cup-winning side) and his United team appeared to be on the threshold of greatness. Frank Swift, a former City goalkeeper who became a journalist, was among the dead.

Anxious, disbelieving crowds gathered on street corners of a city still scarred by German bombing raids in the Second World War, desperate for news of another catastrophe coming out of Germany. Factories stopped work early. Even newspaper sellers were silent. The *News Chronicle* summed up the mood: 'It was as if every family had lost a personal friend. A city staggered under the blow. Manchester became a city of mourning.'[1] When the bodies were flown home, tens of thousands lined the twelve-mile route from Ringway airport to Old Trafford.

This was not the first postwar sporting disaster to strike the region. Thirty-three fans were crushed to death and four hundred injured at Bolton Wanderers' Burnden Park stadium during the second leg of an FA Cup quarter-final tie against Stoke City on 9 March 1946. Authorities had expected about 55,000 at the 70,000 capacity stadium, but an estimated 85,000 managed to find a way in. As the crowd increased, some were crushed against steel barriers that gave way, while others were trampled to death. Play stopped, yet shockingly restarted half an hour later with bodies laid out at the side of the pitch, covered with coats. An inquiry recommended more rigorous control of crowd sizes. The Burnden Park disaster remained Britain's deadliest stadium catastrophe until the Ibrox disaster of 1971.

These tragedies in a city already numbed by war underlined how important sport, both amateur and professional, has been to Manchester and its surrounding towns. Aside from football, cricket and rugby, the Manchester area has at various times been a leading centre for such sports as archery, athletics, cycling, lacrosse, water polo and speedway.

Before the nineteenth century, the term 'sport' generally referred to blood sports and any form of gambling. Hunting by the wealthy in the area dates back to at least the fourteenth century. Race meetings began on Salford's Kersal Moor in the 1680s. People from a wide social spectrum indulged in bull and bear baiting. From the fourteenth century onwards Manchester's ruling elite imposed strict controls on popular sports such as hare coursing, dog fighting and even bowls, fearing that these were distracting men from honing their archery skills and also causing too much gambling and drinking. Football – a mob affair played in the street – created so much disorder that the Court Leet banned it in 1608; not wholly successfully, since there were further banning orders in 1656 and 1657.[2]

Baiting was finally banned in 1835 and cock fighting in 1849, though the latter carried on in secret for years. Sport's growth was shaped by the city's expanding population. Voluntary sports clubs were formed, initially by middle- and upper-middle-class male elites. Manchester Golf Club, reckoned to be England's second after Royal Blackheath, was founded in about 1814 on Kersal Moor by Scottish merchant William Mitchell.

Broughton Cricket Club in Salford was formed in 1823; its rules stated that no fielder be permitted to smoke or lie down during play. Manchester Cricket Club, founded as Aurora CC between 1818 and 1823, moved to the current Old Trafford ground in 1857 and became Lancashire County Cricket Club in 1864. Old Trafford held the first ever Ashes Test match in England in July 1884; the first day was rained off and the match ended in a draw. Famous cricketers from the Manchester area include England captain Archie MacLaren (1871–1944, born in Whalley Range), Worsley-born batsmen Johnny Tyldesley (1873–1930) and younger brother Ernest (1889–1962), fast bowler Brian Statham (1930–2000, born in Gorton) and former England captains Mike Atherton (born in Failsworth, 1968) and Michael Vaughan (born in Eccles, 1974).

Manchester Football Club (which actually played rugby) was formed in Whalley Range in 1860, becoming the first rugby club in the North, followed by Sale a year later. Women began to participate in the more 'respectable' and decorously executed sports such as croquet from the 1850s and later lawn tennis, made possible by the invention of lawn mowers and air-filled rubber balls. Tennis clubs sprang up in almost every suburb, often linked to existing cricket and bowls clubs. They offered safe environments in which members of the opposite sex could mingle. By the 1880s, rising real wages, reductions in working hours and improved public transport were opening sport to a wider public, though class distinctions remained.

Manchester's engineering prowess made it one of the most exciting places to experience the new craze for bicycling. Andrew Muir of Salford in 1868 built and rented out velocipedes, self-propelled vehicles with two wheels, which became known as 'boneshakers' because their solid tyres bumped along cobbled streets. Then came 'penny farthing' bicycles made by the likes of Manchester's William Harrison, in which pedals drove a large front wheel. Swiss engineer Hans Renold set up a company in Salford in 1879 that revolutionised cycling by inventing a chain that drove the rear wheel of new safety bikes. Renold plc remains the oldest transmission chain company in existence, headquartered in Wythenshawe.

By the 1890s Haydon Perry, the *Manchester Guardian*'s 'Wheel notes' correspondent, noted that it was common to see 600 cyclists heading south past Trafford Bar on a fine Saturday afternoon. Cycling offered a sense of freedom to women; American suffragist Frances Willard called her bicycle an 'implement of power'. Rapho Cycle Company of Altrincham was among those that designed bicycles for women, allowing for long skirts, and also tandems designed for the woman to be at the front.[4]

Public houses played a big role in developing professional sport, just as they had once been keen to sponsor bull baiting. They were a springboard for the growth of athletics, often known as 'pedestrianism'. Publicans, possibly starting with Betty Berry of the Snipe Inn, Audenshaw, around 1840, built cinder tracks next to their properties along with bowling greens and facilities for sports such as wrestling and shooting. They created events at which they could charge entrance fees, sell food and drink and promote betting. Manchester became known for mile racing: the world record was broken repeatedly in the 1850s and 1860s at local tracks beside pubs, notably Copenhagen Grounds at the Shears Inn, Newton Heath, and the Royal Oak at Failsworth.

Among other sports, the annual Manchester and Salford Regatta, founded in 1841 and promoted by Pomona Gardens, became a three-day event attracting crowds to the banks of the Irwell and some of the country's leading oarsmen. Horse-racing prospered. Manchester's racecourse moved from Kersal Moor to other parts of Salford – first Castle Irwell in Pendleton and then New Barns near the Ship Canal, before returning to a purpose-built course at Castle Irwell in 1902. It was a boggy, challenging track and finally closed in 1963 after a period of decline.[5]

Clubs formed in late Victorian times include Manchester Wheelers cycling club, Salford Harriers athletics club, the all-conquering Osborne Street Baths water polo team in Collyhurst, and several lacrosse teams, inspired by the visit of two Canadian teams to Longsight in 1876. Manchester's working classes initially showed a liking for rugby, but association football came to predominate, probably because it was relatively simple and – in contrast to earlier times – promoted in schools, boys' clubs and similar agencies for moral and physical self-improvement.

The team that became Manchester United was founded by the dining room committee of the Newton Heath Lancashire and Yorkshire Railway in 1878. Newton Heath was nicknamed 'the Heathens' and played initially on land at North Road, where matches were frequently shrouded in steam from passing locomotives. The team that became Manchester City was founded by two wardens at St Mark's Church in Gorton, east Manchester, and originally called West Gorton St Marks. In an area of high unemployment, it began as an alternative to gang violence. Links with the church were soon severed and it changed its name to Gorton, before moving to a polluted wasteland at Hyde Road, Ardwick, between a viaduct and a boiler works, where it became Ardwick Association FC. The first Manchester derby was played in 1881.[6]

The Football Association initially tried to outlaw professionalism, but accepted it in 1885. The Football League – the world's first national league – was created in April 1888 at a meeting in the Royal

Hotel, Manchester (at the corner of Market Street and Mosley Street). All twelve founder members came from the North and the Midlands, including six from Lancashire. The only one from the Manchester area, however, was Bolton Wanderers, originally founded by a curate and a schoolmaster as Christ Church FC in 1874; it became Bolton Wanderers in 1877, so called because it kept changing grounds. Newton Heath and Ardwick entered the Football League in 1892, Newton Heath in the First Division and Ardwick in the Second. Ardwick reformed as Manchester City in 1894 after a financial crisis and adopted sky-blue shirts.

Elsewhere in the region, Heaton Norris Rovers, founded in 1883, were renamed Stockport County in 1890 and joined the Football League in 1900; they were nicknamed 'the Hatters' after the town's hat-making industry and they have played at Edgeley Park since 1902. Bury FC was formed from two church teams in 1885 at Gigg Lane and entered the Football League in 1894; they were nicknamed 'the Shakers', allegedly because the manager inspired players by saying: 'We shall shake 'em! In fact, we are the shakers.' Pine Villa FC, founded in 1895 (named after Pine Mill), became Oldham Athletic in 1899 when neighbours Oldham County folded; it moved into County's Boundary Park ground. Oldham joined the Football League in 1907. Rochdale AFC was founded in 1907 and joined the Football League in 1921. Wigan Athletic was formed in 1932, the sixth attempt since 1883 to create a stable football club in the town.

Manchester City won its first major trophy, the FA Cup, in 1904, beating Bolton 1–0. The club suffered a major scandal in 1905 when leading player Billy Meredith, the 'Welsh wizard', was fined and suspended for trying to bribe an Aston Villa player. After City refused financial help for Meredith, he publicly accused the club of breaking the league's £4-a-week wage cap. The Football Association suspended the manager for life, fined City £250, and fined and suspended seventeen players. Local journalists felt that City were unfairly punished, since many clubs were breaking the cap. City were forced to sell players. United bought Meredith and three others at an auction, forming the core of the side that won the league championship in 1907–8.[7]

Newton Heath did not flourish at first either. In 1894 they were relegated from the First Division. By 1902 the club was in severe financial difficulties and served with a winding-up order. It was rescued by John Henry Davies, a wealthy brewer who became president and changed its name to Manchester United (having also considered Manchester Central and Manchester Celtic). He adopted red and white colours. United won the FA Cup in 1909 and the next year Davies moved the club to a new, £60,000, 80,000-capacity stadium at Old Trafford, earning it the nickname 'Moneybags United'. In the inaugural match, United lost 4–3 to Liverpool. The club suffered its own match-fixing scandal in 1915 when four Liverpool and three United players were found guilty and banned for life for allegedly fixing a game in United's favour, having bet on the result. All were eventually pardoned.[8]

In rugby, clergyman William Webb Ellis, sometimes portrayed as the game's inventor, came from the Manchester area. The folklore is that Webb Ellis, while a pupil at Rugby School, picked up the ball and ran with it during a football match in 1823, thus creating the 'rugby' style of play. This has been widely challenged on the grounds that the story emerged only after Webb Ellis's death. Nonetheless, the trophy for which teams compete in the Rugby World Cup is named the Webb Ellis Cup. Historians tend to claim that Webb Ellis was born in Salford, though the man himself stated in the 1851 census that he was born in Manchester.[9]

While the Rugby Football Union remained rigidly amateur, industrialists who ran northern clubs wanted to give working-class players 'broken time' payments to compensate them for lost earnings while playing. Representatives of twenty-one Yorkshire and Lancashire sides established the Northern Rugby Football Union at the George Hotel, Huddersfield, in 1895. They included Broughton Rangers, Leigh, Oldham, Rochdale Hornets, Tyldesley and Wigan (plus Stockport, which telegraphed requesting admission to the union and was accepted). Northern Union became a separate code, particularly after 1906 when the sides were reduced from fifteen to thirteen players. It became the Rugby Football League from 1922. The dramatic growth of association football prevented it from expanding beyond the North, though it periodically tried to do so. In the North, Rugby League established itself only in south Lancashire, west Cumbria, and west and east Yorkshire, though it attracted passionate support in its heartlands.

A further example of Manchester's engineering prowess linking with sport is shown in the fact that, from the mid-1890s until at least the 1980s, most turnstiles fitted at Britain's growing number of stadiums, swimming pools, parks, exhibition halls and even public toilets were made by two Salford companies, W.T. Ellison and W.H. Bailey.[10] Sport was drastically curtailed from 1914 to 1918, but there was a boom in attendance after the war. The depression again reduced sporting opportunities for many, but for those in employment there was growth in real wages, especially from the early 1930s, along with shorter hours and paid holidays.

Football saw drops in attendance during the worst years, yet City and United ended the 1930s with average crowds 15 per cent higher than in 1913–14. United performed poorly and spent most seasons in the Second Division. A wealthy local entrepreneur, James Gibson, bailed them out again in 1931. City did better, reaching three Wembley finals and winning the First Division championship in 1936–7. City outgrew its Hyde Road ground and found some cheap land for a new one in 1923, a former clay pit at Maine Road, Moss Side. The choice was to prove a false economy as the pitch frequently turned into a quagmire. It was the largest ground in the country and soon pulled in crowds of more than 70,000. (A researcher for a 1930s street directory knocked on the Hulme front door of Matt Busby, then a City player, and asked his occupation. It appeared in the directory, due to his Lanarkshire accent, as 'fruit broiler'.)[11]

Professional boxing enjoyed a golden age between the wars. Top matches took place at the Free Trade Hall or the New King's Hall at

Belle Vue, regarded by many as Europe's leading venue, and there were many lesser venues. Out of backstreet gyms and boxing booths known as 'blood tubs' came top-class boxers, including 'three cavaliers' trained at Collyhurst and Moston Lads' Club: Jackie Brown, a fast-living boy from Collyhurst who became world flyweight champion; Johnny King, British and Empire bantamweight champion; and middleweight champion Joe Bamford, the 'Rochdale thunderbolt', who fought under the name Jock McAvoy so that his mother did not realise he was boxing.

Lads' clubs originated in the late Victorian era, established by philanthropists in working-class areas as an alternative to being drawn into 'scuttling gangs' common in poor districts. Girls' clubs were also set up, although these were fewer and tended to receive less public attention until the interwar years. The heyday of lads' clubs was the 1930s and many were in sharp decline by the 1960s as a result of redevelopment and wider choices of activity. Salford Lads' Club in Ordsall is a famous survivor, now open to boys and girls and cemented in pop-culture memory by a photo of The Smiths taken in 1986.[12]

Racial prejudice prevented another Manchester boxer, middleweight Len Johnson, from achieving the recognition he deserved. He became de facto British Empire champion briefly in 1926, although this went unrecognised by UK authorities because of a colour bar, which meant he never won a British title. He was born to an English mother of Irish descent and a Sierra Leonian sailor. Prejudices against his mixed family ran deep – his mother was assaulted and received scars on her face for having married a black man. Winston Churchill as home secretary had banned interracial boxing matches in 1911 in response to establishment fears that the Empire could be undermined if a sports tournament even temporarily demonstrated the equality of black and white people. The ban lasted until 1947. Johnson ran a travelling boxing booth after retirement. Modern boxing champions include Wythenshawe-born heavyweight Tyson Fury, Stockport-born super-lightweight/welterweight Terry Hatton, lightweight Anthony Crolla, Bury-born super-bantamweight Scott Quigg, Crumpsall-born lightweight Terry Flanagan and Bolton's super-lightweight Amir Khan.

Manchester entrepreneurs were constantly seeking new attractions. Greyhound racing and speedway were consciously modern forms of excitement. Greyhound racing had roots in coursing and whippet racing, but its modern form began in the US in 1912. The oval track and mechanical hare were introduced to Britain by American businessman Charles Munn, who teamed up with UK investors to create the Greyhound Racing Association. They opened Britain's first track at Belle Vue Stadium, opposite but separate from the leisure park, in July 1926. Others opened at the Albion Ground, Salford, and a revamped White City Stadium in Old Trafford two years later. Within a decade Britain had 200 tracks. Aiming for a wide audience, Salford Albion offered women reduced entry prices and a pram park. Gambling was a big factor: the dogs were a working-class alternative to on-course betting at horse races.[13]

Tracks for speedway, derived from American and Australian grass and dirt-track racing, were established from 1928 at White City, Salford Albion, Kirkmanshulme Lane and Audenshaw Racecourse. All were short-lived, thanks to high expenses and a shortage of top-class riders, and only a new track at Belle Vue, opened in 1929, survived the 1930s. It was home to the Belle Vue Aces, Britain's most successful speedway team of the interwar period. It remains the world's longest continually operating speedway club, racing today at the National Speedway Stadium, opened in 2016 close to former Belle Vue Stadium.

The interwar period also saw voluntary recreational activities organised in opposition to commercial sport. The Co-operative Wholesale Society in 1928 formed Manchester Sports Association, which acquired grounds, formed two football leagues and sponsored competitions in bowls, swimming and women's cricket. Working-class rambling was strong. The Communist Party-inspired British Workers Sports Federation was responsible for the mass trespass on

Kinder Scout in 1932. There were more than a hundred clubs in Manchester and District Federation of Ramblers. It was hard, however, to resist the rising tide of commercial leisure.[14]

In tennis, Fred Perry (1909–95), one of the game's greatest players, was born to a working-class family in Portwood, Stockport, where his father was a cotton spinner. The family later lived in Bolton, Wallasey and Ealing. Perry won ten majors including three consecutive Wimbledon championships from 1934 to 1936. Dismayed by the class-conscious nature of the Lawn Tennis Club of Great Britain, Perry turned professional at the end of the 1936 season and moved to the US, where he became a naturalised citizen. Full recognition of his achievements by Britain's tennis authorities did not come until late in life; a statue was unveiled at Wimbledon in 1984. Memorials in Stockport include a blue plaque at his birthplace and a designated walking route called the Fred Perry Way, opened in 2002.

The immediate postwar years saw attendances at professional sport reach their zenith. Gates of 80,000 and more were common at City's Maine Road, where United also played until 1949 because of bomb damage at Old Trafford. Crowds began to fall from the 1950s, however, as televisions, cars, foreign holidays and other activities diluted sport's attraction. Declining revenues and lack of reinvestment led to a spiral of decline for various stadiums. Three of the city's four greyhound and speedway stadiums closed during the 1980s. Closure of Castle Irwell in 1963 left Manchester without its own racecourse for the first time since at least 1681. The Ice Palace in Cheetham Hill, opened in 1910 and one of the world's finest skating rinks, closed in 1967. Swinton Rugby League club lost its ground in 1992. Many swimming baths also closed, including Victoria Baths in 1993.[15]

Manchester United bucked the trend of declining attendances as it made its way to becoming a global super-club. Busby rebuilt his shattered Babes as the 'Red Devils' (a nickname previously acquired by Salford Rugby League club during a visit to France in 1934 when

French journalists labelled them '*Les Diables Rouges*'). In 1968 United became the first English club to win the European Cup, beating Benfica 4–1 in the final with a team that contained three European Footballers of the Year: Bobby Charlton, Denis Law and George Best. Charlton, from Ashington in Northumberland, survived the Munich disaster after being dragged from the plane by goalkeeper Harry Gregg. Aberdeen-born Law also played for City early and late in his career. Belfast-born Best, a hugely talented winger, suffered personal problems, notably alcoholism, as a result of extravagantly embracing the Swinging Sixties lifestyle. 'I spent a lot of money on booze, birds and fast cars – the rest I just squandered,' he once said.[16]

Three members of England's 1966 World Cup-winning team, playing alongside Charlton, were born in the region: Manchester United's Nobby Stiles in Collyhurst, Alan Ball in Farnworth, near Bolton, and Geoff Hurst in Ashton-under-Lyne. Other England footballers include Bolton-born Nat Lofthouse (Bolton Wanderers), Westhoughton-born Francis Lee (Bolton Wanderers and Manchester City), Farnworth-born Tommy Lawton (whose clubs included Everton, Chelsea and Arsenal) and United's Paul Scholes (from Salford), Gary and Phil Neville (from Bury) and Nicky Butt (from Gorton).

After a modest spell in the 1970s and 80s, United, under the successful management of Sir Alex Ferguson, benefited from globalisation of the game stimulated by the Premier League's creation in 1992 and its penetration of world markets via digital TV. United's global following is estimated to have grown to more than 300 million, attracted by the club's success and by stars such as David Beckham. United have won a record twenty League titles, twelve FA Cups and the European Cup/UEFA Champions League three times, though they have had less success since Ferguson retired in 2013. Members of Ferguson's 'Class of 92' – Gary and Phil Neville, Ryan Giggs (raised in Salford), Scholes and Butt – went on to co-found University Academy 92, an institution in Old Trafford aimed at widening access to higher education.

One of City's biggest postwar heroes was goalkeeper Bernhard (Bert) Trautmann, a former German prisoner of war, who signed for the club in 1949.[17] Trautmann had been a Nazi-sympathising paratrooper and strongly anti-British, but his opinion changed after being captured and interned. After the war he declined to be repatriated. There were demonstrations against his signing, but he soon became popular. In 1956 he was injured during the FA Cup final and played to the end, not realising he had a broken neck. In that year he was named the Football Writers' Association Footballer of the Year. He stayed with City for fifteen years.

City had a mixed record in the postwar years. There was success in the late 1960s and early 1970s under the management of Joe Mercer and Malcolm Allison, winning the league title, FA Cup, League Cup and European Cup Winners Cup. After a period of decline in which City were relegated to the third tier in 1998, they climbed back and have been in the Premier League since 2002. City were bought by former Thai prime minister Thaksin Shinawatra in 2007 and then by the United Arab Emirates vice president, Sheikh Mansour bin Zayed Al Nahyan, through the Abu Dhabi United Group in 2008. Since then the club has won seven League titles, three FA Cups and six League Cups, though there has also been criticism – contested by the club – that the Abu Dhabi ownership amounts to 'sportswashing' by members of an autocratic regime. In 2023 City won their first UEFA Champions League title, beating Inter Milan 1–0.

City topped the Deloitte Football Money League in 2023 as the club with the world's highest revenue, estimated at €731 million, with United fourth at €688.6 million. Forbes in 2023 rated United the world's second most valuable club, worth $6 billion, with City fifth at $4.99 billion. Top-level players today include Wythenshawe-born Marcus Rashford, the Manchester United and England striker praised for his anti-poverty campaigning, and Manchester City and England midfielder Phil Foden, born in Stockport.

Life has been tougher for other Greater Manchester clubs. Bury were expelled from the Football League in 2019 after financial difficulties and went into administration in 2020; they returned to play the North West Counties League in 2023 after merging with Bury AFC. Stockport County tumbled to the sixth tier in 2013 but have recovered to the fourth, securing promotion back to League Two in 2022. Bolton Wanderers entered administration in 2019, but were acquired by new owners. Oldham Athletic was a founder member of the Premier League in 1992, but fell to the third tier by 1997. In 2022 they were relegated from League Two, making them the first former Premier League team to play non-League football. The club was bought that year by businessman Frank Rothwell. Rochdale, after 102 years as a Football League club, were relegated to the National League in 2023. Wigan Athletic were on the rise after being bought by Dave Whelan, local millionaire and owner of JJB Sports, in 1995; they reached the top division in 2005 for the first time in their seventy-three-year history. In 2013 they won the FA Cup for the first time, beating Manchester City 1–0, but they were relegated from the Premier League. Whelan sold the club in 2019 and it entered administration in 2020, ostensibly because of the impact of the Covid pandemic on its finances, but it has survived.

In Rugby League, of the Northern Rugby Football Union's original founders, Tyldesley folded in 1901, Stockport in 1903 and Broughton in 1955 (after becoming Belle Vue Rangers in 1946). By contrast, Wigan, now known as Wigan Warriors, are the most successful club in British Rugby League history, having won twenty-two league championships, twenty Challenge Cups and four World Club Championships. After decline in the 1970s, Rugby League – located largely in small industrial and mining towns – achieved an improbable resurgence despite industry's collapse in the 1980s. The top-tier Super League was created in 1996, switching from winter to a summer game, since when Wigan Warriors have won the title five times compared with ten for St Helens and eight for Leeds Rhinos. Leigh (now Leigh Leopards) are also in the Super League, as are Salford (now Salford Red Devils), who joined the Northern Union a few months after its foundation. Oldham, known as the Roughyeds, and Rochdale Hornets are in RFL League 1, the third tier. In Rugby Union, Sale Sharks, a professional offshoot of Sale founded in 1999, are the only Manchester area team in the English Premiership.

All the major professional sports have created women's teams in recent years. Out of twenty-eight players in the England lionesses' squad for the UEFA Women's Euro 2022, nine were from Manchester City and three from United. England beat Germany 2–1 in the final, with goals by United's Tyldesley-born Ella Toone and City's Chloe Kelly. The 2023 Women's World Cup squad contained six from City and four from United; England lost the final 1–0 to Spain. A blue plaque was unveiled in 2023 to honour a pioneering group who defied an FA ban on women's football to form a team, Manchester Corinthians, in 1949. They won a major European trophy in Germany and played on international tours in front of more than 50,000 people. In Rugby League's Women's Super League, Wigan Warriors are in Group 1, and Salford Red Devils and Leigh Leopards in Group 2. Lancashire's women's cricket team played their first game in 1930 and joined the County Championship in 1998, which they went on to win in 2017. Lancashire's England players have included Manchester-born Kate Cross as well as Alex Hartley, Sophie Ecclestone and Emma Lamb. England captain Heather Knight was born in Rochdale.

In athletics, Diane Modahl (born 1966) was raised in Longsight by parents who had emigrated from Jamaica, her mother being a nurse and father a labourer. Modahl ran for Sale Harriers and went on to win gold in the 800 metres at the 1990 Commonwealth Games. She also won six Amateur Athletics Association titles and a silver and bronze in other Commonwealth Games. She held the English, British and Commonwealth records at 600 and 800 metres. Her career was disrupted, however, when she was sent home from the Commonwealth Games in Canada in 1994 and banned by the

British Athletics Foundation after her urine sample tested positive for performance-enhancing drugs. It later proved that her sample had been kept in a room at a temperature of thirty-five degrees Celsius for three days, which would result in a false positive. She was exonerated, though legal battles for compensation led to her and her husband losing their house and coming close to bankruptcy. In 2010 they established the Diane Modahl Sports Foundation, a charity that brings athletics coaching opportunities to young people, particularly those living in disadvantaged areas.[18]

A big local cycling star was Bury-born Reg Harris (1920–92), who won the world amateur sprint title in 1947, two Olympic silver medals in 1948 and four professional titles. He had a ferocious will to win and made a surprise comeback twenty years later, winning a British title in 1974 at age fifty-four. Also notable was Jack Sibbit, a butcher's son from Ancoats who won a silver medal at the 1928 Olympics and twelve national titles. Rochdale's Mandy Jones won the women's world road race championship in 1982 at Goodwood, Sussex, aged twenty. She said: 'I won by accident. It was just plain daft. We were going downhill and I just rode past them. Then I looked back, saw I had a gap and kept going. I was praying my legs wouldn't collapse. But with around half a lap to go, I started thinking "Hey, I could win this!"'[19]

Track cyclist Sir Jason Kenny (born in Bolton in 1988), with seven gold and two silver medals, is the most successful British Olympian, most successful British cyclist and most successful cyclist in Olympic history. His wife Dame Laura Kenny (née Trott), born in Essex and raised in Hertfordshire, holds the same records on the female side (five gold and one silver). They live near Knutsford with their two children.[20] Dame Sarah Storey, born in 1977 in Eccles, is Britain's most successful Paralympian, having won seventeen gold medals. She began her Paralympic career as a swimmer before switching to cycling in 2005. She was born without a functioning left hand after her arm became entangled in the umbilical cord in the womb. Also in swimming, Longsight-born Ethel 'Sunny' Lowry

(1911–2008), a second cousin of L.S. Lowry, became in 1933 one of the earliest women to swim the English Channel.

Manchester's embrace of sport as a means of economic regeneration has created a rich crop of new facilities. Although bids to host the 1996 and 2000 Olympics failed, Manchester managed to attract the 2002 Commonwealth Games. This led to the building of the 146-hectare Sportcity, a complex of six arenas (including the cycling velodrome, already opened in 1994) combined with commercial outlets and housing on an industrial wasteland in the east Manchester district of Bradford. Manchester City moved into the athletics stadium – built partly on a former coalmine – in 2003 on a 250-year council lease and subsequently renamed it the Etihad after a sponsor. Manchester Aquatics Centre near the city centre also opened in 2000. Sport seems destined to play as big a part in Manchester's future as it did in its past.

14

THE POSTWAR ERA

Manchester's story since the Second World War is one of decline, near-death and miraculous rebirth. Many doubted whether the city would ever recover. 'It reminds me of Berlin after the war. Everything was broken and falling down,' said German chanteuse Nico, Andy Warhol's muse, who came to live in the city in 1981 (the attraction for her had probably more to do with a reliable supply of heroin).[1] It is not a simple narrative, however. Resurrection was hampered by a disastrous twenty-year experiment with modernist architecture. Despite what has been achieved, recovery is still a work in progress.

City leaders were determined to improve life for its citizens. More than 60,000 houses were declared unfit after the war, with a further 53,000 thought overdue for demolition. Manchester Corporation published the wildly ambitious *City of Manchester Plan 1945*, drawn up by city surveyor Rowland Nicholas and his team, proposing 'to enable every inhabitant of this city to enjoy real health of body and health of mind'. It envisaged a city centre of tree-lined boulevards; zones for commerce, housing, industry and recreation; a city liberated from nineteenth-century grime. Little was ever implemented because of the cost, which is perhaps as well because, along with Victorian slums, it proposed to sweep away Manchester's mills, warehouses, offices, banks and even Alfred Waterhouse's Town Hall.[2]

Cotton saw a modest recovery after the war, but decline soon accelerated as Lancashire's producers lost out to those from the Indian subcontinent, Hong Kong and China. By the late 1950s Britain was importing more cotton cloth than it exported for the first time in two centuries. That also affected Manchester's merchants and brokers; Rylands, one of the largest merchants, was taken over in 1953 by Isaac Wolfson's Great Universal Stores, best known for mail order and furniture. Peter Thorneycroft, Conservative president of the Board of Trade, was dubbed the 'hangman of Lancashire' for his reluctance to protect the industry. Prime minister Harold Macmillan, nervous about losing north-west seats after a by-election defeat in Rochdale, hurriedly negotiated voluntary import quotas in 1958 with India, Pakistan and Hong Kong. These did not stem the decline and neither did the Cotton Industry Act 1959, which sought to reorganise the industry and provided grants to replace equipment.[3]

Engineering remained strong, including companies such as Mather and Platt, founded in 1845 and based at the Park Works, Newton Heath; the firm became a leader in making fire-fighting equipment, electric motors and food machinery. Trafford Park remained important, though its workforce declined from its peak of 75,000 in 1945 to 50,000 by 1967 as industrial growth shifted to the western end of the Ship Canal at Ellesmere Port and Runcorn.[4]

Many of the finer buildings damaged in the Blitz were reconstructed. The Free Trade Hall, little more than a shell, was rebuilt behind the remaining façade and reopened as a concert hall in 1951. The Royal Exchange was repaired and reopened in 1953, though it was a scaled-down version, reflecting cotton's decline. There were things to cheer Mancunians up. Manchester United under manager Matt Busby won the FA Cup final against Blackpool in 1948; *Manchester Evening News* journalist Tom Jackson coined the nickname 'Busby Babes' in 1951. In 1952 they won the First Division, United's first league title for forty-one years, then back-to-back titles in 1956 and 1957. Manchester City beat Birmingham City in the 1956 FA Cup final.[5]

Researchers at Manchester University made breakthroughs in science and technology that would have a global impact. Max Newman, Freddie Williams, Tom Kilburn and Geoff Tootill produced their Small-Scale Experimental Machine, nicknamed Baby, in 1948, the first time a programme was stored in a computer memory, rather than on paper or other mechanism. It heralded the arrival of modern computing. Manchester's Science and Industry Museum has a working replica of Baby. Alan Turing worked on the Mark I model. His statue is in Sackville Park, near the university's Sackville Street campus. Bernard Lovell's Jodrell Bank achieved an honoured place in the study of astronomy.

Health minister Aneurin Bevan chose to mark the creation of the National Health Service on 5 July 1948 by attending a ceremony at Park Hospital, Davyhulme (renamed Trafford General in 1988), where he symbolically received the keys to the hospital. Also joining the NHS in 1948 was the Christie Hospital, which has become a world leader in cancer care. It was founded at the end of the nineteenth century as the Cancer Pavilion and Home for Incurables from money bequeathed by Sir Joseph Whitworth to his friend Richard Christie, lawyer and academic. Manchester Royal Infirmary and Manchester Royal Eye Hospital were also among those joining the NHS.

The Air Force released Ringway airport for civil use in 1946 and the old terminal was quickly swamped by growth in traffic. Adaptation of an adjacent hangar helped for a while. Intercontinental flights began with a Sabena service to New York in 1953. A new terminal opened in 1962 and the airport was renamed Manchester International in 1975. Terminal 2 opened in 1993 and a second runway in 2001, despite protests. Terminal A, opened in 1989, was expanded as Terminal 3 in 1998. Manchester Airport Holdings is majority owned by the ten Greater Manchester local authorities and also owns London Stansted and East Midlands airports. The UK's third-busiest airport has enjoyed huge commercial success, but has also had disasters. In 1957 a British Airways Viscount crashed into houses on approach, killing twenty-two people. In 1967 a British Midland plane carrying holidaymakers back from Palma crashed in Stockport, killing seventy-two. In 1985 a British Airtours plane suffered engine failure during take-off, killing fifty-five.

Manchester barrister Charles Gandy, chairman of the National Smoke Abatement Society, proposed the world's first smokeless zones in 1935. The war delayed consideration, and residents continued to suffer a high death rate from respiratory diseases. The corporation introduced the first smokeless zone in the city centre in 1952, but that was not where most smoke came from. After the London smog that year, the Clean Air Act 1956 aimed to reduce air pollution by 80 per cent over twenty years. Manchester and other authorities grouped together to tackle it on a regional basis. By the act's twenty-fifth anniversary in 1981, smoke pollution had fallen to one-fifteenth of its previous level, aided by slum clearances.[6]

In Labour's 1945 general election landslide, the party won nine of Manchester's ten seats, with only Withington remaining Conservative. The picture was more balanced in the 1950s, but with Labour always in the ascendant. From the 1960s to 1990s there was a flow away from the Tories across larger northern cities. Factors included industrial decline and loss of population to the suburbs. Manchester's last Tory seat was lost when Withington fell in 1987. It has been a broadly similar pattern on the city council, barring a brief period of Tory control in the late 1960s. Withington-born mathematician Kathleen Ollerenshaw (1912–2014), lecturer at Manchester University and grandchild of the founder of the Timpson shoe repair business – and deaf from age eight – was Conservative councillor for Rusholme from 1956 to 1981, including a year as lord mayor in 1975–6, and became an adviser on education to Margaret Thatcher's government. The party lost its two remaining councillors in 1996.

Labour's Ellen Wilkinson (1891–1947) was born in Ardwick to a working-class but ambitious Methodist family and won a history scholarship to Manchester University. Nicknamed 'Red Ellen' or the

'Fiery Particle', she started out on the hard left and was a founder
member of the Communist Party of Great Britain. Later she became
Labour MP for Jarrow, played a big part in the 1936 Jarrow March
of the unemployed to London to petition for the right to work, and
eventually became minister of education in the 1945 Labour government. As minister, she raised the school-leaving age from fourteen to
fifteen and oversaw the creation of grammar schools and secondary
moderns under the wartime coalition's Education Act 1944.
Wilkinson has been accused of resisting the introduction of comprehensive schools, favoured by some in Labour (they were initially
known as 'multilateral' schools; the first was created at Windermere
in 1945). She believed such a major change was unachievable at that
time and focused on what she saw as attainable reforms. Others
included free school milk, improvements in the school meals system,
more university scholarships and an expansion of part-time adult
education through county colleges. During the bitter winter of
1947, Wilkinson succumbed to a bronchial disease and died after an
overdose of medication, which the coroner at her inquest declared
was accidental.[8]

By 1954 Manchester Corporation could move on from war
damage repairs to slum clearance, slowly at first but becoming more
ambitious in the 1960s. At first it stuck to its preference for low-rise,
low-density development, which created a need for more suburban
overspill estates. The government rejected a proposal to build what
would have been two more 'Wythenshawes' in Cheshire, at
Mobberley and Lymm. From 1953 to 1973 Manchester built almost
twenty-three and a half thousand homes in twenty-two places, the
largest being at Hattersley (east of Hyde) and Langley (south of
Rochdale).[9] These tended to be isolated from jobs and services. Folk
singer Mike Harding summed up a common feeling in 'The
Hattersley Lament':[10]

Oh dear, what can the matter be,
Some silly bugger has sent us to Hattersley,

We've been up Hattersley three weeks on Saturday,
Oh how I wish we weren't here

Hulme, Beswick, Longsight and Harpurhey were singled out as the first areas for 'comprehensive development'. The need to increase densities led the council to look to medium-height, deck-access blocks as a compromise between their low-rise ideals and the high-rise alternative. The notion was that these would be 'streets in the sky', recreating traditional street life above the dangers and pollution of traffic. By the time Hulme was completed in 1972, about 5,000 homes had been built in less than eight years, 3,000 of them deck-access, Britain's largest concentration of these.[11]

The crescents at Hulme – four south-facing u-shaped blocks, seven storeys high – were designed by Hugh Wilson and J. Lewis Womersley; the latter was also in charge of delivering Sheffield's Park Hill flats. Each crescent was named after a distinguished architect – Adam, Nash, Barry and Kent – which seemed insensitive once the crescents' failings surfaced. Womersley said: 'We feel that the analogy we have made with Georgian London and Bath is entirely valid. By the use of similar shapes and proportions, large-scale building groups and open spaces, and, above all, by skilful landscaping and extensive tree planning, it is our endeavour to achieve at Hulme a solution to the problems of twentieth-century living which would be the equivalent in quality that reached the requirements of eighteenth-century Bloomsbury and Bath.'[12]

The flats were poorly designed, manufactured and constructed. Concrete cracked, communal waste chutes clogged, lifts broke down, poor insulation and high energy costs generated health problems. Crime and graffiti abounded. In 1974 a five-year-old child died after falling from a balcony, leading the council to agree to rehouse families and replace them with students and all-adult households. The crescents were described by *Architects' Journal* as 'Europe's worst housing stock ... hideous system-built deck-access blocks which gave Hulme its unsavoury reputation'.[13] They were demolished between

1993 and 1995. Similar problems occurred on a smaller scale in other inner-city developments. By the mid-1970s large-scale schemes were coming to an end and there was a shift back to refurbishing what remained of the older housing stock.

It was not only in public housing that modernism took hold. The twenty-five-storey CIS Tower, erected by the Co-operative Insurance Society on Miller Street in 1962 and inspired by Chicago's skyline, was said to be the tallest office block in Europe when it opened and remained Manchester's tallest building for three decades. The Arndale, designed as Europe's largest covered shopping centre, was constructed in phases between 1972 and 1979, replacing an area of narrow medieval-patterned streets and alleys. It was built by Town & City Properties, successor to the Arndale Property Trust, created in the 1950s by Arnold Hagenbach and Sam Chippindale from Yorkshire. The architects again were Wilson and Womersley, but they did not have a free hand: the developers demanded a closed building with little natural light and no external window displays.[14] The result was an exterior of concrete panels faced with yellow tiles, which Mancunians derided as 'the biggest toilet block in the world'.

By the 1970s the result of all this was to leave Manchester stranded between a crumbling redbrick past and a failing modernist future. A year before L.S. Lowry died in 1976, writer Phil Griffin bumped into the artist staring at the windowless Arndale. 'Oh no,' Lowry sighed. 'Who let them do that?'[15]

Manchester's economic decline accelerated. Tonnage on the Ship Canal peaked in 1958 and shrank after containerisation made it harder to use. The port closed in 1982. Trafford Park's workforce plummeted from 50,000 in 1967 to 15,000 by 1976. There were savage cutbacks at firms including GEC (formerly Metropolitan-Vickers, subsequently becoming Associated Electrical Industries), which shrank from 22,000 in 1964 to 3,000 by 1976. It made turbines, switchgear and traction control gear.[16]

In the early 1960s there were hopes that the region might benefit from Harold Wilson's 'white heat of technology'. Heavy engineering was declining, but electrical engineering looked promising. Even the stagnant textile industry was rejuvenated by ICI and Courtaulds' manufacture of synthetic fibres. Wilson opened the Mancunian Way, one of the country's first 'aerial motorways', in 1967. The age of steam was ending – British Rail's final steam-hauled train ran from Carlisle to Liverpool via Manchester in 1968 and Central Station closed in 1969 – but a new Piccadilly Station replaced London Road and the Manchester–London line was electrified.

It was a false dawn. Overall, jobs in Manchester declined by 22 per cent between 1951 and 1981; jobs in engineering and electrical goods nearly halved, while those in textiles declined by 86 per cent.[17] The Royal Exchange closed in 1968. The inner industrial belt of factories and workshops was devastated. By the 1980s, 'like lumbering dinosaurs who suddenly met their meteorite, the big heavy industries of east Manchester toppled into extinction', wrote Paul Taylor in the *Manchester Evening News*.[18]

The *Guardian*'s dropping of Manchester from its title in 1959 and move to London in 1964 was a portent of the city's decline as the Fleet Street of the North. Away from the city, however, a son of Salford became one of Britain's most celebrated journalists. Sir Harold Evans (1928–2020), born in Patricroft, Eccles, to Welsh parents – his father was a train driver and his mother ran a small grocery shop from home – won plaudits as editor of the *Sunday Times* from 1967 to 1981. He started as a reporter in Ashton-under-Lyne before studying at Durham University, then forged a reputation at the *Manchester Evening News* and became editor of the *Northern Echo* in Darlington. At the *Sunday Times* he was noted for investigative journalism, including campaigning for greater compensation for those damaged by Thalidomide, a drug to control morning sickness that led to children being born with deformities.[19]

By 1985 almost three-quarters of Manchester's workforce was employed in services, though even here there was pressure: commercial offices were moving to the suburbs for better motorway access and lower rents.[20] On the brighter side, Manchester still had a sizeable banking and insurance sector and was important as a retail centre and in newer industries such as television.

During the early 1980s recession, unemployment reached crisis proportions in some inner-city districts. By 1986, 59 per cent of adult males in Hulme were unemployed. In Miles Platting the figure was 46 per cent, while Cheetham Hill and Moss Side both registered 44 per cent. Hulme had the highest youth unemployment at 68 per cent.[21] Migrants from the West Indies, India and Pakistan who arrived in the 1950s and 60s were mostly concentrated in the inner city. Rioting in Moss Side in 1981, sparked off by alienation among young people, followed similar outbreaks in London and Liverpool.

Prime minister Margaret Thatcher, blamed by many for high unemployment, visited Manchester in 1986 to speak at a black-tie dinner held by the Chamber of Commerce in the Peacock Room of the Piccadilly Hotel, another 1960s modernist building. Chamber president John Morris, a retired insurance broker, attacked her employment secretary, Norman Tebbit, for claiming the North's wounds were self-inflicted. Criticising her government's perceived south-east bias, Morris declared: 'We search in vain for some indication that the government is adapting its policies to take account of the problem.' Taken aback, she replied: 'You are telling me what I have got to do and I am telling you what you have got to do.'[22]

The 1980s were Manchester's darkest time, yet also when the seeds of recovery were sown. Major shifts in politics and culture were afoot. The city's transformation was to require pragmatism, leadership, public–private partnership and a degree of co-operation across the wider region.

Among the first stirrings was regeneration of the formerly derelict Castlefield basin, site of the Roman fort and terminus of the Bridgewater Canal and original Liverpool–Manchester railway. It began in the 1970s with a few apartments, then Castlefield was designated a conservation area in 1980 and the UK's first urban heritage park in 1982. That was also the year in which the legendary Haçienda nightclub opened in a former city-centre warehouse, destined to play an often controversial role in Manchester's flowering music scene (see next chapter). According to writer Andy Spinoza, the Haçienda can be viewed not only as 'the first project of today's Manchester', but also as 'the point at which the modernist period concluded'.[23]

Edward Heath's government in 1974 created Greater Manchester County Council (GMC) with responsibilities such as transport, planning and refuse. It was the third largest of six new metropolitan counties, after Greater London and the West Midlands, and the only one outside the capital to be named after its core city. It shared power with ten metropolitan borough councils – Manchester, Wigan, Bolton, Bury, Rochdale, Oldham, Salford and Stockport, plus two new inventions, Trafford (including Altrincham, Sale and Stretford) and Tameside (including Ashton-under-Lyne, Denton, Hyde and Longdendale). The GMC covered almost 500 square miles and 2.7 million people in the historic counties of Lancashire, Cheshire and Yorkshire (the boundaries of all three meet in Mossley, Tameside). The concept of Greater Manchester enraged some in the city's surrounding towns, who felt it rode roughshod over traditional identities. 'Lancs not Mancs' read graffiti post-1974. Feelings about this remain strong in some quarters.

The GMC was instrumental in creating the Museum of Science and Industry (now the Science and Industry Museum) on the site of the world's first passenger railway station in 1983. Originally the museum had been the initiative of academics at UMIST. As almost its last act, the GMC also converted former Central Station in 1986 into the Greater Manchester Exhibition Centre or GMex (now Manchester Central), an exhibition hall and concert venue that in recent years has hosted political party conferences. In that year the GMC, along with the other metropolitan county councils, was abolished by the Thatcher government. Metropolitan boroughs survived, however, and the ten districts formed the Association of Greater Manchester Authorities to carry on working together. Manchester borough accounts for only 19 per cent of the city-region's population, so it pays to work with its neighbours.

In 1974, idealistic young left-wingers won control of Manchester City Council under the leadership of thirty-three-year-old Graham Stringer on a platform to confront the government with all means at his disposal. Stringer, raised in inner-city Beswick, was an analytical chemist in the plastics industry with a degree from Sheffield University. According to Spinoza, he 'had a dour demeanour which stood him in good stead as "one of us" on the doorstep, in party meetings and with the unions'. The new regime was notable for radical gestures such as trying to abolish the lord mayor role and support for gay and lesbian groups. The queen's portrait was taken down from the Great Hall, the council voted to express solidarity with Irish republicanism and it set up a committee to monitor the police. The chief constable was controversial Wigan-born James Anderton, labelled 'God's copper' for his belief that God was using him to speak out against gay rights, feminism, debauchery and social nonconformism. The council's parks boss, unenthusiastic about the leadership's insistence on gay- and lesbian-themed flower beds in Piccadilly Gardens, left after a dispute about homosexual content at Manchester Fair stalls.[24]

All this led to a stream of 'loony left' headlines in the *Manchester Evening News* aimed at its traditional working-class readership. The national media bracketed Manchester with left-led Liverpool, Sheffield and the Greater London Council, though there were differences. Manchester's leadership, resisting pressure for spending cuts, tried to refuse to set a budget in 1985, but was defeated by Labour moderates and Conservative councillors. After Labour failed to win the 1987 general election, the council faced a stark choice. Rate rises were capped and, despite its previous 'no cuts' promise, the council either had to slash budgets to balance the books or stage an illegal Liverpool-style revolt, which was likely to be crushed.

Stringer and the leadership changed tack dramatically. They accepted that they had to play by government rules and acknowledged that they needed the private sector to create jobs. An early act was to break with fifty years of policy and sell council land for a new Siemens headquarters on Princess Road, Didsbury, which became one of the city's most successful landmark buildings. Manchester entered an entrepreneurial period, driven by Stringer, senior councillor Richard Leese and deputy chief executive Howard Bernstein, and embraced collaboration with private business. Manchester needed a vision and sense of purpose to promote itself as a major European city-region. Stringer said: 'About a dozen of [Europe's forty or fifty second-tier cities] will become the cities where decisions are made ... We have to try and get there, because the alternative is to gradually decline.'[25] Revival involved a sequence of prestige projects focused on leisure, culture and lifestyle, a path also followed by cities including Barcelona and Bilbao.

A key aim was to win government funding competitions and European grants, particularly important in the early years of Manchester's turn-round. An important decision was to work with the Central Manchester Development Corporation created by the government in 1988, one of the urban development corporations with private- and public-sector staff that ministers used to intervene in problem locations. The CMDC had a £100 million budget to stimulate commercial property investment.

One success was in Castlefield where the CMDC opened up the canal complex, made environmental improvements to the basins and introduced leisure, tourism and residential developments. Salford-born entrepreneur Jim Ramsbottom, a former bookmaker, converted derelict properties such as Merchants' Warehouse into offices and flats and turned a former stable block into the Dukes 92 pub. In the Whitworth Street area of the city centre, the CMDC oversaw refurbishment of empty or underused warehouses and other listed buildings. Most became apartments, while Alfred Waterhouse's former Refuge Assurance building became a hotel. The CMDC part-funded the Bridgewater Hall, a concert hall completed in 1996, alongside the city council and the European Regional Development Fund. The CMDC had less success in areas such as Pomona and Piccadilly. By the time it closed in 1996, the agency had attracted almost £400 million of investment.[26]

Another such agency, the Trafford Park Development Corporation, existed from 1987 to 1998 and succeeded where a previous enterprise zone had achieved little. Its area included not only Trafford Park but also parts of Stretford, Salford Quays and a former steelworks at Irlam. The corporation attracted 1,000 companies and generated 28,000 jobs and £1.76 billion of private-sector investment.[27] Trafford Park was once again a major employment centre. Salford City Council in 1983 bought part of the docks, which had closed the year before, from the Ship Canal Company and rebranded the area Salford Quays. Though this at first seemed bleak and unpromising, improvements were made to water quality and infrastructure, and investment was attracted for a hotel and apartments. Lottery funding was secured to build the Lowry Centre, which opened in 2000 with two theatres and a permanent collection of paintings by L.S. Lowry. The area's revival was further helped by the opening in 2002 of the Imperial War Museum North on the Trafford side, designed by Polish-American architect Daniel Libeskind.

With tourism increasing, Granada ran tours of its site at Castlefield from 1988 to 1999 in which visitors could walk down Coronation Street and enjoy a drink in a replica of the Rovers Return. The Cornerhouse cinema and visual arts centre opened in 1985 next to Oxford Road Station. Manchester and Salford had four universities by the early 1990s, giving the cities the largest concentration of students in western Europe – the University of Manchester, University of Salford, UMIST and Manchester Metropolitan University. Manchester Metrolink, the tram/light-rail system, was approved for government funding in 1988, with the first phase linking Bury, Manchester and Altrincham opening in 1992. Now it is the UK's most extensive light-rail system.

Manchester bid unsuccessfully to stage the Olympic Games of 1996 and 2000, an ambition pursued by businessman Sir Bob Scott from the mid-1980s. Scott was administrator of the Royal Exchange Theatre Trust and had revived the Palace Theatre and Opera House. The first bid generated limited enthusiasm (the London *Evening*

Standard talked flippantly of holding the Games 'among the rusting cranes of Mancunia'), but the second was impressive and generated central government support of £55 million for a stadium and £20 million to purchase the site.[28] The council had chosen a site called Eastlands in an area ravaged by industrial closures as part of its East Manchester Regeneration Strategy, launched in 1992.

Tory environment secretary Michael Heseltine, known for his role in Liverpool's revival, also played an important part in Manchester. Fortuitously, Graham Stringer had been at university with Heseltine's private secretary Phil Ward and had been best man at Ward's wedding. Stringer and Scott outlined the second Olympic bid to Heseltine at a meeting at Manchester Airport. Howard Bernstein recalled that Heseltine, at first cool on sport as a regeneration lever, ended by shouting, 'I love it, I love it!'[29] Funding came through rapidly for the stadium site and a velodrome that opened in 1994. Manchester Arena, which opened in 1995 near Victoria Station, was built as part of the second Olympic bid. These bids laid the groundwork to win the Commonwealth Games in 2002, delivering the stadium and other facilities at Sportcity.

In the late 1980s, however, talk of city-centre regeneration remained strictly aspirational. Anyone hoping for a café culture and 'twenty-four-hour city' faced difficulty in getting outdoor seating and late drinking licences. Regulations had been applied since the 1960s to curb the seething backstreet scene of clubs, bars and casinos. Police and magistrates limited the number of venues, but things began to change after a new chief constable, David Wilmot, replaced Anderton in 1991. Licence numbers expanded and by 1997 police estimated that the city centre was hosting an average 75,000 visitors a weekend, more than double the figure five years before.[30]

Repopulating the city centre has been a central objective. Despite UK media chatter about New York-style 'loft living' in the late 1980s, it would take a few years to transform Manchester's empty redbrick buildings into living spaces in significant numbers. Growth accelerated, though. Manchester, down to a few hundred residents in its central core by the start of the 1990s, had 65,000 in the wider city-centre area by 2019 and was projected to reach 100,000 by 2025, with big growth also in Salford.[31] Many were students and young professionals with high earning potential.

One consequence of these arrivals was development of the 'Gay Village' around Canal Street. Before the 1970s, gays would meet in semi-secrecy in pubs such as the Rembrandt and the Union, facing public hostility and a real legal threat. The North West Homosexual Law Reform Committee was started in Manchester in 1964, co-founded by Alan Horsfall, a National Coal Board employee from Atherton near Wigan. By 1972 it had morphed into the Campaign for Homosexual Equality, one of the UK's leading gay rights organisations. Homosexual acts were partially decriminalised in 1967, but prejudice remained. In the late 1970s and early 1980s police raided gay clubs such as Napoleon's in Bloom Street using a nineteenth-century byelaw that prohibited men from dancing together. 'We've been trying to close these queer places for years,' remarked an officer after a 1984 raid. Such actions were supported by Anderton, who in 1986 described Aids sufferers as 'swirling around in a human cesspit of their own making'.[32]

Attitudes were changing by the mid-1980s, however. The city council under Stringer gave grants to gay and lesbian organisations. A key moment was when a new club, Manto, was opened on Canal Street by entrepreneurs Carol Ainscow and Peter Dalton in 1990. It had a glass wall frontage enabling customers to see and be seen. 'I felt sick of having to knock on doors and hide,' said Ainscow. Other bars followed and soon Canal Street was described as one of the world's top gay locations. Manto was the first city-centre venue permitted to put out street chairs and tables. Ainscow had started in property development by converting a Victorian house in her native Bolton into a nursing home. She went on to own more bars, restaurants and flats, and was a key figure in the Gay Village's growth. Her company, Artisan, also breathed new life into the former Daily Express building on Great Ancoats Street.

Luchia Fitzgerald, a teenage runaway from Ireland, and Angela Cooper became doughty campaigners for lesbian and women's rights in the 1970s. Both were born to single mothers in Ireland's Catholic Magdalene homes; Cooper was adopted by a Salford family. Fitzgerald, struggling to survive on Manchester's streets, narrowly escaped bring sent for a lobotomy to cure her 'deviant sexual tendencies'. They formed the Manchester branch of the Gay Liberation Front, formed a rock band, opened a printing press, ran the Manchester Women's Liberation Centre and started the city's first women's refuge. In the 1980s they gathered 20,000 people to march through Manchester in protest against Margaret Thatcher's legislation prohibiting schools teaching about same-sex relationships, known as Section 28.[33]

Julia Grant (1954–2019), a transgender activist raised in Fleetwood, owned cafés and bars in the Gay Village, including the Hollywood Show Bar. She was the first person to have her transition chronicled on mainstream television in *A Change of Sex*, a documentary series that ran from 1979 to 1999. A further boost to the Gay Village came in 1999 with the Channel 4 drama series *Queer as Folk*, written by Russell T. Davies, chronicling the lives of three gay men in the area (originally it was to be titled *Queer as Fuck*, but that was deemed too risqué).[34]

The influx of young people also led to what became known as the Northern Quarter, an area of bohemian bars and independent record shops north of Piccadilly that did not have a name before the early 1990s. Oldham Street had previously been a bustling retail thoroughfare, but lost trade to the Arndale. Influential new businesses included Dry Bar, opened by the Factory Records team, and Afflecks Palace, opened in 1982, an indoor market for independent traders. It became known for selling fashion gear to music fans such as t-shirts with the legend 'And on the sixth day God created Manchester', designed by Leo Stanley. A key point in the Northern Quarter's creation was Urban Splash's conversion of Smithfield

Buildings, the former Affleck & Brown store, into apartments. Lord Richard Rogers in his landmark 1999 Urban Task Force report *Towards an Urban Renaissance* praised the Smithfield flats as 'a catalyst for entrepreneurial and creative activity, attracting people to live in the area and locate new businesses'.[35]

Urban Splash, founded by entrepreneur Tom Bloxham and designer Jonathan Falkingham in 1993, set the style for regeneration development in Britain, becoming known for sympathetic conversions of mills and warehouses. The Castlefield-based company has invested more than a billion pounds into sixty-plus projects, including Fort Dunlop in Birmingham, the Midland Hotel in Morecambe, Royal William Yard in Plymouth, Park Hill in Sheffield and the Ropeworks in Liverpool. In Manchester, it was lead developer of the New Islington scheme on the city centre's edge. Bloxham, born in Hampshire and raised in Kingston-upon-Thames, studied politics and history at Manchester University and began selling music posters in Afflecks Palace; he sub-let part of his space there, allowing him to glimpse prospects in the property market. For long a familiar figure on Manchester's nightclub scene, wearing a trilby hat outdoors and in, he was chancellor of the University of Manchester from 2008 to 2015 and became the founding chairman of Manchester International Festival. Bloxham is fond of the ancient Athenian oath: 'We will leave this place not less, but greater, better and more beautiful than it was left to us.'[36]

Hulme, meanwhile, had become a mix of 'artists, musicians, drop-outs, ex-students and the unemployed' in the last days before the crescents' demolition. Some saw it as Manchester's version of Copenhagen's Christiana or Berlin's Kreuzberg, a creative hub left to its own devices by officialdom. But with only 8,000 living on an estate designed for more than 20,000 it was draining council resources. The answer came in the government's City Challenge funding competition. Heseltine, environment secretary again under John Major, took a helicopter tour of Hulme before the contest was announced. From 1992 to 1997 the programme injected £35 million into Hulme, followed by further funding from the government's Single Regeneration Budget and the European Commission.[37]

After City Challenge, some £400 million is estimated to have been spent on the area, creating a mix of 2,000 social and private homes. Marking the emergence of a 'Manchester model' for regeneration, it was led by an arm's-length company, Hulme Regeneration Ltd, on which secondees from the city were joined by private-sector developers such as Amec and Bellway Homes. The Hulme design guide, later extended across the city with mixed success, required varied communities in low-rise housing on connected streets. Houses fronted on to pavements to generate 'eyes on the street' and discourage crime and vandalism. Generally regarded as successful, though at some cost in gentrification, it was achieved by attracting incomers as much as by improving things for existing residents.

Not everything was going smoothly in Manchester's revival. Gun-related crime, fuelled by drugs and unemployment, became a serious problem in the 1990s, with rival gangs competing in areas such as Moss Side, Longsight and Hulme. The media dubbed the city 'Gunchester', and Moss Side 'the Bronx of Britain'. Police tried to take gang members out of circulation, mainly for drugs offences, but found they were easily replaced by new recruits. Eventually, measures such as heavy sentencing of main offenders, prohibitions on firearms and a multi-agency approach bore fruit, and gang-related gun crime was greatly reduced by the late 2000s.

On Saturday 15 June 1996 Manchester city centre was slightly busier than usual. No one paid much attention to a white and orange truck parked between Marks & Spencer and the Arndale, apart from a traffic warden who put a ticket on it. At 9.40am a man with an Irish accent phoned Granada Television and warned of a bomb. It was one of four coded warnings, allowing time for police to seal off the city centre and evacuate almost 80,000 people. At 11.20 an explosion ripped through the centre – the biggest bomb detonated in Britain since the Second World War. No one died, but

220 were injured in the IRA bombing and the damage to the city's retail and commercial core was extensive.[38]

Manchester's response was impressively rapid. The disaster was treated as an opportunity not just to restore the centre, but to reinvigorate it. A task force was created under Howard Bernstein's leadership comprising secondees from the private sector, local authority and central government. Heseltine, now deputy prime minister, visited the city centre and promised £21 million of government aid. With his encouragement, the city launched an international design competition and announced the winner, EDAW, in early November.

The design involved creating New Cathedral Street to link the retail area of St Ann's Square with the cathedral and the heart of medieval Manchester, previously cut off from the busiest areas. The new street attracted high-profile retailers, including Harvey Nichols. A new Exchange Square was created in front of the Corn Exchange, which had suffered structural damage. Previous tenants of the Corn Exchange's indoor market, small independent stallholders, were displaced, with many moving to the Northern Quarter, and were replaced by high-end retail businesses. The sixteenth-century Old Wellington Inn and its neighbour Sinclair's Oyster Bar were dismantled and moved across the road to a site next to Exchange Square. The area around the cathedral and Chetham's School of Music was refurbished as the Millennium Quarter.[39]

As the century's end approached, Manchester's revival was gathering pace. Richard Leese took over as council leader from Stringer a month before the bombing. (Stringer was elected MP for Blackley and Broughton in 1997 and later he became a leading Brexiteer.) Leese, a maths graduate and former teacher from Mansfield, had worked as a youth worker in Crumpsall. He had a talent for grasping detail and getting things done. He formed a formidable partnership with Bernstein, who became chief executive in 1998.

Challenges remained, including the opening of the Trafford Centre in 1998, a huge out-of-town shopping destination that posed a potential threat to city-centre retailers just as they were recovering from the bomb. It was built by Peel Group, created by John Whittaker, a Bury-born developer who lived in tax exile on the Isle of Man; it was opposed by Manchester City Council and opened only after a ten-year planning battle. Whittaker began business life at the family quarry but soon started buying troubled mills for their land. His group grew to manage assets worth more than £6 billion in infrastructure, transport, property, energy, media, airports, ports, hotels and utilities.

The Trafford Centre was built in riotously gaudy Rococo/Baroque architectural style, with elements of Art Deco and Egyptian Revival, and decorated in white, pink and gold with marble in ivory, jade and caramel colours, along with fake palms and neoclassical pillars. It was a one-off design aimed at avoiding redesign headaches that bedevilled modern malls. Whittaker called it a 'people's palace' with 'the Dallas effect'. Despite a reputation for being media-shy, Whittaker abseiled into the Trafford Centre when it opened as if he were Richard Branson. The centre was a popular success, drawing visitors from across the North. Fears that it would undermine city-centre retail proved exaggerated, though it did hit nearby towns such as Altrincham.[40]

Manchester was becoming an international exemplar of reinvention, though its transformation was far from complete. Social regeneration was much harder than physical and economic regeneration. The dramatic shift from industry to services meant that, like many cities, Manchester was relying on precarious part-time jobs in bars, hotels and restaurants. A poverty belt still encircled the city core, a pattern that Engels would have recognised. A quarter of the city's housing was unfit or in need of renovation. Skills and educational achievement were poor and there were high levels of ill health. In 2000 Manchester was the sixth most deprived local authority in the country on the government's Index of Multiple Deprivation.[41] There was work still to do.

15

MUSIC

Music, perhaps even more than sport, has come to define Manchester. The highbrow end was led by the Hallé Orchestra, once described by Guy Garvey of rock group Elbow as 'the first Manchester band'.[1] In popular music the city has been even more influential, from the 1960s beat era of the Hollies, Freddie and the Dreamers and Herman's Hermits to the punk and post-punk years of Joy Division, New Order, The Smiths and soul artists Simply Red. The ecstasy-fuelled dance club scene of the late 1980s coincided with 'Madchester' and the Stone Roses, Happy Mondays and Inspiral Carpets. The 1990s saw the rise of Britpop, notably Oasis. The city also has a long-standing black music tradition, often ignored by commentators and the media.

Manchester's pop music was shaped by post-industrial devastation and in turn helped to inspire the city's recovery, burnishing an international reputation that has echoes of its nineteenth-century glory days. 'The kind of anger that punk was about was very suited to a post-industrial wasteland like Manchester,' said Tony Wilson, the television presenter who co-founded Factory Records and the legendary Haçienda nightclub. He added: 'Manchester has been Britain's immigrant city since 1200, and that openness is essential.'[2] As writer and disc jockey Dave Haslam puts it: 'Just as the city used to import raw material – cotton – and turn it into something else, so modern Manchester finds itself importing, refashioning and exporting pop music.'[3]

Charles Hallé (1819–95), conductor and pianist, was born as Carl Halle in Hagen, Westphalia, not far from where Friedrich Engels was born the following year. Hallé was living in Paris when its 1848 revolution prompted him to escape to Britain with his French wife and two children. He was invited to Manchester by calico printer and music patron Hermann Leo, who said the city was 'quite ripe to be taken in hand'.[4] Hallé became conductor of the Gentlemen's Concerts, established about 1770. He created an orchestra for the Art Treasures exhibition in 1857 and then began weekly Hallé winter concerts the following year.

Over thirty-seven years, Hallé and the citizens who backed him built one of Europe's greatest orchestras. He introduced the works of contemporary composers such as Wagner and Brahms and especially championed Berlioz. His lowest price of one shilling allowed some of the less well-off to attend, though inevitably the Thursday-night concerts were grand occasions for the wealthy. Railways ran special trains from the suburbs. In 1893, Hallé helped to found the Royal Manchester College of Music on Ducie Street, of which he was principal. After he died, the Hallé in 1899 engaged Hans Richter, principal conductor of the Vienna Opera and Philharmonic, as musical director, who secured its reputation for symphonic music. There were other Manchester orchestras too, including one started by Hallé flautist Edward de Jong. And in 1895, five different opera companies played for a total of seventeen weeks at three separate venues.[5]

Popular music was heard in singing rooms of public houses from the 1830s and 1840s, which developed into music halls. The city's raucous nightlife was celebrated in the ballad 'Victoria Bridge on a Saturday Night'; the stone arch bridge connecting Salford and Manchester was thronged with drunks, gangs, thieves and prostitutes. Another popular song was 'Manchester's Improving Daily', a cynical commentary contrasting the reality of city life with the hype, and wondering where the revolutionary, fighting spirit of Manchester's people had gone. However, many music hall songs were repetitive and derivative. Robert Roberts, in his account of Salford life *The Classic Slum*, complained that the bulk of songs were 'of wretched quality, with airs painfully banal and lyrics of an inanity that even the sub-literate rejected'.[6] Brass bands also became important in Manchester and its surrounding region: Saddleworth's Whit Friday contests date back to 1884.

The 1920s brought a boom in jazz and dancing as, for the young, the First World War had blown away buttoned-up ways of behaving. It was loud, used unconventional instruments such as saxophones and trumpets, and grew out of Afro-American black culture. Such dancehalls offered a relatively cheap night out even in the depression years and were embraced enthusiastically by the unmarried, including working women. Ragtime was the first form of jazz to reach England, but there was a frenetic turnover of styles, including dances such as the Black Bottom and the Charleston. Band leader Jack Hylton (1892–1965), known as the 'British King of Jazz', was born in Great Lever near Bolton, the son of a millhand. A wide range of Manchester venues included the upmarket Ritz in Whitworth Street West, opened in 1927. Young people ventured from their neighbourhoods in search of a good night out; girls from Salford travelled to Manchester or Sale, for example. The adventurous took the 'dance train' to Blackpool for half a crown return.[7]

In classical music the 2ZY Orchestra, formed in 1922 for the Manchester radio station of the same name, was part-funded by the British Broadcasting Company and renamed the Northern Wireless Orchestra in 1926. It became part of the Manchester-based BBC Northern Orchestra, created in 1934, now the BBC Philharmonic. The Hallé's traditional venue, the Free Trade Hall, was virtually destroyed in the 1940 Blitz, after which the orchestra moved to various locations, including Belle Vue. The Hallé was in danger of extinction for lack of players when John Barbirolli became its conductor in 1943.

Barbirolli, born in London to Italian and French parents, was a cellist who had succeeded Arturo Toscanini as musical director of the New York Philharmonic. He narrowly avoided death before taking up the Hallé challenge: en route from New York he changed flights at Lisbon with actor Leslie Howard, who wanted to postpone his own flight by a few days; Barbirolli's plane landed safely, but Howard's was shot down. In Manchester Barbirolli had a month to recruit forty players to add to thirty-five under contract. He scoured the country for talent and launched a virtually new orchestra, soon acclaimed as the nation's best. He was knighted in 1949 and served for twenty-seven years until his death in 1970. The orchestra returned to the Free Trade Hall when it reopened in 1951. Barbirolli took the Hallé from strength to strength, touring the UK and overseas. Ralph Vaughan Williams dedicated his Eighth Symphony to Barbirolli, whose nickname 'Glorious John' comes from an inscription at the head of the score: 'For glorious John, with love and admiration from Ralph.'[8]

Composer Sir William Walton (1902–83), born into a musical family in Oldham, wrote music in genres from film scores to opera. He went to choir school in Oxford and said he started composing because 'I must make myself interesting somehow or, when my voice breaks, I'll be sent home to Oldham.' Nonetheless, he was awarded the freedom of the borough in 1960.[9] The Manchester School is a name given to composers Sir Peter Maxwell Davies (1934–2016, born in Langworthy, Salford), Sir Harrison Birtwhistle (1934–2022, born in Accrington) and Alexander Goehr (born in Berlin in 1932) who studied together at Royal Manchester College of Music in the 1950s under Richard Hall, professor of composition. They formed a group dedicated to contemporary music called New Music Manchester together with pianist John Ogdon, who had been a pupil at Manchester Grammar School, and conductor and trumpeter Elgar Howarth. Its members played a significant role in reshaping the landscape of British classical music in the later twentieth century. Maxwell Davies became Master of the Queen's Music.

Ewan MacColl (1915–89), folk singer, labour activist and actor, born as James Miller to Scottish parents in Broughton, Salford, wrote his famous song 'Dirty Old Town' about his home city in 1949. A lifelong communist, he was under surveillance by MI5 from age seventeen. His beliefs were rooted in social inequalities in Salford: 'All the time I was living on a thread of anger, which was eating me away.'[10] He deserted from the army in 1940 but was never caught or charged. After the war he became a leading figure in the folk revival. He made eight 'radio ballads' with producer Charles Parker for the BBC between 1958 and 1964, dealing with the everyday lives of workers from railwaymen to fishermen, using a montage of interviews and new songs written by MacColl. 'Dirty Old Town' has been covered by artists including The Dubliners and The Pogues. His song 'The First Time Ever I Saw Your Face' was a number-one hit in America for Roberta Flack in 1972. Other prominent folk musicians from the Manchester region include Mike Harding, singer, comedian and broadcaster, born in Crumpsall in 1944, and the Oldham Tinkers, a trio formed in 1965.

Commercial jazz continued to dominate dancehalls into the 1950s, though listeners could also hear cutting-edge styles such as be-bop and rhythm and blues on the American Forces Network. John Mayall, an art student in Manchester who had been brought up in Cheadle Hulme, taped all the important shows; in 1963 he formed the Bluesbreakers, viewed as Britain's premier R&B band. Contemporary jazz could also be heard in Moss Side black clubs such as the Reno, Nile and Western.[11] Calypso music had been brought to the UK by Lord Kitchener (Aldwyn Roberts) who arrived on the *Empire Windrush* in 1948 from Trinidad and was filmed singing 'London Is the Place for Me'; he lived in Stretford with his first wife from 1957 to 1962 and opened a nightclub in Manchester.[12]

As rock and roll followed jazz, Mancunians struggled to hear it. Before Manchester's first import record shop – One Stop – opened in 1957, the main means of getting records were via sailors or American servicemen. The arrival of coffee bars with jukeboxes playing Bill Haley or Little Richard started to change things. Also in 1957, Bill Haley and his Comets played at the Odeon. Jimmy Savile, later labelled a prolific sex offender, was credited with rejuvenating music played at Mecca's Plaza Ballroom on Oxford Street when he became manager there in the late 1950s.[13]

Liverpool was the first main focus of the beat boom in the early 1960s. The Beatles' first Manchester appearance, at the Oasis Coffee Bar in 1962, attracted just thirty-seven people, but when they returned there a year later the place was packed.[14] British bands became less slavishly imitative of American music and sang about their own lives in their own accents. Liverpool's success sparked competition in Manchester. The Hollies, formed in 1962 by Salford's Allan Clarke and Graham Nash, had a three-part vocal harmony style. Freddie and the Dreamers, formed the same year in West Didsbury, including vocalist Freddie Garrity, performed wacky dance routines. Wayne Fontana, born in Levenshulme as Glyn Geoffrey Ellis, formed his backing group the Mindbenders in 1963. Herman's Hermits came along in 1964, fronted by Peter Noone from Davyhulme and Stretford; they were known for a jaunty style and Noone's tongue-in-cheek vocals.

The BBC's *Top of the Pops* came from Manchester's Dickenson Road Studios for its first two years from 1964. Freddie and the Dreamers, Wayne Fontana and the Mindbenders, and Herman's Hermits together held the top three positions in the US Billboard 100 in spring 1965.[15] The Bee Gees also had Manchester origins: brothers Barry, Robin and Maurice Gibb lived in Chorlton in the 1950s and formed a skiffle/rock and roll group called the Rattlesnakes, before their family moved to Australia in 1958 and they formed the Bee Gees. R&B musician Georgie Fame, born as Clive Powell in Leigh, had three UK number ones with his band the Blue Flames.

Manchester had a taste for R&B, alongside the beat boom. The Twisted Wheel opened in 1963 as a blues and soul club, initially in Brazennose Street and then in Whitworth Street. Elton John wrote in his autobiography: 'Those kids in the Twisted Wheel were so clued-up, so switched-on, so much hipper than anyone else in the country.'[16] According to musician and author C.P. Lee: 'Black music was always big in Manchester. It was a tradition that came from when we supported the North in the American Civil War, fighting against the slave trade ... Mancunian bands had a hardcore R&B edge that doesn't come across in the recordings.'[17] The genre label 'Northern Soul' was originated by music journalist Dave Godin in 1970 after a visit to the Twisted Wheel, before the venue closed in 1971. Soul fans in Lancashire, West Yorkshire and North Staffordshire enjoyed the heavy beat and fast tempo of music from Detroit and Chicago. Other venues around the North kept the scene going and Wigan Casino, which opened in 1973, emerged as Northern Soul's spiritual home. It peaked later in the decade and closed in 1981.[18]

The early 1960s seem like an innocent age, but times were changing. At the Free Trade Hall in 1965, a heckler shouted 'Judas!' at Bob Dylan in protest at his switch from acoustic guitar to electric rock – described by journalist Richard Williams as 'the most electrifying single moment in postwar culture'.[19] Graham Nash left the Hollies for America in 1968, a move that was to bring him fame as part of Crosby, Stills, Nash & Young. John Mayall moved to Los Angeles.

In the classical world, a merger had been mooted since 1955 between the Royal Manchester College of Music and the Northern School of Music, originally founded by Hilda Collens as Matthay School of Music in 1920. A joint committee was established in 1966 and they merged as the Northern College of Music in 1972, becoming the Royal Northern College of Music (RNCM) – one of Europe's leading music colleges – when it moved to its present site on Oxford Road in 1973. In 1969 Chetham's Hospital School, a boys' grammar school, became Chetham's School of Music, a co-educational music school catering for pupils from eight to eighteen. Manchester Camerata, one of the few freelance chamber orchestras outside London, was formed in 1972.

Pop music continued to evolve. Soft rock group 10cc was formed in Stockport in 1972. They had five consecutive UK top-ten albums between 1972 and 1978, mostly recorded at their own Strawberry Studios. Their song 'I'm Not in Love' was a worldwide hit in 1975. The progressive rock era also produced Barclay James Harvest from Oldham and Van der Graaf Generator, formed by students at Manchester University. Manchester soul group Sweet Sensation had a number-one hit in 1974 with 'Sad Sweet Dreamer'. Nonetheless, the verdict of Tony Wilson in 1975 was that the city's music 'wasn't worth shit ... I just felt like we were waiting for something to happen.'[20]

That something was two concerts at the Lesser Free Trade Hall in 1976 by little-known London punk rockers the Sex Pistols – regarded as among the most influential gigs in pop music history. They were invited by two students at Bolton Institute of Technology, Howard Trafford and Pete McNeish, who saw the Pistols twice in London. The pair wanted their own band, christened Buzzcocks during the trip, to be the support act. They also changed their names to Howard Devoto and Pete Shelley. Most sources say only about forty people attended the first gig on 4 June (Devoto reckoned about a hundred), though many more later claimed to have been there. Their first thought was to hold it at Bolton Institute, but they decided to try somewhere else. Tickets were fifty pence. The audience included Salford council clerk Peter Hook and his friend Bernard Sumner, a pair who later formed Joy Division, and Steven Morrissey from Stretford who had just done his O Levels, later to be singer for The Smiths.

Word spread about the Pistols' insane energy ('we're into chaos') and the second gig on 20 July was busier. Those present included Tony Wilson and Mark E. Smith, an unhappy shipping company clerk at Salford docks who was spurred into forming The Fall. He was a complex maverick whose band involved sixty musicians over forty-two years before he died in 2018. Several other young Mancunians were inspired to start bands. Says Dave Haslam: 'Punk was disturbing, subverting and liberating ... Manchester was an ideal breeding ground for punk. There was boredom, plenty of it, and poverty.' According to author Dave Nolan, the attitude of many after hearing the Pistols was: 'That's rubbish! We could do so much better.'[21]

Buzzcocks did not play the first gig because they lacked a drummer, but appeared at the second. Also playing were Wythenshawe's Slaughter and the Dogs, who performed in full glitter regalia. Buzzcocks took their name from a headline, 'It's the Buzz, Cock', in a review of TV series *Rock Follies* in *Time Out* magazine. They became a quintessential punk band and led the creation of the independent record label movement. By January 1977 they had released the EP *Spiral Scratch* on the New Hormones label run by their manager Richard Boon. Devoto soon left and formed the band Magazine, after which Shelley became Buzzcocks' main singer-songwriter. They broke up in 1981 but reunited in 1989 and released six more albums before Shelley's death in 2018. The band has remained active and Steve Diggle, guitarist and co-founder, is now the singer.

The 1970s were also a big time for reggae. The roots of reggae and dub arrived with the *Windrush* generation from the late 1940s, bringing Jamaican culture to Moss Side, Hulme and Old Trafford. Sound systems – a DJ with mixer, turntables, amp and speakers – played local venues and supported live bands. Singer Sylvia Tella, one of the world's biggest reggae stars, was brought up in Hulme, born in 1961 to a Nigerian father and English mother of Polish/Romanian heritage. She first found fame backing Boney M before hitting her stride as a solo artist in the 1990s, specialising in 'lovers rock', a romantic form of reggae. Tella's road to independence was not easy. After winning ITV's *Opportunity Knocks* with her band The Romantics at age thirteen, she says she was propositioned by presenter Hughie Green and another man in return for promising to make her a star. She refused and poured a litre of wine over Green's head.[22]

Phil Lynott, songwriter, singer and bassist with Thin Lizzy – of Irish and British Guianan parents – attended school briefly in Moss Side before his single-parent mother, Philomena, sent him to be brought up by his grandparents in Dublin. It is said that he was inspired to write 'The Boys Are Back in Town' in 1976 in part about the Quality Street Gang, a loose affiliation of Manchester business-men of dubious repute, regulars at the Biz nightclub at the Clifton Grange Hotel, a haunt of celebrities that his mother ran in Whalley Range.[23]

For Pendleton-born Cambridge graduate Tony Wilson (1950–2007), an anchor of ITV's *Granada Reports* and presenter of culture programme *So It Goes*, seeing the Sex Pistols was 'nothing short of an epiphany'. He entered the music business with actor friend Alan Erasmus in 1978 by launching 'Factory' nights at the Russell Club, a bus drivers' social club in Hulme, featuring local bands such as The Durutti Column, which the pair managed. The Factory name was not a nod to Andy Warhol's New York Factory, but thought up by Erasmus, who saw a 'factory closing' sign and thought 'let's have a Factory opening instead'.[24] A few months later they created Factory Records by releasing *A Factory Sample*, an EP of music by acts at the club. The label also involved record producer Martin Hannett and designer Peter Saville, who created enigmatic graphic art for Factory's record sleeves. Saville had created the original Factory night poster, which he called FAC 1, the first in a series of catalogue numbers given to anything associated with the label. When Wilson died, his coffin was FAC 501.

Factory was in the forefront of creating post-punk, a genre that experimented with varying musical styles and avant-garde art. Whereas major labels paid a large advance to acquire ownership of an artist's work, Factory artists received no advance but owned the rights. Signings included A Certain Ratio, a Flixton band that drew on funk. In June 1979 Factory released its first LP, *Unknown Pleasures*, the debut album of Joy Division, created by Hook (bassist) and Sumner (guitarist/keyboardist) after the Sex Pistols gig along with singer Ian Curtis and eventually drummer Stephen Morris. Initially the band was called Warsaw, but it renamed itself Joy Division to avoid confusion with London punk band Warsaw Pakt; the new name was borrowed from the sexual slavery wing of a Nazi concentration camp.

17. Havana-born Enriqueta Rylands, founder of John Rylands Library.
Smabs Sputzer / Wikimedia Commons CC BY 2.0

18. Emmeline Pankhurst,
founder of the Suffragettes,
c.1880s. Wikimedia Commons

19. Annie Kenney and Christabel Pankhurst, Suffragette leaders.
Wikimedia Commons

20. Central Library, which opened in 1934 (photo by Michael Beckwith).
Michael D Beckwith / Wikimedia Commons CC0

21. Ellen Wilkinson leading Jarrow marchers, 1936.
Associated Press / Alamy Stock Photo

22. Manchester Blitz, December 1940. Piemags / Alamy Stock Photo

23. Alan Turing, Sackville Gardens. Paul Hermans / Wikimedia Commons

24. Author Anthony Burgess appearing on After Dark on 21 May 1988.
Wikimedia Commons

25. Ian Curtis of Joy Division took his own life in 1980 (mural by Akse). Gerard Noonan / Alamy Stock Photo

26. The Haçienda nightclub recreated for the film *24 Hour Party People*, 2002. Photo 12 / Alamy Stock Photo

27. IRA bombing, 1996. PA Images / Alamy Stock Photo

28. Curry Mile, Rusholme, 2010. Wikimedia Commons

29. Victoria Wood,
Library Gardens, Bury.
Wikimedia Commons

30. Tony Wilson mural, Northern Quarter. Stu / Alamy Stock Photo

31. Cyclists Jason and Laura Kenny, Britain's most successful Olympians.
PA Images / Alamy Stock Photo

32. Manchester skyline, evening, 2020.
Chris Clarke / Wikimedia Commons

Joy Division developed a sparse sound reflecting industrial desolation. Sumner later said their music came 'from within', in his case a response to 'the death of my community' when his Lower Broughton terraced streets were torn down and his family swept up into tower blocks. DJ Rob Gretton became their manager and also a Factory director. Nineteen seventy-nine was Joy Division's year, but Curtis – born in Stretford, raised in a working-class household in Macclesfield – struggled with personal problems, including a failing marriage, depression and epilepsy. His condition made it increasingly difficult to perform and he sometimes had seizures on stage. He killed himself by hanging in May 1980, aged twenty-three. In doing so Curtis became a mythical figure, feeding global fascination with Manchester and its music scene. Joy Division's second and final album, *Closer*, was released two months later; it and the single 'Love Will Tear Us Apart' became their highest-charting releases. Peter Saville later said: 'Much of the aura of Manchester today is founded on the charisma of Factory, and Factory's charisma was founded on Ian.'[25]

Sumner, Hook and Morris formed New Order, joined later in 1980 by Gillian Gilbert on keyboards. They became one of the era's most acclaimed bands, incorporating dance rhythms and electronic instrumentation into their work. Their 1983 hit 'Blue Monday' became a popular club track and several successful albums followed. The band's name was taken from a newspaper headline, 'The New Order of the Kampuchean Front', but controversy erupted because they were unaware the term had been used by Adolf Hitler in *Mein Kampf* to describe the effect of his planned Holocaust. Nonetheless, the name stuck.

New Order's profits bankrolled the creation in 1982 of the Haçienda by the Factory team, driven forward by Wilson and Gretton, in a former warehouse on Whitworth Street West that had previously been a yacht builder's showroom. Displaying a lack of business acumen, they conceived it as an avant-garde live events venue for what Wilson called 'the interesting community'. It lost money for several years. The name was inspired by a 1953 prose-poem essay by French Situationist Ivan Chtcheglov about reimagining the city, including the line 'The Haçienda must be built'. (Chtcheglov was later jailed for five years for plotting to blow up the Eiffel Tower, complaining that its lights ruined his sleep, and he had spells in psychiatric hospitals.)

The club was oversized and cold, acoustics were bad and gigs often poorly attended. Programming, including literary readings and conceptual art events, could be eclectic. Comedian Bernard Manning, invited to perform on the opening night, remarked to the audience: 'I've played some shit-holes during my time, but this is really something.' His jokes went down badly and he returned his fee. Northern chauvinism sometimes showed through, such as when female strippers performed at Christmas 1983. 'There are no happy women in the Factory story,' observed writer Richard Witts. Nonetheless, it was the venue for Madonna's first UK appearance in 1984, broadcast live on Channel 4's *The Tube*. After the show she was forced to spend the night in a Chorlton front porch after a mix-up over door keys with club DJ Mike Pickering.[26]

The Smiths performed three times at the Haçienda in 1983. They had formed the previous year when guitarist Johnny Marr, brought up in Ardwick Green and Wythenshawe, knocked on Steven Morrissey's Stretford door. They had met at a Patti Smith gig; both were of Irish heritage and bonded over a love of poetry and literature. After being turned down by Factory they signed with Rough Trade and became one of the decade's most influential bands. All their albums reached the top five, including the number-one *Meat Is Murder*. Singer-songwriter Morrissey struck a chord with lyrics of emotional isolation and anti-establishment views – 'like epistles from one loner to another,' says Haslam.[27] Tension between the pair grew and the band split in 1987. In later years, some people consider Morrissey to have embraced far-right, anti-Islamic views.

Simply Red were formed in 1985 by red-headed soul singer and Manchester United fan Mick Hucknall. His mother abandoned the family when he was three and he was brought up in Denton by his father Reginald, a barber in Stockport. The band's debut album *Picture Book* also came out in 1985 and a year later the single 'Holding Back the Years', inspired by the upheaval of his early years, became a global hit. Their 1991 album *Stars* was one of the best-selling albums in UK chart history. Even after that success, Hucknall was still getting the bus into town from his Victorian semi in Old Trafford, as if he were an aspiring musician. Unlike some other stars, Hucknall invested his earnings substantially in Manchester property, aiding city-centre regeneration.[28]

The Haçienda's fortunes improved temporarily when it shifted from live gigs to dance as part of the rave revolution of the late 1980s. In 1986 it became one of the first British clubs to start playing house music, a dance style that originated in Chicago. Events such as Pickering's legendary house night Nude filled the dancefloor, while DJs such as Dave Haslam took over other nights and drew in youths from widely around the Manchester region. House morphed into acid house, with a driving tempo and distorted synthesised sound effects and an association with the drug ecstasy. Drugs gave the scene a colourful intensity, but the inevitable burnout came quickly. The Haçienda became infiltrated by gangsters seeking to profit from the drugs, bringing with them stabbings and shootings. In July 1989, the UK's first ecstasy-related death happened at the Haçienda when sixteen-year-old Clare Leighton collapsed and died after her boyfriend gave her an ecstasy tablet.

Madchester exploded in 1988–9, linked with the indie dance scene – 'the sound of young guitar bands with their roots in rock music but their hearts won over by the energy of house, their sense of rhythm unlocked and their creativity liberated by immersion in E culture', wrote Haslam. The name is said to have been initially coined by video directors the Bailey Brothers, working with Factory, in an unsuccessful pitch to Hollywood about a Manchester-set crime movie. In 1990, US magazine *Newsweek* put 'Stark Raving Madchester' on its front cover and explained the new phenomenon: 'Punk was menacing; the new music is buoyant, almost goofy. The fashion grafts British football gear onto American hippy glad rags – with a soupçon of the Jetsons' futurism. The philosophy is simplistic, the politics nil. And the whole package, still nameless and leaderless, was created in Manchester, England. The kids call it Madchester.'[29]

The Happy Mondays, featuring vocalist Shaun Ryder from Little Hulton, Salford, and dancer Mark 'Bez' Berry from Bolton, were reaching their commercial peak with rhythm-heavy music influenced by punk, house and psychedelia. Ryder gained a reputation as an expletive-ridden troublemaker and prankster. He was an early user of ecstasy and later a heroin addict. In 2020 he was belatedly diagnosed with attention deficit hyperactivity disorder (ADHD), which he said was the cause of some of his 'nutty behaviour'.[30]

The Stone Roses released their eponymous debut album in 1989 to critical acclaim, regarded by many as one of the greatest British albums ever recorded. Singer Ian Brown – who had an assured and cocky onstage presence – and guitarist John Squire had met at Altrincham Grammar School for Boys. The band played an outdoor concert at Spike Island in Widnes in 1990; regarded as a failure at the time because of sound problems and poor organisation, it became legendary in retrospect as a 'Woodstock for the baggy generation'.

Other bands at the time included Inspiral Carpets from Oldham, who used organs and distorted guitars, influenced by psychedelic rock. The Charlatans formed in the West Midlands but relocated to Northwich, where singer Tom Burgess was brought up; they became associated with Madchester. James, originally from Whalley Range, had a popular hit in 1991 with the single 'Sit Down'. Electronic dance group 808 State took their name from a drum machine. Dance group M People were formed in 1990 by Mike Pickering; soul singer Heather Small became their distinctive vocalist. Electronic music duo The Chemical Brothers was formed by two Manchester University students, Tom Rowlands and Ed Simons, in 1989. Lisa Stansfield, a soul singer-songwriter from Crumpsall and

Rochdale, had a breakthrough with her first solo album *Affection* in 1989 and its worldwide chart-topping single 'All Around the World'.

Manchester produced a number of black female singers in the 1990s, notably Diane Charlemagne from Moss Side, who sang jazz, soul, funk and electronic music with chart success. Hers are the vocals on Goldie's 'Inner City Life' in 1994, which helped to take the drum and bass genre mainstream. She also toured the world extensively with Moby. She died of kidney cancer in 2015, aged fifty-one. Others include Denise Johnson, raised in Hulme, best known for her vocals on Primal Scream's 1991 album *Screamadelica*. She also worked with Manchester bands including A Certain Ratio and New Order. She died in 2020, aged fifty-six.[31]

At the Haçienda, violent incidents were becoming the norm and the club was losing money, in part because drug-takers drank water to slake their thirst, denting income from selling alcohol. Greater Manchester Police tried to get its licence revoked, but the club hired George Carman QC and won a reprieve. The club closed voluntarily in early 1991 and reopened in May, after discussions with police, but shootings and stabbings continued. Madchester was dying.

The Stone Roses' second album was a long time arriving after the band fought a protracted legal battle to terminate their contract with the Silvertone label. When *Second Coming* was released in 1994, it had mixed reviews. The group soon disbanded after several line-up changes. The making of the next Happy Mondays album *Yes Please!* was also problematic; the band flew to Barbados to record it and went 'crack crazy', according to bassist Paul Ryder, Shaun's brother. Shaun and Bez caused a storm in November 1991 when they voiced hostility to gays in an interview with *New Musical Express*. 'Faggots are disgusting,' said Bez, oblivious to the fact that he was showing people how to dance to music produced by gay men in the US for gay nightclubs.[32] Ryder and Bez formed Black Grape in 1993 after the Mondays disintegrated. Factory Records went into receivership in 1992, having lost money for several years. New Order disbanded in 1993 to work on individual projects, then reunited in 1998; Hook left in 2007 after disputes with other members.

After Madchester came Britpop, a term that writer and musician John Robb 'shamefacedly' admitted he had originally coined in 1988.[33] Among the biggest bands was Oasis, fronted by brothers Liam and Noel Gallagher, raised in Longsight and Burnage. Their album *Definitely Maybe* in 1994 became the fastest-selling debut album in UK history at the time. The next year they recorded *(What's the Story) Morning Glory?* amid chart rivalry with Blur; the album became an international success. Tabloid newspapers had a field-day with the brothers' disputes and wild lifestyles. Liam became famed for his swagger, a gait of Mancunian insouciance similar to that of Ian Brown. The group disbanded when Noel left in 2009.

It was not all Britpop and Madchester. Boy band Take That (originally Kick It) were formed in Manchester in 1990 by manager Nigel Martin-Smith. The line-up included Howard Donald from Droylsden, Mark Owen from Oldham and Crumpsall-born Jason Orange alongside better-known Gary Barlow from Frodsham and Robbie Williams from Stoke-on-Trent. They achieved many number-one singles and albums. Rock band The Verve, including lead vocalist Richard Ashcroft, were formed in Wigan in 1990. They became commercially successful later in the decade with singles such as 'Bitter Sweet Symphony' before breaking up in 1999.

The Haçienda closed in 1997, burdened by debts. Its story was told in Michael Winterbottom's 2002 film *24 Hour Party People* starring Steve Coogan as Tony Wilson. Filming required reconstructing the Haçienda as a temporary set in a factory, opened to ticket holders over three nights. Gangs that used to terrorise the club door tried storming the gates and the police were called, just like old times. The Haçienda was demolished in 2002 and replaced with apartments. The club and its music made a significant contribution to building modern Manchester's global reputation and assisting its economic regeneration. Whether commercially savvy Manchester today lives up to that original Situationist dream is another matter.

Since then, Manchester's pop music scene has been more fragmented, though it was always more varied than stereotypes allow. As writer David Scott puts it: 'Manchester music doesn't exist. At least, not in the way you think. The city has undoubtedly created some of the greatest songs of all time, yet there is nothing sonically that ties them all together.'[34] Indie singer-songwriter Damon Michael Gough, raised in Bolton and known as Badly Drawn Boy, won the 2000 Mercury Music Prize, beating Manchester contemporaries Doves. Rock band Elbow, formed in Bury in 1997, won the Mercury in 2008 for their album *Seldom Seen Kid* and the Brit Award for Best British Group in 2009.

In classical music, the Hallé moved to the Bridgewater Hall as its main venue when it opened in 1996 and the Free Trade Hall was converted into a Radisson hotel. The Bridgewater's stage and organ lie on 270 giant foundation springs usually used in earthquake zones, to prevent vibration from traffic and trains. The Hallé had a difficult time in the 1990s. Principal conductor Kent Nagano was criticised for expensive and ambitious programming, while weak financial management led to threatened bankruptcy in 1998. The situation was turned round by improved financial discipline, cuts in the number of musicians, public fund-raising and an Arts Council grant. Sir Mark Elder, who became music director in 2000, is seen as having restored the orchestra to high critical and musical standards. Singapore's Kahchun Wong is due to become principal conductor from the 2024-5 season.[35] In December 2023, English National Opera announced that it had chosen Manchester as its new headquarters, after being told to leave London or lose its Arts Council funding.

The two sides of Manchester's music history came together when Elbow played with the Hallé in 2009 as part of Manchester International Festival. In 2019 Peter Hook and the Manchester Camerata collaborated on a show reworking the music of Joy Division, which has been performed a number of times. It seems a fitting tribute to the musical energy that Manchester brought to the world.

16

TWENTY-FIRST CENTURY

Manchester, while no longer exactly the 'shock city' of early Victorian times, once again finds itself a test case for the future of urban living. Jobs, economic output and population have grown strongly so far this century despite a recession, pandemic and European war. Dozens of skyscrapers have sprung up in the city centre. For some, the pace of change has been disconcerting. It is a startling turn-round from industrial decline, yet debate rages about whether 'Manctopia' or 'Manc-hattan' and its embrace of private-sector investment – also known as the 'Manchester model' – benefits ordinary citizens or has become a 'neoliberal' playground for property developers and affluent newcomers.

The city's renaissance gained its own momentum by the mid-2000s. The Commonwealth Games in 2002 were carried off with panache, though the city had to squeeze extra funding out of Tony Blair's government. It was an opportunity to show how Manchester had changed since the 1996 IRA bombing and breathe new life into parts of post-industrial east Manchester. Howard Bernstein, Manchester City Council's chief executive, was knighted in 2003 and council leader Richard Leese in 2006. Over the next two decades Manchester's leadership – widely known as 'The City' while Bernstein and Leese were around – continued its pragmatic, partnership-building approach.

An impressive array of new and refurbished buildings was created in the city centre. The former newspaper printing site at Withy Grove was sympathetically restored and reopened in 2000 as the Printworks, an entertainment venue with a cinema, clubs and eateries. Allied London, led by Mike Ingall, developed the 23-acre Spinningfields business district between the Irwell and Deansgate as an alternative to the historic King Street area for financial and professional services firms. The national media dubbed Spinningfields, named after a narrow old street, the 'Canary Wharf of the North'. By 2007 all three million square feet of commercial space were filled by corporate occupiers, though its shops and restaurants were less successful. US bank BNY Mellon also created a regional centre in Manchester in 2005, with its main base at 1 Piccadilly Gardens.

In 2006 the forty-seven-storey Beetham Tower was completed on Deansgate, containing a Hilton hotel and displacing the CIS Tower as Greater Manchester's tallest building. The Beetham Tower became a visual symbol of the new Manchester, soaring upwards. It was built by Merseyside's Frost family, operating as the Beetham Organisation; the scheme's architect Ian Simpson occupied the penthouse. Beetham went into administration in 2011, but the tower set the template for Manchester's embrace of skyscrapers. It scotched any notion that Manchester should stay resolutely Victorian and signalled to landowners the value of putting a tower on their plot. It is now called the Hilton Tower and owned by a London-based company, but locals still call it the Beetham Tower.

In the early 2000s it seemed likely that the Labour government would hold a referendum on creating a North West regional assembly as part of its devolution plans. The idea was enthusiastically championed by Tony Wilson, who had become keenly interested in politics. Manchester's leadership was cool on the proposal, fearing that an assembly would be a rival for funds and influence and might tip projects and public cash towards needier Merseyside. It came to nothing, however. A proposed assembly for North East England was rejected by almost four-to-one in a referendum in October 2004, after which Labour dropped further plans for English regional assemblies. Wilson died in 2007, aged fifty-seven.

In 2006 Manchester hosted the Labour Party conference for the first time since 1917, part of a shift from traditional seaside locations, though relations between the party and the city's leadership have sometimes been strained. From Heseltine onwards, Manchester, although dominated by Labour councillors, has felt it tended to get a better deal from Conservative ministers, impressed by the city's entrepreneurial nous.[1]

Not everything went smoothly for The City. In 2006 Manchester lost out to Salford when the BBC chose Salford Quays as the site for relocating five departments and 1,800 staff from London. Manchester had offered a site near the Oxford Road corridor, but the Salford plot was bigger and cheaper. MediaCityUK's developer was John Whittaker's Peel Holdings, a thorn in Manchester's side whose Trafford Centre was already competing for Mancunian shoppers. ITV's Manchester operations also moved to MediaCityUK in 2013.

In 2007 Manchester won a government-led contest to award a Las Vegas-style supercasino to one English location. The scheme dismayed many in the Labour movement, who saw gambling as an immoral way to create jobs, but Blair's government saw it as a way to revive problem areas. A site next to the City of Manchester Stadium was put forward and selected as the winner by an advisory panel, but the supercasino was killed off when Gordon Brown became prime minister.

More dramatically still, in 2008 Greater Manchester pledged to introduce a congestion-charging scheme in return for a government offer of £3 billion public transport funding. Vehicles entering an area bounded by the M60 motorway would be charged £2 in the morning peak, with a further £1 for those entering the inner cordon, roughly at the Inner Ring Road; in the evening, a further £1 would have been charged on exit from each cordon. The proposal provoked huge opposition, including from former city council leader Graham Stringer, and was defeated by four-to-one in a referendum. The affair had an echo in 2022 when Andy Burnham, mayor of Greater Manchester, paused the implementation of a clean air zone after initially supporting it. It would have seen non-compliant vans, taxis, buses and lorries paying between £7.50 and £60 a day to drive around the city-region, but Burnham said its introduction would be unfair after hardships caused by the Covid pandemic.

More encouragingly, the biennial Manchester International Festival was launched in 2007 presenting new works across the performing and visual arts. Aiming to build on the Commonwealth Games momentum, the city council hired Alex Poots, English National Opera's artistic director, to be the first artistic director. The aim was to enhance Manchester's global reputation. Less successful was Urbis, an underwhelming 'museum of urban life' that opened in 2002 in a building designed by Ian Simpson as part of the Exchange Square redevelopment. Urbis closed in 2010 and was replaced in the same building two years later by the National Football Museum, relocated from Preston.

The 2008 downturn saw many property developments halted or delayed. There was a crisis at Spinningfields, including the collapse of Halliwells, a large local law firm, which went into administration in 2010 partly as a result of its role as an anchor tenant. Allied London almost withdrew from the whole project. However, the city council bought some of the freeholds to allow the development to proceed. Manchester's growth soon picked up again. The Co-operative Group announced plans for NOMA (a contraction of north Manchester), an ambitious 20-acre development stretching from Shudehill to Angel Meadow, an area historically poor. At its heart was One Angel Square, a new headquarters for the Co-op Group, opened by Queen Elizabeth in 2013.

Home, a £25-million arts complex, opened in 2015 to replace the Library Theatre and the Cornerhouse cinemas and galleries. The city council provided £19 million of the funding. The building was located in Tony Wilson Place, part of a new creative quarter off Whitworth Street West, which also includes a 1970s statue of Friedrich Engels transported from eastern Ukraine. Meanwhile in the suburbs, entrepreneur Nick Johnson, formerly Urban Splash's deputy chief executive, revived Altrincham's town centre – hard-hit by competition from the Trafford Centre – by transforming its market in 2014 into an artisan food and drink hub. The project won national awards and Johnson opened further food halls in Macclesfield and Manchester, while the idea was copied by others in Stockport and elsewhere.

In June 2014, Tory chancellor George Osborne – many of whose Tatton constituents were Manchester commuters – stood up at Manchester's Science and Industry Museum and proposed the creation of a 'Northern Powerhouse' with investments in science and transport aimed at realising the potential for connecting cities from Liverpool to Hull. He backed a new high-speed rail link between Manchester and Leeds – initially known as HS3, later Northern Powerhouse Rail – and held out the prospect of 'serious devolution of powers and budgets' to city-regions that opted for an elected mayor.[2]

According to Bernstein, Osborne realised that centralised governance was not working. Manchester's leaders saw an opportunity. When Labour HQ called Leese and asked him to criticise Osborne's speech, he is said to have told them to get lost, with an expletive.[3] In November a deal was signed that would give Greater Manchester control of transport, planning, housing and the £500-million further education and skills training budget. It would also be the first place to integrate health and social care budgets. Osborne went on to approve a Metrolink extension to the airport, funded a £235-million centre for advanced materials at Manchester University named after Sir Henry Royce, co-founder of Rolls-Royce, and pledged £78 million for an arts venue to be known as The Factory.

Groundwork for 'Devomanc' had been laid over several years. Greater Manchester Combined Authority was created in April 2011, the first in the UK, under which the ten district councils pooled some resources and exercised various powers jointly. A key figure driving the agenda forward was Lord Peter Smith, leader of Wigan Council and chairman of the Association of Greater Manchester Authorities, who saw that boroughs had much to gain from working together. Not that the region's citizens were always united. In the 2016 Brexit referendum, Manchester, Trafford and Stockport voted to stay in the EU, while the other seven boroughs voted to leave; about 55 per cent of the city-region's residents backed Brexit.[4]

Andy Burnham, former Labour cabinet minister under Gordon Brown and twice an unsuccessful candidate for the party leadership, was elected Greater Manchester's first mayor in 2017 with 63 per cent of the vote, after a campaign focused on efforts to tackle home-lessness. Burnham was born in Aintree, Merseyside, and raised in Culcheth; he became MP for Leigh in 2001 and is seen as belonging to the soft left. After his win, Burnham informed Twitter followers of his favourite Manchester bands: Stone Roses in top spot, followed by The Smiths, The Courteeners, The Verve and New Order ('a selection skewed towards melodic guitar bands, rather than the city's more experimental music heard in early Factory and The Fall', says Andy Spinoza).[5] Bernstein stood down as chief executive of Manchester City Council in 2017 and was replaced by Joanne Roney, previously chief executive of Wakefield Council. Leese stepped down as council leader in 2021 and was succeeded by Bev Craig, councillor for Burnage. Born and raised near Belfast, she is the city council's first female and first gay leader.

The mayoralty's creation was not without friction. There were mutterings from the Bernstein–Leese camp that Burnham was slow to appreciate Manchester's partnership way of doing things. Some business leaders complained that they could not get the mayor on speed-dial.[6] Burnham, however, has achieved a national profile as spokesman for the region. His A Bed Every Night campaign, a £6-million emergency accommodation scheme, is credited with bringing the number of people sleeping rough in Greater Manchester down from 250 in 2018 to double digits by 2022, though demand has recently been rising.[7] In 2020 Burnham was dubbed 'King of the North' by social media users for his role in securing more money for northern communities during the pandemic. He was re-elected in 2021 with 67 per cent of the vote and has driven forward a plan to make Greater Manchester the first area outside London to have a regulated bus system since privatisation in 1986, creating the Bee Network. Other prominent politicians from the region include Lisa Nandy, Wigan MP and shadow minister for international development, and Angela Rayner, Ashton-under-Lyne MP and deputy leader of the Labour Party.

In May 2017 Manchester had to cope with the trauma of the Arena bombing, in which twenty-three died (including the attacker) and more than a thousand were injured when Salman Ramadan Abedi, an Islamist, detonated a bomb as people were leaving a concert by American singer Ariana Grande. Poet Tony Walsh encapsulated the city's outpouring of love and grief in a public reading of his poem 'This is the Place'. Grande returned in June with other global stars for a tribute concert for the victims at Old Trafford cricket ground. In 2023, a public inquiry led by Sir John Saunders concluded that there was a 'realistic possibility' that the bomber could have been thwarted if MI5 had acted more decisively on intelligence. Ken McCallum, MI5's director-general, said he was 'profoundly sorry' the security service did not prevent the attack.[8]

Meanwhile the city centre carried on expanding upwards and outwards. The old centre has spilled out into Ancoats, Castlefield and Salford's Greengate along with central Salford, Salford Quays and parts of Old Trafford around the football and cricket grounds. The city of Manchester's population had grown by 30 per cent over two decades to 549,000 in 2021, while Greater Manchester's population was up 14 per cent at 2.87 million (closer to the 13.4 per cent national average rise). Salford's growth was second fastest among the ten boroughs, up 25 per cent, and Stockport slowest at less than 4 per cent.[9] More than a hundred and fifty languages are spoken in Greater Manchester, according to Manchester University researchers.[10]

The 201-metre South Tower of Deansgate Square – apartments with a pool, gym, yoga studio and rooftop garden – overtook 169-metre Beetham Tower in 2018 as Manchester's tallest tower and was also said to be the tallest building in the UK outside London.[11] It is part of a four-tower development by Renaker and designed by SimpsonHaugh, founded in 1987 by Ian Simpson and Rachel Haugh. According to property data firm Urbinfo, as of August 2022 there were fifty-five buildings in central Manchester above twenty storeys, forty-one of which had been built since 2000, with thirty completed since 2010. A further twenty-three were under construction and five at pre-construction phases, while thirty-five more had planning approval. If all are built, there will be one hundred and eighteen tall buildings, double the number today.[12]

One of the world's most celebrated architects, Lord Norman Foster (born in 1935 in Reddish), grew up in modest circumstances in Levenshulme. His father was a machine-painter at Metropolitan-Vickers in Trafford Park and his mother worked in a bakery. Foster drew inspiration from Manchester Town Hall, where he started work as a clerk aged sixteen before training as an architect. Foster is known for sleek modern buildings of steel and glass, including the Reichstag in Berlin and 30 St Mary Axe (known as 'the Gherkin') in London. His practice has, though, done a relatively modest amount of work in Manchester, notably the Hardman Square office scheme in Spinningfields.

The development boom continued through the Covid pandemic. This startling change in the city's skyline allows more people to share in its growth, but it has been discomfiting for many Mancunians. Folk singer Mike Harding raged that 'the big money moved in and the dream was hijacked. Now Manchester looks like a city designed by a schizophrenic drunk with attention deficiency disorder.'[13] Many complain that the skyscrapers are not distinctively Mancunian, though the city has had a tradition of building big and bold since the Industrial Revolution with its factories and 300-foot chimneys.

Criticism of the influence of property developers on Manchester has grown, notably over a lack of affordable housing in new apartment blocks. A sign of the changing mood came when Gary Neville, former Manchester United and England full-back, pundit and entrepreneur, was forced into a U-turn in 2017 on his St Michael's scheme, a plan to create two towers linked by a split-level public plaza, two 'sky bars' and a shopping centre at a 1.5-acre site on Jackson's Row, just off Albert Square and Manchester Town Hall. It provoked strong opposition because it would have destroyed former Bootle Street police station and the Sir Ralph Abercrombie pub, where wounded protesters at Peterloo were reputed to have been carried. Neville revised his plan so as to retain the pub and the police station frontage and reduced the towers from two to one. The scheme went ahead.

There is no sign, however, of the Craig/Roney regime at the city council wanting to halt or slow the wave of development or reduce building heights, although Craig is seen as being to the left of Leese. In Salford, Labour's Paul Dennett, a left-wing gay man from a working-class background in Warrington, was elected city mayor, in effect council leader, in 2016 and re-elected in 2021. He has reconciled the property boom with his beliefs using slogans such as 'no ghetto rich or poor', 'sensible socialism' and 'putting growth to use'. He calculated that from 2017 to 2019, a billion pounds of new development had raised the council tax base, injecting £40 million into council coffers. In 2021 Dennett created a council-owned social housing organisation called Dérive aimed at building several hundred homes, the largest council-house-building programme in Salford for fifty years. Manchester followed with its own social housing arm: This City.[14]

Questions about whether the 'Manchester model' benefits ordinary Mancunians have become more persistent, particularly as the city has depended more on international capital over the past decade.

A report by Sheffield university researchers in 2022 argued that the city council had 'sold the family silver too cheap' in a joint venture with Abu Dhabi United Group, majority owners of Manchester City. This has delivered almost one and a half thousand homes, mainly for rent, in Ancoats and New Islington since 2004, but the report said 999-year leaseholds had been sold at 'below comparable rates', yet no affordable housing had been provided.[15]

Isaac Rose, organiser for a pressure group, the Greater Manchester Tenants Union, wrote in *Tribune* that despite all the new apartments, 'the city's housing crisis is only getting worse. In 2021, rents in the private sector were up nearly 24 per cent. Homelessness and temporary accommodation are rocketing, while 13,000 wait for social housing.'[16] Sam Wheeler, left-wing councillor for Piccadilly, warned in the *Morning Star* that Manchester had made a 'Faustian pact' with developers yet still had 'the second worst life expectancy in England after Blackpool, the second worst rate of child poverty in England after Tower Hamlets, wages that have fallen since 2002 and 15,000 families on its housing waiting list'.[17]

Daniel Timms, data journalist at *Manchester Mill*, an online journal, examined the evidence in July 2023 and found that concerns about Manchester's growth solely benefiting middle-class people or pushing out working-class people did not seem supported by the data. Far from being displaced, the number of people living in the centre who work in lower-paid roles such as cleaners and bar workers had increased. Displacement was occurring more in suburbs such as Reddish, Cheadle and Altrincham. Timms found more evidence for the criticism that ripple effects of growth in the centre were not permeating significantly into the outer boroughs. While Trafford and Salford seemed to have benefited, Oldham, Tameside and Rochdale all took a long time to recover from the financial crisis and had only marginally more jobs than in 2000. Most Greater Manchester boroughs had fallen behind UK jobs growth while the city had surged ahead.[18]

There is no doubt that Manchester still suffers significant poverty. The city is the second most deprived, after Blackpool, of England's

317 local authorities according to the government's 2019 Indices of Deprivation (based on population-weighted ranks of all the neighbourhoods within it).[19] The pattern of relative deprivation has changed little; swathes of north and east Manchester and parts of Wythenshawe remain poor. Across Greater Manchester there are stark differences in health, employment, pay and skills. Like other cities, it is grappling with the prevalence of low-paid, insecure jobs.

Burnham sees part of the answer in building Atom Valley, a planned hub for innovation in advanced materials, manufacturing and green technologies aimed at creating 20,000 jobs across three sites in Bury, Rochdale and Oldham. He hopes the scheme will be 'the engine room of Greater Manchester's next industrial revolution'.[20] Under a 'trailblazer' devolution deal with the government, leaders across the region will have a single pot of money to spend as they see fit, rather than having to make separate bids over different projects. Burnham also plans a Greater Manchester Baccalaureate offering students the option of studying technical subjects instead of going to university.

In the city centre, ID Manchester is a £1.7 billion plan by the University of Manchester and Bruntwood SciTech to regenerate the university's north campus near Piccadilly Station, creating an 'innovation district' focusing on advanced materials, health, digital technology and biotechnology. It will include offices, work spaces, homes and shops, aiming to create ten thousand jobs over fifteen years. The university celebrates its bicentenary in 2024 (tracing its origin to the foundation of Manchester Mechanics' Institute). The £211-million Factory International arts centre – renamed Aviva Studios – opened in 2023, four years late and £100 million over budget, giving Manchester International Festival a purpose-built home on the site of former Granada Studios. Co-op Live, a £365-million music arena next to Manchester City's Etihad Stadium, is due to open in 2024.[21]

Transport remains an issue, despite expansion of the Metrolink tram network. The opening of the Ordsall chord, a rail link between

Victoria and Piccadilly, in 2017 improved capacity for trains running through Manchester, but promises of doubling the number of through platforms at Piccadilly to four have not been kept. Boris Johnson as prime minister downgraded Northern Powerhouse Rail in 2021, with plans to be delivered through new track and upgrades to existing infrastructure rather than an entirely new line between Manchester and Leeds. The planned Birmingham to Manchester leg of the High Speed 2 line was scrapped by Prime Minister Rishi Sunak in 2023.

The scale of Manchester's challenge remains huge. Friedrich Engels wrote about the separation of Manchester's classes in *The Condition of the Working Class in England* in the 1840s: 'The town itself is peculiarly built, so that a person may live in it for years, and go in and out daily without coming into contact with a working-people's quarter or even with workers, that is, so long as he confines himself to his business or to pleasure walks.'[22] He would recognise today's division between rich and poor and its geographical spread of deprivation. Bev Craig said in 2023: 'For the vast majority, the economy simply isn't good enough.'

As in the nineteenth century, Manchester is at a crossroads. Like then, its growth is breathtakingly rapid. It has become an experiment in how to turn round the economy of an ailing former industrial colossus. The city – and its region – needs now to show that it can broaden and deepen its revival. If it can spread the benefits widely among the bulk of its population, it will have earned the world's admiration.

REFERENCES

Introduction

1. Benjamin Disraeli, *Coningsby* (William Blackwood 1844), Book IV, Ch. I
2. Friedrich Engels, *The Condition of the Working Class in England* (Oxford World's Classics), 65
3. Multilingual Manchester 2010–21, University of Manchester, manchester.ac.uk
4. Emmeline Pankhurst, *Suffragette: My Own Story* (Solis 2015, originally published 2014), 3
5. Stuart Maconie, *Pies and Prejudice* (Random House 2008), 112–13
6. Granada's David Plowright, described in Andy Spinoza, *Manchester Unspun: Pop, Property and Power in the Original Modern City* (Manchester University Press 2023), 135
7. ONS population estimates 2021, nomisweb.co.uk
8. Jonathan Schofield, '"The unlikeliest looking transvestites on the planet" – 35 great quotes about Manchester', *Manchester Confidential*, 14 December 2017
9. Philippe Auclair, *Cantona: The Rebel Who Would Be King* (Pan Macmillan 2009), 422
10. Schofield, *Manchester Confidential*, 14 December 2017
11. '"He was a recklessly generous soul." Frank Cottrell-Boyce on Tony Wilson and the 20-year anniversary of *24 Hour Party People*', 16 April 2022, northernsoul.me.uk; Michael Taylor, 'Trust me, Tony Wilson never said: "This is Manchester, we do things differently here"', linkedin.com; Tony Wilson, *24 Hour Party People: What the Sleeve Notes Never Tell You* (Channel 4 Books 2002), 29

Chapter 1: Beginnings

1. P. Holder and J. Walker, 'The Northgate reconstruction' in Bryant, Morris and Walker, *Roman Manchester: A Frontier Settlement* (The Archaeology of Greater Manchester, Volume 3, Greater Manchester Archaeological Unit 1986), gmau.manchester.ac.uk; RIB 575, 577, 579, 580, romaninscriptionsofbritain.org; W.H. Thomson, *A History of Manchester to 1852* (John Sherratt 1967), 11–14; Michael Nevell, *Manchester: The Hidden History* (History Press 2008), 21; Norman Redhead, 'A guide to Mamucium', 2008, bbc.co.uk; Alan Kidd, *The Origins of Manchester, from Roman Conquest to Industrial Revolution* (Carnegie 2023), 10–12; Deborah Woodman, *The Story of Manchester* (Phillimore 2017), 23, 26–7
2. Brian Groom, *Northerners: A History, from the Ice Age to the Present Day* (HarperNorth 2022), 4
3. Nevell 13–16; Glynis Cooper, *Salford: An Illustrated History* (Breedon 2005), 18–19
4. Alan Kidd, *Manchester: A History* (Carnegie 2006, first published 1993), 2; Kidd, *The Origins of Manchester* 4–5; Denise Kenyon, *The Origins of Lancashire* (Manchester University Press 1991), 39–40; Woodman 12
5. Kenyon 47–8; David Mason, *Roman Chester: City of the Eagles* (Tempus 2001), 41–2; Woodman 14
6. Richard Gregory, *Roman Manchester: The University of Manchester's Excavations within the Vicus* 2001–5 (Oxbow 2007), 1–3; Woodman 14–15
7. Kidd, *The Origins of Manchester* 4; David Mills, *A Dictionary of British Place Names* (Oxford 2011, first published 1991), 316; 'Manchester' in Victor Watts (ed.), *The Cambridge Dictionary of English Place-Names Based on the Collections of the English Place-Name Society* (Cambridge 2004); Andrew Breeze, 'Manchester's ancient name', *The Antiquaries Journal* 84: 353–7 (2004)
8. E. Ekwall, *Place Names of Lancashire* (Manchester University Press, Longmans Green 1922), 225, 246; N.J. Frangopulo (ed.), *Rich Inheritance: A Guide to the History of Manchester* (Manchester Education Committee 1962), 12–13; Kenyon 88
9. Nevell 30–1; Gregory 3; Redhead; Steven Dickens, *Manchester's Military Legacy* (Pen and Sword 2017), 13; Woodman 15–17
10. Nevell 34; Redhead; Kidd, *The Origins of Manchester* 9–14
11. David Shotter, *Romans and Britons in North-West England* (Centre for North-West Regional Studies, University of Lancaster 2004, first published 1993), 129–30; Kidd, *The Origins of Manchester* 11, 14
12. Nevell 321; Kidd, *The Origins of Manchester* 14; Woodman 27
13. Kidd, *The Origins of Manchester* 5–6; Stuart Hylton, *A History of Manchester* (Phillimore 2003), 4; Barri Jones, *Roman Manchester* (Manchester Excavation Committee, John Sherratt 1974), 11; Thomson 14
14. Thomson 18; Woodman 31
15. Nevell 38–9; Kenyon 78

16. Kidd, *The Origins of Manchester* 15–16; Anne Savage (ed.), *Anglo-Saxon Chronicles* (Salamander 2002), 118
17. Historic England Research Records, monument number 1348592, heritagegateway.org.uk; Hylton 8; Woodman 32
18. Frangopulo 14; Hylton 8; Kidd, *Manchester: A History* 3
19. Kidd, *The Origins of Manchester* 17; Hylton 9; Frangopulo 14
20. Hylton 10
21. James Tait, *Medieval Manchester and the Beginnings of Lancashire* (Manchester University Press 1904), 9–11; Frangopulo 15–16; Hylton 11; Kidd, *Manchester: A History* 3; Kenyon 167.
22. Hylton 11–13; Nevell 41; Kidd, *The Origins of Manchester* 18, 22–4; Woodman 41
23. Hylton 12–13; Kidd, *Manchester: A History* 4; Tait 42–6; Woodman 33–4; 38–9
24. Nikolaus Pevsner, *The Buildings of England: South Lancashire* (Penguin 1969), 265; Kidd, *The Origins of Manchester* 29–32; Woodman 37–8
25. Hylton 16–17; Frangopulo 19–22
26. Tait 51; Hylton 16; Woodman 39–40
27. Frangopulo 19–21; Hylton 6–20; Thomson 43–7; Tait 45–52, 60–119
28. Thomson 48–52; Hylton 20; Frangopulo 21–2; Kidd, *The Origins of Manchester* 28
29. Frangopulo 24–5; Nevell 39–41; Thomson 56–62; Hylton 14–15; Woodman 34–5
30. Kidd, *The Origins of Manchester* 36–8
31. Kidd, *Manchester: A History* 5–6; Kidd, *The Origins of Manchester* 38–44; Hylton 25; Frangopulo 25–7; Woodman 54–7
32. Hylton 25; quote from Attorney General v Earl of Stamford 1839 in T.J. Phillips, *Report of Cases Argued and Determined in the High Court of Chancery during the time of Lord Chancellor Lyndhurst, with a few during the time of Lord Chancellor Cottenham* (Vol. I, William Benning and Co. 1847), 738; Woodman 55
33. Hylton 29
34. Frangopulo 25; Woodman 50
35. Stephen Bowd, 'In the labyrinth: John Dee and Reformation Manchester', *Manchester Region History Review*, Vol. 19 (2008), 17–43, research.ed.ac.uk
36. Tait 37; Hylton 21; Frangopulo 27; Thomson 98; Nevell 52–5; Woodman 54
37. Frangopulo 28

Chapter 2: Civil War to Georgian Boom Town

1. Stephen Bull, *'A General Plague of Madness': The Civil Wars in Lancashire, 1640–1660* (Carnegie 2009), 90; Dickens 38; Thomson 110; Hylton 33
2. T.S. Willan, *Elizabethan Manchester* (Manchester University Press 1980), 39; Nevell 64

3. Bull 78
4. Dickens 36; Thomson 111
5. Dickens 39–41; Kidd, *The Origins of Manchester* 56–7
6. Dickens 41–54; Bull 97–104; Hylton 33–4; Thomson 109–14; F.A. Bruton, *A Short History of Manchester and Salford* (Sherratt & Hughes 1924), 109–13; Kidd, The Origins of Manchester 57; Woodman 58–9
7. Bull 213–25; Hylton 34; Bruton 109, 113–14; Kidd, *The Origins of Manchester* 35
8. Hylton 34; Thomson 120, 128; Bruton 121
9. Bull 401–4; Hylton 36–7; Thomson 129–30
10. Hylton 35–6; Thomson 107, 131; Nevell 55; Woodman 52
11. Bruton 116; Thomson 106
12. Frangopulo 31, 211–13; Hylton 37; Thomson 133; Bruton 131
13. Kidd, *Manchester: A History* 5–7; Kidd, *The Origins of Manchester* 61–9
14. Daniel Defoe, *A Tour Thro' the Whole Island of Great Britain* (London 1762), Vol. III, 249, 252; Thomson 148, 152, 157–8; Hylton 42; Nevell 63
15. Stephen Duxbury, *The Brief History of Lancashire* (History Press 2011), 86–8; Hylton 37; Thomson 143; Bruton 132
16. Hylton 37–8; Frangopulo 32–3; Thomson 133, 137, 144, 150–1; Bruton 122–3; Woodman 59–63
17. Thomson 175; Hylton 43; Bruton 151
18. Hylton 39; Thomson 153; Bruton 133–4; Kidd, *The Origins of Manchester* 108–9; Woodman 63–4
19. Hylton 43–5; Thomson 175–85; Bruton 151–7; Kidd, *The Origins of Manchester* 109–12; Woodman 64–5
20. Hylton 42; Kidd, *The Origins of Manchester* 89
21. Hylton 45–6; Bruton 158–9
22. Elizabeth Raffald, *The Experienced English Housekeeper* (J. Harrop 1769); Thomson 208; Kidd, *The Origins of Manchester* 98–100
23. Hylton 46, 50; Frangopulo 37; Thomson 250; Bruton 160
24. Hylton 50–2
25. Thomson 199–200; Hylton 46–7, 56; Kidd, *The Origins of Manchester* 92–7
26. Hylton 52–4, 58–60; Frangopulo 37–8; Thomson 191–2, 220, 226
27. James Ogden, *A Description of Manchester, 1783* (British Library reprint), 3; quoted in Kidd, *Manchester: A History* 9, Nevell 72

Chapter 3: Rise of Cottonopolis

1. Nevell 82–4
2. Joel Mokyr, *The Enlightened Economy: Britain and the Industrial Revolution 1700–1850* (Penguin 2009), 302
3. Quotes from Thompson 237, 240–1
4. John Aikin, *A Description of the Country from Thirty to Forty Miles Round Manchester* (first edition 1795, republished by David & Charles 1968), 191

5. Nevell 74–6; Hylton 40

6. Alan Kidd and Terry Wyke (eds), *Manchester: Making the Modern City* (Liverpool University Press 2016), 59–60, 76–8; Kidd, *Manchester: A History* 25; Hylton 63–7; Nevell 76–81, 105–11; Woodman 80

7. Kidd and Wyke, *Manchester* 60–2; Kidd, *Manchester: A History* 21; Hylton 61; Woodman 77–9

8. Roger Osborne, *Iron, Steam & Money: The Making of the Industrial Revolution* (Bodley Head 2013, Pimlico 2014), 161–2; Alfred P. Wadsworth and Julia de Lacy Mann, *The Cotton Trade and Industrial Lancashire, 1600–1780* (Manchester University Press 1931), 449–71; Duxbury 127–9

9. Robert C. Allen, *The British Industrial Revolution in Global Perspective* (Cambridge 2009), 188–93; Edward Baines, *History of the Cotton Manufacture in Great Britain* (H. Fisher, R. Fisher and P. Jackson 1835), 155–63; Wadsworth and Mann 476–82; Duxbury 129–32; C. Aspin and S.D. Chapman, *James Hargreaves and the Spinning Jenny* (Helmshore Local History Society 1964), 48–9, cited in Allen 193

10. Osborne 175–8; Allen 206–7; Duxbury 140–6

11. Osborne 196–7; Kidd, *The Origins of Manchester* 73

12. R.S. Fitton, *The Arkwrights: Spinners of Fortune* (2012 edition, Derwent Valley Mills Educational Trust , first published 1989 Manchester University Press), 219; Allen 202

13. Nevell 82–93; Hylton 70; Kidd, *Manchester: A History* 16

14. Nevell 95–105; Kidd and Wyke, *Manchester* 13–15, 72; Thomson 240; Kidd, *Manchester: A History* 28

15. D. Bythell, *The Handloom Weavers* (Cambridge University Press 1968), 254, cited in Mary B. Rose (ed.), *The Lancashire Cotton Industry: A History Since 1700* (Lancashire County Books 1996), 13; Hylton 70; Thomson 240

16. R. Lloyd-Jones and M.J. Lewis, *Manchester and the Age of the Factory* (Croom Helm 1988), 30, 105; cited in Kidd, *Manchester: A History* 17; Ian Miller and Chris Wild, *A & G Murray and the Cotton Mills of Ancoats* (Oxford Archaeology North 2007), 77; Nevell 95

17. Thomson 235; John J. Parkinson-Bailey, *Manchester: An Architectural History* (Manchester University Press 2002), 87–95

18. Harold Pollins, *Economic History of the Jews in England* (Associated University Presses 1982), 91; Frangopulo 114

19. Hylton 75; Thomson 269–70; Woodman 74–5

20. Osborne 224; Kidd and Wyke, *Manchester* 72, 80–1; Kidd, *Manchester: A History* 23; Nevell 130

21. Jane Carlyle, *Letters*, ed. Alexander Carlyle (John Lane 1903), Vol. I, No. 78; quoted in Norman Atkinson, *Sir Joseph Whitworth: 'The World's Best Mechanician'* (Sutton 1996), 119; David Waller, 'Why we should never listen to the Luddites', 23 August 2017, davidwallerwriter.com; Simon Winchester, *Exactly: How Precision Engineers Created the Modern World* (William Collins 2018), 119–25

22. Kidd and Wyke, *Manchester* 83
23. Mokyr 361–2, 366; Osborne 14–15, 222
24. Kidd, *Manchester: A History* 34
25. Hylton 71
26. Sue Wilkes, *Narrow Windows, Narrow Lives: The Industrial Revolution in Lancashire* (Tempus 2008), 56, 61
27. Wilkes 58–60; Hylton 71
28. Thomson 238, Hylton 71–2
29. Aikin 193; L.D. Bradshaw, *Visitors to Manchester: A Selection of British and Foreign Visitors' Descriptions of Manchester from c.1538–1865* (Neil Richardson 1987), 24; Thomson 271, also quoted in Asa Briggs, *Victorian Cities* (Penguin 1968, first published 1963), 69
30. Hylton 96–100, Bruton 183
31. Osborne, 277–9; David Ross, *George & Robert Stephenson: A Passion for Success* (History Press 2018), 110–20, Bruton 183–4
32. Hylton 38–9; Bruton 184–5
33. Hylton 99–101
34. Nevell 115–16
35. Hylton 107–8

Chapter 4: Riots and Radicals

1. Jacqueline Riding, *Peterloo: The Story of the Manchester Massacre* (Head of Zeus 2018), 1, 6, 9, 14, 235–56, 275–6, 303–10; Colin Brown, *The Scum of the Earth: What Happened to the Real British Heroes of Waterloo* (The History Press 2019, originally published 2015), 169–92; Robert Reid, *The Peterloo Massacre* (Windmill 2018, originally published 1989), 257–8, 273, 293–5, 306
2. Robert Poole, *Peterloo: The English Uprising* (Oxford 2019), 1–2
3. Kidd, *Manchester: A History* 14
4. Kidd, *Manchester: A History* 60–1; Michael E. Rose in Kidd and Wyke (eds), *Manchester* 179–80
5. Hylton 56–7; Kidd, *Manchester: A History* 61; Thomson 246; Woodman 65–6
6. Hylton 75; Kidd, *Manchester: A History* 84; Frangopulo 38; Bruton 169
7. Hylton 82, Kidd, *Manchester: A History* 77
8. Kidd, *Manchester: A History* 77–9
9. Duncan Bythell, *The Handloom Weavers* (Cambridge 1969), 96–106, cited in Poole 42, 205
10. Tom Hazeldine, *The Northern Question: A History of a Divided Country* (Verso 2020), 52–3; Dickens 58; Kidd, *Manchester: A History* 84–5; Hylton 81
11. Kidd, *Manchester: A History* 85
12. Poole, *Peterloo* 80–1

13. Thomson 235
14. Kidd, *Manchester: A History* 85–7; Hylton 83–5
15. Riding 167–85; Poole 237–46
16. Kidd, *Manchester: A History* 87
17. Kidd, *Manchester: A History* 87–8; Poole 360; Hylton 87; Riding 233; Dickens 68
18. Riding 233–52; Poole 285–97; Dickens 66–70; Reid 230–48
19. Poole 297–300, 349; Riding 254–70; Dickens 70–6; Reid 249–54; Kidd, *Manchester: A History* 88–9; Hylton 87
20. Poole 300–19, 348; Riding 270–83; Dickens 76–82; Reid 255–68; Kidd, *Manchester: A History* 89–90; Hylton 87–8; Samuel Bamford, *Passages in the Life of a Radical* (1840–44, published initially in parts), Ch. 35; 'Who were the victims of the Peterloo Massacre and what are their stories?', *Manchester Evening News*, 16 August 2019
21. Riding 285–9, 318–19; Poole 1–2, 333–9, 344, 383–4; Reid 270–1, 275–6; Hylton 88–9, 91–5
22. Poole 391; Hylton 90; Bruton 202–3
23. Dickens 82
24. Hylton 109–17, 142; Rose in Kidd and Wyke (eds), *Manchester* 181–2; Frangopulo 48–9; Thomson 337–8, 340–1; Bruton 203–5
25. Kidd, *Manchester: A History* 79–80; Rose in Kidd and Wyke (eds), *Manchester* 177–8
26. Kidd, *Manchester: A History* 92–7; Rose in Kidd and Wyke (eds), *Manchester* 175–7
27. John Saville, 'Jones, Ernest Charles (1819–69)', *Oxford Dictionary of National Biography*, oxforddnb.com; Kathryn Coase, *2000 Years of Manchester* (Pen and Sword 2019), 35

Chapter 5: Shock City of the 1840s

1. Asa Briggs, *Victorian Cities* (Penguin 1968, first published 1963), 56
2. Disraeli, *Coningsby*, Book IV, Ch. I
3. Alexis de Tocqueville, *Journeys to England and Ireland* (1835), trans. George Lawrence and K.P. Mayer, ed. K.P. Mayer (Yale 1958), 107–8
4. Anthony Howe, *The Cotton Masters 1830–1860* (Oxford University Press 1984), 46; cited in Kidd, *Manchester: A History* 17; Andrew Marrison, 'Indian Summer, 1870–1914' in Rose (ed.), *The Lancashire Cotton Industry* 244; Robina McNeil and Michael Nevell, *A Guide to the Industrial Archaeology of Greater Manchester* (Association for Industrial Archaeology 2000), 3–7; 'Oldham history', visitoldham.co.uk; Peter Arrowsmith, *Stockport: A History* (Stockport Metropolitan Borough Council 1997), 67–9, 70, 97–105, 125–57, 218–26, 258–9
5. Charles Dickens, *Hard Times* (Penguin 1969, first published 1854), 58
6. Kidd, *Manchester: A History* 67–75

7. Briggs 114; Gary S. Messinger, *Manchester in the Victorian Age: The Half-Known City* (Manchester University Press 1985), 22–3

8. Briggs 118–33; Kidd, *Manchester: A History* 63–7; Messinger 65–71; Hylton 134–6; Frangopulo 49–50; Bruton 209–11

9. A.J.P. Taylor, *Politicians, Socialism and Historians* (Hamish Hamilton 1980), 75; Woodman 102–4

10. Messinger 86–8; Bruton 214–15

11. Jenny Uglow, *Elizabeth Gaskell* (Faber and Faber 1993), 192–3

12. Hylton 122–5; Messinger 36–44; Nevell 161

13. James Phillips Kay, *The Moral and Physical Condition of the Working Classes Employed in the Cotton Manufacture of Manchester* (Cass & Co. 1970, first published 1832), 22–3

14. Quoted in Messinger 36

15. Edwin Chadwick, *Report to Her Majesty's Principal Secretary of State for the Home Department from the Poor Law Commissioners, on an Inquiry into the sanitary condition of the labouring population of Great Britain: with appendices* (HMSO 1842), 157

16. Thomas Carlyle, *Past and Present* (Chapman and Hall 1843), Book 1, Ch. 1

17. *Manchester Guardian*, 20 August 1845; quoted in Tristram Hunt, *Building Jerusalem: The Rise and Fall of the Victorian City* (Weidenfeld & Nicolson 2004, Phoenix 2005), 132

18. Messinger 55–64; Hylton 125–6

19. Engels, *The Condition of the Working Class in England* 65, 75

20. Engels, *The Condition of the Working Class in England* 31

21. Engels, 'England in 1845 and in 1885', *Commonweal* (March 1885), 12–14

22. Hylton 152–4; Kidd, *Manchester: A History* 39; Frangopulo 56–7; Nevell 161

23. Kidd, *Manchester: A History* 39–43; Hylton 143–50, 154–5

24. Hylton 160–4; Messinger 132–9; Briggs 136; Kidd, *Manchester: A History* 52; Frangopulo 59

25. Hylton 156–60; Frangopulo 73–8; Bruton 241–6; Messinger 131–2

26. Hylton 138–40; Messinger 139–49; Woodman 134–5

27. Briggs 112–13

28. Samuel Sidney, *Rides on Railways* (W.S. Orr 1851), 255

29. Thomas Carlyle to W.B. Baring, 8 February 1848, *The Collected Letters of Thomas and Jane Welsh Carlyle*, Vol. 22 (Duke University Press 1993), 241

30. Briggs 136–7; Hunt 189–91, 224–6; Hylton 166–8; Messinger 120–6; Woodman 132–3

31. Briggs 111–12; 137–8

Chapter 6: Migrant Tales

1. Manchester City Council, Census 2021, www.manchester.gov.uk/info

2. Hunt 20

3. Kay 21–2, 27; quoted in Mervyn Busteed, *The Irish in Manchester c.1750–1921: Resistance, Adaptation and Identity* (Manchester University Press 2016), 26–7

4. Dean Kirby, *Angel Meadow: Victorian Britain's Most Savage Slum* (Pen and Sword History 2016), 51

5. Busteed, *The Irish in Manchester* 30–1; Tristram Hunt, *The Frock-Coated Communist: The Revolutionary Life of Friedrich Engels* (Allen Lane 2009, Penguin 2010), 232–3

6. *Cowdroy's Weekly Gazette and Manchester Advertiser*, 18 July 1807; quoted in Busteed, *The Irish in Manchester* 88–9

7. Pauline Millward, 'The Stockport riots of 1852: A study of anti-Catholic and anti-Irish sentiment', in R. Swift and S. Gilley (eds), *The Irish in the Victorian City* (Croom Helm 1985), 207–25; Busteed, *The Irish in Manchester* 63

8. Busteed, *The Irish in Manchester* 211–18; Graham Davis, *The Irish in Britain, 1815–1914* (Gill and Macmillan 1991), 193–5; Donald MacRaild, *The Irish Diaspora in Britain, 1750–1939* (Palgrave Macmillan 2011), 126–7

9. Mervyn Busteed, 'A cosmopolitan city', in Kidd and Wyke (eds), *Manchester* 221

10. Hylton 228

11. Hylton 228–30

12. Busteed in Kidd and Wyke (eds), *Manchester* 223

13. Manchester City Council, 'Migration and ethnic history – Welsh', www.manchester.gov.uk; Busteed in Kidd and Wyke (eds), *Manchester* 216–17

14. Busteed in Kidd and Wyke (eds), *Manchester* 217–19

15. Pierre Lieuillot, *La 'biographie industrielle' de F.C.L. Albert (1764–1831), Contribution à l'histoire de l'introduction du mechanisme en France* (offprint from the *Annales historiques de la Révolution française*, 1952); cited in Barrie M. Ratcliffe (ed.), *Great Britain and Her World 1750–1914: Essays in Honour of W.O. Henderson* (Manchester University Press 1975), 91

16. *Wheeler's Manchester Chronicle*, 24 March 1814; quoted in Frangopulo 112

17. Bill Williams, *Jewish Manchester: An Illustrated History* (Breedon 2008), 16; Busteed in Kidd and Wyke (eds), *Manchester* 227; Pollins 93–4

18. Busteed in Kidd and Wyke (eds), *Manchester* 229

19. Busteed in Kidd and Wyke (eds), *Manchester* 230

20. Frangopulo 114; Todd M. Endelman, *The Jews of Britain 1656 to 2000* (University of California 2002), 80

21. Salis Schwabe, www.jewishlivesproject.com; Williams 22

22. Endelman 128–30, 132; Busteed in Kidd and Wyke (eds), *Manchester* 232

23. Frangopulo 115; Williams 110–11; Busteed in Kidd and Wyke (eds), *Manchester* 233

24. Endelman 196–203, 223–5; Williams 49–50, 140–56; Busteed in Kidd and Wyke (eds), *Manchester* 234

25. Busteed in Kidd and Wyke (eds), *Manchester* 235

26. Busteed in Kidd and Wyke (eds), *Manchester* 235–9; Eve Henley, 'Manchester's "Little Italy" and the pioneers of Britain's ice cream industry' (*Manchester Historian* 21 April 2022), manchesterhistorian.com

27. Manchester City Council, 'Migration and ethnic history – Chinese', www .manchester.gov.uk; Busteed in Kidd and Wyke (eds), *Manchester* 240–2; 'China diplomats wanted over Manchester assault outside consulate "not welcome back", says minister', *Manchester Evening News*, 20 December 2022

28. Migrant Manchester, www.movingpeoplechangingplaces.org

29. Marika Sherwood, *After Abolition: Britain and the Slave Trade Since 1807* (I.B. Tauris 2007), 45–6; 'Manchester and slavery', www.ucl.ac.uk; 'The Greg family of Styal', revealinghistories.org.uk; 'Guardian owner apologises for founders' links to transatlantic slavery', *Guardian*, 28 March 2023; Kidd, *The Origins of Manchester* 76–81

30. Adam Hochschild, *Bury the Chains: The British Struggle to Abolish Slavery* (Macmillan 2005, Pan 2006), 117–21; Busteed in Kidd and Wyke (eds), *Manchester* 243

31. David Olusoga, *Black and British: A Forgotten History* (Macmillan 2016), 362–4

32. Steve Turner, *A Hard Day's Write* (HarperCollins 1994); www.arthur whartonfoundation.org; Busteed in Kidd and Wyke (eds), *Manchester* 243–4

33. Busteed in Kidd and Wyke (eds), *Manchester* 244–6

34. Hylton 225–6; Busteed in Kidd and Wyke (eds), *Manchester* 246–7

35. Busteed in Kidd and Wyke (eds), *Manchester* 247–9

36. Ahmed Iqbal Ullah Race Relations Resource Centre, 'Stories of South Asian migration', www.racearchive.org.uk

37. Michael H. Fisher, Shompa Lahiri and Shinder Thandi, *A South-Asian History of Britain* (Greenwood 2007), 178–9

38. Busteed in Kidd and Wyke (eds), *Manchester* 252

Chapter 7: Science and Technology

1. Henry Enfield Roscoe, *The Life & Experiences of Sir Henry Enfield Roscoe* (Macmillan 1906), 404

2. Allan Chapman, 'Under a Lancashire heaven: William Crabtree, Jeremiah Horrocks and their circle, and the origins of research astronomy in seventeenth-century England' in John Pickstone (ed.), *The History of Science and Technology in the North West, Manchester Region History Review*, Vol. 18 (Manchester Centre for Regional History 2007), 19–40; James Sumner, 'Science, technology and medicine' in Kidd and Wyke (eds), *Manchester* 120; Coase 115

3. Sumner in Kidd and Wyke (eds), *Manchester* 120–1; Pickstone 2–3; Kidd, *Manchester: A History* 70; Frangopulo 38; Messinger 22

4. Sumner in Kidd and Wyke (eds), *Manchester* 121–2

5. 'John Dalton: Atoms, eyesight and auroras', 16 April 2019, scienceandindustrymuseum.org.uk; Sumner in Kidd and Wyke (eds), *Manchester* 123–5; Coase 115–16; Hylton 59, 156; Messinger 23

6. Albert Musson and Eric Robinson, *Science and Technology in the Industrial Revolution* (Manchester University Press 1969), 427–72

7. Winchester 119–25; Coase 120–1; Richard Hills, 'Richard Roberts (1789–1864), pioneer of production engineering in Manchester' in Pickstone 41–62

8. Donald Cardwell, *James Joule: A Biography* (Manchester University Press 1991); Sumner in Kidd and Wyke (eds), *Manchester* 127–8; 'James Joule: From establishment irritant to honoured scientist', 28 January 2019, scienceandindustrymuseum.org.uk

9. Jenny Wetton, 'John Benjamin Dancer: Manchester instrument maker', *Bulletin of the Scientific Instrument Society*, 29 (1991), 4–8; Cardwell 63; Sumner in Kidd and Wyke (eds), *Manchester* 133; Coase 117

10. Leucha Veneer, 'How Manchester Museum joined arguing societies together', 27 October 2010, bbb.co.uk; 'How to make a museum', 10 November 2013, storiesfromthemuseumfloor.wordpress.com; Sumner in Kidd and Wyke (eds), *Manchester* 128

11. Sumner in Kidd and Wyke (eds), *Manchester* 129–32; Coase 123; Pickstone 3

12. 'Early history of the Vegetarian Society', vegsoc.org

13. Coase 119–20; 'About James Braid', jamesbraidsociety.com

14. Coase 121–2; Andrew Lambert, 'Garrett, George William Littler (1852–1902)', *Oxford Dictionary of National Biography*

15. Sumner in Kidd and Wyke (eds), *Manchester* 135–40; Pickstone 4–7

16. Sumner in Kidd and Wyke (eds), *Manchester* 142–5; Samuel Alberti, 'Molluscs, mummies and moon rock: The Manchester Museum and Manchester science' in Pickstone 130–54

17. 'J.J. Thomson: Biographical', nobelprize.org

18. 'Rutherford's legacy – the birth of nuclear physics in Manchester', University of Manchester, 2 November 2017, manchester.ac.uk; Sumner in Kidd and Wyke (eds), *Manchester* 1454–6

19. Sumner in Kidd and Wyke (eds), *Manchester* 147, 150–1, 153; Pickstone 9

20. E.H. Burrows, 'Paterson (James) Ralston Kennedy (1897–1981), also including Edith Isabel Myfanwy Paterson (1900–95)', *Oxford Dictionary of National Biography*; Sumner in Kidd and Wyke (eds), *Manchester* 152

21. Hylton 189–92; Coase 124–5; Jean and John Bradburn, *A–Z of Manchester: Places, People, History* (Amberley 2019); Sumner in Kidd and Wyke (eds), *Manchester* 151

22. Anthony K. Cheetham, 'Kroto, Sir Harold Walter (1939–2016)', *Oxford Dictionary of National Biography*

23. Sumner in Kidd and Wyke (eds), *Manchester* 154–7; Hylton 219–20; Coase 126–7; Sarah Turing, *Alan M. Turing: Centenary Edition* (Cambridge University Press 2012, first edition 1959), 132

24. Bradburn 39–40; Sumner in Kidd and Wyke (eds), *Manchester* 157; Coase 127–8; 'Sir Bernard Lovell feared "poisoning to remove memories"', 21 September 2012, bbc.co.uk; 'Sir Bernard Lovell (1913–2012)', 24 September 2012, rylandscollections.com
25. Sumner in Kidd and Wyke (eds), *Manchester* 160–1
26. 'Graphene is less wonderful as an investment material', *Financial Times*, 21 July 2019; 'Graphene: Pencil it in', *Financial Times*, 1 January 2020
27. 'Our Nobel Prize winners', manchester.ac.uk

Chapter 8: Words and Pictures

1. Elizabeth Gaskell, *North and South* (Penguin edition 1970, first published 1854), 96
2. Shelley Rohde, *A Private View of L.S. Lowry* (Collins 1979), 61
3. Anthony Burgess, *Little Wilson and Big God* (Vintage 2012, first published 1987), 156
4. Jeanette Winterson, *Why Be Happy When You Could Be Normal?* (Vintage 2012, first published Jonathan Cape 2011), 13
5. Coase 174–5
6. Robert Morrison, 'De Quincey's wicked book', 21 February 2013, oupblog.com; Bradburn 66–8; Coase 178
7. Thomas Carlyle, *Collected Works: Vol. XIII, Past and Present* (Chapman and Hall 1843), 283, 327
8. Elizabeth Gaskell, *Mary Barton* (Oxford University Press World's Classics 1987, first published 1848), xxxv
9. Uglow, *Elizabeth Gaskell* 361
10. Coase 186–7
11. 'Anthony Burgess's fictional Manchesters', The International Anthony Burgess Foundation (29 September 2020), anthonyburgess.org
12. 'Howard Jacobson wins Booker Prize 2010 for The Finkler Question', *Guardian*, 12 October 2010
13. *Desert Island Discs*, BBC Radio 4, 11 October 2015
14. Hilary Mantel, *Giving Up the Ghost* (Harper Perennial 2004, first published Fourth Estate 2003), 114
15. Dave Russell, 'Culture, media and sport' in Kidd and Wyke (eds), *Manchester* 270; James Harding, *Agate: A Biography* (Methuen 1986), 33; Jonathan Croall, *Sybil Thorndike: A Star of Life* (Haus 2009), Ch. 7
16. Janet Wolff and John Seed (eds), *The Culture of Capital: Art, Power and the Nineteenth-Century Middle Class* (Manchester University Press 1988), 57; Kidd, *Manchester: A History* 71
17. Russell in Kidd and Wyke (eds), *Manchester* 266–7; Messinger 152–4
18. 'Annie Swynnerton: Painting light and hope', Manchester Art Gallery, manchesterartgallery.org
19. Coase 195

REFERENCES

Chapter 9: Victorian, Edwardian Expansion

1. Robert Vaughan, *The Age of Great Cities* (Jackson and Walford 1843), 1
2. Briggs 59
3. *Architect*, XV (1876), 9–10; quoted in Hunt 218
4. Kidd, *Manchester: A History* 104–5; Jonathan Schofield, 'A short history of Manchester: The rise and fall of Cottonopolis', 22 June 2018, confidentials. com/manchester
5. Kidd, *Manchester: A History* 105–7; Kidd and Wyke (eds), *Manchester* 16
6. Paul Burnell and Chris Long, 'The weekend: The campaigning duo who helped get workers two days off', 24 September 2022, bbc.co.uk; 'Sir Ian McKellen's great-great-grandfather helped invent the weekend', *Daily Telegraph*, 15 January 2017
7. Alan Kidd, 'From township to metropolis', in Kidd and Wyke (eds), *Manchester* 299–315; John Stanley Gregson, *Gimcrackiana or Fugitive Pieces on Manchester Men and Matters Ten Years Ago* (Wilmot Henry Jones 1833), 88–98; Nevell 162–6
8. Kidd, *Manchester: A History* 142–6; Kidd and Wyke (eds), *Manchester* 315–26; Woodman 128
9. C.W. Sutton, revised by Philip S. Bagwell, 'Watkin, Sir Edward William, first baronet (1819–1901)', *Oxford Dictionary of National Biography*; 'Sir Edward Watkin – king of railways', Chetham's Library, 9 October 2019, library.chethams.com
10. Kidd, *Manchester: A History* 157–9, 171–4; Briggs 130–3; Michael E. Rose, 'Voices of the people' in Kidd and Wyke (eds), *Manchester* 195–6; Messinger 120
11. Kidd, *Manchester: A History* 167–71; Rose in Kidd and Wyke (eds), *Manchester* 178, 197–9
12. Kidd and Wyke (eds), *Manchester* 93, 178–9, 209; Bruton 256–7
13. Kidd, *Manchester: A History* 175–8; Hylton 186–7
14. Kidd, *Manchester: A History* 179–80; Rose in Kidd and Wyke (eds), *Manchester* 197; Michael Herbert, 'Women's history walk around radical Manchester', *HerStoria* magazine (autumn 2010), 38; Woodman 137
15. Messinger 188–92; Hylton 91–5; Kidd, *Manchester: A History* 160–1; Kidd and Wyke (eds), *Manchester* 98, 281, 311; Frangopulo 153; Woodman 159–60
16. Russell in Kidd and Wyke (eds), *Manchester* 281–4
17. Kidd, *Manchester: A History* 119, 124–7, 151; Hylton 145–8, 149, 184–5; Frangopulo 60–2, 65–6, 68; 'History of heath visiting', Institute of Health Visiting, ihv.org.uk, accessed 27 March 2023
18. Kidd, *Manchester: A History* 133–5; Frangopulo 78–92; Messinger 132
19. Frangopulo 82
20. Andrew Davies, *The Gangs of Manchester: The Story of the Scuttlers, Britain's First Youth Cult* (Milo 2008); 'Manchester's real-life Peaky Blinders only feared one thing', *Manchester Evening News*, 23 April 2023

21. Coase 227–8
22. Frangopulo 82; Michael Sanderson, 'Literacy and social mobility in the Industrial Revolution', *Past and Present*, 56 (1972), 84–5; Kidd, *Manchester: A History* 46–7, 135–6
23. Messinger 151–8; Kidd, *Manchester: A History* 153–7; Hylton 163; Kidd and Wyke (eds), *Manchester* 17–18; Frangopulo 61; Bruton 262; Coase 291; Woodman 138–41
24. Margaret Beetham 'Heywood, Abel (1810–93)', *Oxford Dictionary of National Biography*; Joanna Williams, *Manchester's Radical Mayor: Abel Heywood, the Man Who Built the Town Hall* (History Press 2017); Coase 373–8
25. Hylton 171–2, 183–4; Kidd, *Manchester: A History* 153–7; Kidd and Wyke (eds), *Manchester* 8–9, 99, 329; Frangopulo 62–5
26. Hylton 175–9; Kidd, *Manchester: A History* 113–16; Kidd and Wyke (eds), *Manchester* 95–6; Jonathan Schofield, *My Guide to Manchester* (Manchester Books 2015), 225; Woodman 130–1
27. Kidd, *Manchester: A History* 115–16; Hylton 165, 179, 182–3; Kidd and Wyke (eds), *Manchester* 97; C.B. Phillips and J.H. Smith, *Lancashire and Cheshire from AD 1540* (Longman 1994), 245; Michael Nevell, *The Archaeology of Trafford* (Trafford Metropolitan Borough with University of Manchester Archaeological Unit 1997), 130–3
28. Kidd, *Manchester: A History* 103
29. D.A. Farnie, 'Rylands, John (1801–88)'; D.A. Farnie, 'Rylands [*née* Tennant], Enriqueta Augustina (1843–1908)', *Oxford Dictionary of National Biography*
30. Kidd, *Manchester: A History* 107–9, 138–9; Hylton 180; Kidd and Wyke (eds), *Manchester* 16–17, 94–5; Michael Winstanley, 'Brooke, Arthur (1845–1918)', *Oxford Dictionary of National Biography*; Coase 262–6, 269–73; Woodman 141
31. 'The body in a cart and a horsewhipping in Kendals: Terrifying tales from Manchester's Christmas past', *Manchester Evening News*, 25 December 2020
32. 'Meet the Timpsons', Timpson-group.co.uk; Coase 259–60
33. Hylton 189–92; Messinger 192–3; Bradburn 69–70; Frangopulo 70; Woodman 149–51
34. Hylton 187; Rose in Kidd and Wyke (eds), *Manchester* 198–9
35. Andrew Marrison, 'Indian summer, 1870–1914' in Rose (ed.), *The Lancashire Cotton Industry* 238–64; Marguerite Dupree, 'Foreign competition and the interwar period' in Rose (ed.), *The Lancashire Cotton Industry* 265; Anita McConnell, 'Pender, Sir John (1816–96)', *Oxford Dictionary of National Biography*

REFERENCES

Chapter 10: Votes for Women

1. June Purvis, *Emmeline Pankhurst: A Biography* (Routledge 2002), 74–6
2. James Wroe, *Peterloo Massacre, Containing a Faithful Narrative of the Events which preceded, accompanied and followed the fatal Sixteenth of August 1819* (third edition, printed by James Wroe, Manchester 1819), 21
3. Rose in Kidd and Wyke (eds), *Manchester* 188
4. Sandra Stanley Holton, 'Elmy, Elizabeth Clarke Wolstenholme (1833–1918)', *Oxford Dictionary of National Biography*
5. Linda Walker, 'Becker, Lydia Ernestine (1827–90)', *Oxford Dictionary of National Biography*; Joanna Williams, *The Great Miss Lydia Becker: Suffragist, Scientist and Trailblazer* (Pen and Sword 2022)
6. City Jackdaw, 31 December 1875; quoted in Kidd, *Manchester: A History* 181
7. J. Parker, 'Lydia Becker: Pioneer orator of the women's movement', *Manchester Region History Review*, 5.2 (1991–2), 16; Rose in Kidd and Wyke (eds), *Manchester* 189; Harold L. Smith, *The British Women's Suffrage Campaign* (Longman 2010, first published 1998), 10
8. Kidd, *Manchester: A History* 181–2; Margaret M. Jensen, 'Roper, Esther Gertrude (1868–1938)', Gifford Lewis, 'Booth, Eva Selina Gore- (1870–1926)', *Oxford Dictionary of National Biography*
9. Rose in Kidd and Wyke (eds), *Manchester* 189–91
10. Rose in Kidd and Wyke (eds), *Manchester* 191–2
11. June Purvis, 'Pankhurst [*née* Goulden], Emmeline (1858–1928)', *Oxford Dictionary of National Biography*; Emmeline Pankhurst, *Suffragette: My Own Story*
12. June Hannam, 'Pankhurst, (Estelle) Sylvia (1882–1960)', Verna Coleman, 'Walsh, Adela Constantia Mary Pankhurst (1885–1961)', *Oxford Dictionary of National Biography*
13. Peter D. Mohr, 'Ashton, Margaret (1856–1937)', *Oxford Dictionary of National Biography*; Rose in Kidd and Wyke (eds), *Manchester* 190
14. Brian Harrison, 'Kenney, Annie (1879–1953)', *Oxford Dictionary of National Biography*
15. Coase 39; Rose in Kidd and Wyke (eds), *Manchester* 195
16. Tessa Boase, *Mrs Pankhurst's Purple Feather: Fashion, Fury and Feminism – Women's Fight for Change* (Aurum 2018), 62–6; Molly Baer Kramer, 'Williamson [*née* Bateson], Emile (1855–1936)', *Oxford Dictionary of National Biography*
17. Purvis, *Emmeline Pankhurst* 194
18. Martin Pugh, *The Pankhursts* (Vintage 2008, first published Allen Lane 2001), 287–8; Purvis, *Emmeline Pankhurst* 248–9

19. Purvis, *Emmeline Pankhurst* 316, 318–35, 341, 361–3; June Purvis, 'Pankhurst, Dame Christabel Harriette (1880–1958)', *Oxford Dictionary of National Biography*; Paula Bartley, *Emmeline Pankhurst* (Routledge 2002), 231–7; Smith 34, 60–1

Chapter 11: Popular Culture

1. Coase 157
2. Dave Haslam, *Manchester, England: The Story of the Pop Cult City* (Fourth Estate 1999), xxx
3. Joseph Aston, *The Manchester Guide* (privately printed 1804), 245; Kidd, *Manchester: A History* 44; Coase 158–61
4. J. Ginswick (ed.), *Labour and the Poor in England and Wales 1849–51*, Vol. I (Frank Cass 1983), 80–2
5. Kidd, *Manchester: A History* 45
6. Woodman 114–15; Coase 145–6
7. Coase 168; Kidd, *Manchester: A History* 46; Chris Aspin, *Lancashire: The First Industrial Society* (Helmshore Local History Society 1969), 166
8. Coase 169–71; Lee Jackson, *Palaces of Pleasure: From Music Halls to the Seaside to Football, How the Victorians Invented Mass Entertainment* (Yale 2019), 122, 124, 146; Robert Nicholls, *The Belle Vue Story* (Neil Richardson 1992), 5; 'The world on fire … pyrodramas at Belle Vue, Manchester, c. 1850–1950' in David Mayer and John M. MacKenzie (eds), *Popular Imperialism and the Military: 1850–1950* (Manchester University Press 1992), 180
9. Coase 169, 171–2; Kidd, *Manchester: A History* 46
10. Woodman 116; Coase 165–6
11. Frances A. Bailey, 'The origin and growth of Southport', *Town Planning Review*, 1 January 1951
12. Jackson 56; 'Circus keeper killed by Barney the leopard', *Bolton News*, 10 October 2002, theboltonnews.co.uk
13. Kidd, *Manchester: A History* 128; Richard Anthony Baker, *British Music Hall: An Illustrated History* (Pen and Sword 2014), 114–15, 154; Haslam 3–5
14. Jackson 90; Kidd, *Manchester: A History* 131–2
15. Russell in Kidd and Wyke (eds), *Manchester* 272; Kidd, *Manchester: A History* 128–9
16. Baker, *British Music Hall* 244–5
17. Obituary, 'Eric Sykes', 8 July 2012, independent.ie
18. A.J.P. Taylor, *Essays in English History* (Hamilton 1976), 312
19. Walter Greenwood, *Lancashire* (Robert Hale 1951), quoted in Charles Nevin, *Lancashire, Where Women Die of Love* (Mainstream 2004), 10
20. Jeffrey Richards, 'Randle, Frank (1901–57)', *Oxford Dictionary of National Biography*
21. Kate Fox, *Where There's Muck, There's Bras: Lost Stories of the Amazing Women of the North* (HarperNorth 2022), 32–9

22. 'Victoria Wood', imdb.com; 'Victoria Wood obituary', *Guardian*, 20 April 2016
23. Kidd, *Manchester: A History* 129; Russell in Kidd and Wyke (eds), *Manchester* 273
24. Burgess 30
25. *Sing as We Go!* (1934), British Film Institute, screenonline.org.uk; David Bret, *Gracie Fields: The Authorized Biography* (Robson 1995), 76
26. Robert Murphy, *Realism and Tinsel: Cinema and Society in Britain, 1939–1948* (Routledge 1989), 193
27. Kidd, *Manchester: A History* 227–8; Bradburn 49–52
28. Dominic Sandbrook, *Never Had It So Good: A History of Britain from Suez to the Beatles* (Little, Brown 2005, Abacus 2006), 409–10; Laurence Kitchin, *Mid-Century Drama* (Faber 1960), 177; Haslam xxviii
29. Linda Grant, 'Mike Leigh comes out on his Jewishness', *Guardian*, 18 April 2006; Vanessa Thorpe, 'My home life was a battlefield: Mike Leigh tells of early traumas', *Observer*, 16 November 2014; Tim Lewis, '"Silly question", Mike Leigh interviewed by our readers and famous fans', *Observer*, 21 October 2018
30. Kidd, *Manchester: A History* 228
31. Russell in Kidd and Wyke (eds), *Manchester* 278–9; Graham Turner, *The North Country* (Eyre and Spottiswood 1967), 74–6; *Manchester Evening News*, 17 March 1965; Dave Russell, 'Going with the mainstream: Manchester cabaret clubs and popular music in the 1960s', *Manchester Region History Review*, 25 (2014), 1–19
32. Russell in Kidd and Wyke (eds), *Manchester* 284–5; Paddy Scannell, 'Shapley, Olive Mary (1910–99)', *Oxford Dictionary of National Biography*
33. Sandbrook 399–401
34. 'Greater Manchester night time economy strategy', 25 March 2022, democracy.greatermanchester-ca.gov.uk

Chapter 12: World Wars and Depression

1. 'First world war: How the Manchester Guardian fought to keep Britain out of conflict', *Guardian*, 2 August 2014
2. Hylton 192–4; Woodman 151; 'New book remembers Greater Manchester's Victoria Cross heroes of World War One', *Manchester Evening News*, 12 December 2015; *London Gazette*, 22 December 1914
3. Rose in Kidd and Wyke (eds), *Manchester* 199–200
4. 'The war is over! How the Guardian reported the signing of the armistice – November, 1918', *Guardian*, 2 November 2018
5. 'Coronavirus: Boris Johnson hospital stay and parallels to Lloyd George', bbc.co.uk, 8 April 2020
6. Benjamin Bowker, *Lancashire under the Hammer* (Leonard and Virginia Woolf 1918), 32–42

7. Marguerite Dupree, 'Foreign competition and the interwar period' in Mary B. Rose (ed.), *The Lancashire Cotton Industry: A History Since 1700* (Lancashire County Books 1996), 265

8. Kidd, *Manchester: A History* 187–8; Woodman 149

9. 'PG Tips: A Manchester brew', bbc.co.uk, 24 September 2014; Coase 262–3

10. 'Our heritage', inperialleather.co.uk, accessed 13 June 2023; Coase 264

11. Barbara Clegg, 'Moores, Sir John (1896–1993)', *Dictionary of National Biography*; 'Littlewoods' John Moores, the father of home shopping', bbc.co.uk, 17 March 2010

12. Coase 275–7

13. Burgess, *Little Wilson and Big God* 121

14. Ewan McColl, *Journeyman: An Autobiography* (Sidgwick & Jackson 1990), 201; Woodman 153–5

15. Sharman Kadish, 'Sunlight, Joseph (1889–1978)', *Oxford Dictionary of National Biography*; Coase 298; Ed Glinert, *Manchester Compendium: A Street-by-street History of England's Greatest Industrial City* (Penguin 2009), 47

16. J.S. Middleton, revised by Marc Brodie, 'Clynes, John Robert (1869–1949)', *Oxford Dictionary of National Biography*

17. Kidd, *Manchester: A History* 206–8

18. J.V. Beckett, *City Status in the British Isles, 1830–2002* (Ashgate 2005), 81

19. Salford University, Greenwood papers, WPG 3/1, review in the *Evening Chronicle*, 21 June 1933, quoted in Richard Overy, *The Morbid Age* (Penguin 2010), 74; Ibid., WPG 3/5/1, review in *The People* quoted in Overy 73; Chris Hopkins, *Walter Greenwood's Love on the Dole: Novel, Play, Film* (Liverpool University Press 2018), 214–15

20. GB Historical GIS/University of Portsmouth, visionofbritain.org,uk; cited in Kidd and Wyke (eds), *Manchester* 330–1

21. 'Manchester's historic population' and 'Census results 2021', manchester.gov.uk

22. GB Historical GIS/University of Portsmouth, visionofbritain.org,uk

23. Arthur Redford and Ina Stafford Russell, *The History of Local Government in Manchester*, Vol. III (Longman Greens 1939), 246; cited in Kidd and Wyke (eds), *Manchester* 337–8

24. Hylton 196–7; Kidd, *Manchester: A History* 217–21

25. Hylton 195–6; Kidd and Wyke (eds), *Manchester* 336–7; Brendon Jones, 'Simon, Ernest Emil Darwin, first Baron Simon of Wythenshawe (1879–1960)', *Oxford Dictionary of National Biography*

26. Kidd, *Manchester: A History* 209

27. Hylton 200–2

28. Kidd and Wyke (eds), *Manchester* 107–8; Hylton 203–4

29. Hylton 203–11; Woodman 165–8

30. 'VE Day 75: How Manchester celebrated in 1945 and what it still means to veterans', *Manchester Evening News*, 7 May 2020

REFERENCES

Chapter 13: Sporting Passion

1. David Hall, *Manchester's Finest: How the Munich Air Disaster Broke the Heart of a Great City* (Bantam 2008), 110
2. Simon Inglis, *Played in Manchester: The Architectural Heritage of a City at Play* (English Heritage 2004), 15–17; Russell in Kidd and Wyke (eds), *Manchester* 288; Dave Russell (ed.), *Sport in Manchester* (*Manchester Region History Review*, Vol. 20, Manchester Centre for Regional History 2009), 3
3. Inglis 17–19; Russell in Kidd and Wyke (eds), *Manchester* 288–9; Russell (ed.), *Sport in Manchester* 3–5
4. 'Manchester's cycling story', 27 January 2022, scienceandindustrymuseum .org.uk
5. Russell in Kidd and Wyke (eds), *Manchester* 288; Russell (ed.), *Sport in Manchester* 4; Samantha-Jayne Oldfeld, 'The Manchester Milers 1950–1870', 15 May 2020, playingpasts.co.uk
6. Inglis 19; Russell in Kidd and Wyke (eds), *Manchester* 290–1; Hylton 172–4
7. Gary James, *Manchester: A Football History* (James Ward 2008), 111–18; Hylton 172; Coase 301; Woodman 162
8. Jim White, *Manchester United: The Biography* (Sphere 2009), 23–35; Coase 302; Hylton 173–4; Woodman 161–2
9. James 23
10. Inglis 64–9
11. Russell in Kidd and Wyke (eds), *Manchester* 291; Hylton 173; Spinoza 67
12. Inglis 48; Russell in Kidd and Wyke (eds), *Manchester* 291–2; Melanie Tebbutt, '100 years and still fighting: Manchester's amateur boxing heritage', 26 July 2019, visitmanchester.com
13. Keith Laybourn, *Going to the Dogs: A History of Greyhound Racing in Britain, 1926–2017* (Manchester University Press 2019), Ch. 1; Russell in Kidd and Wyke (eds), *Manchester* 292–3; Kidd, *Manchester: A History* 230; Russell (ed.), *Sport in Manchester* 9–10
14. Kidd, *Manchester: A History* 231–2; Russell in Kidd and Wyke (eds), *Manchester* 293; Russell (ed.), *Sport in Manchester* 10
15. Inglis 21; Russell in Kidd and Wyke (eds), *Manchester* 293; Russell (ed.), *Sport in Manchester* 12
16. 'Best: Decline of the Golden Boy', 14 June 2005, bbc.co.uk
17. Coase 301
18. Fox 121–3
19. Fox 110–11
20. 'Jason Kenny: Great Britain's most successful Olympian retires', 24 February 2022, bbc.co.uk; 'Tokyo 2020: Historic win for Laura Kenny as she and Katie Archibald secure gold for Team GB', 6 August 2021, itv.com; 'Cheshire Olympians Laura and Jason Kenny welcome baby boy', 24 July 2023, cheshire-live.co.uk

Chapter 14: The Postwar Era

1. Richard Witts, *Nico: The Life & Lies of an Icon* (Virgin 1993), 302
2. Hylton 212–14; Woodman 168; Jonathan Schofield, 'The biggest Manchester development plant of all time', 7 July 2017, confidentials.com
3. Geoffrey Timmins, *Four Centuries of Lancashire Cotton* (Lancashire County Books 1996), 74–86; John Singleton, *Lancashire on the Scrapheap* (Oxford 1991), 130; David Kynaston, *Family Britain 1951–57* (Bloomsbury 2009), 120
4. Kidd, *Manchester: A History* 189
5. Woodman 179–81; '"Busby Babes" writer has died, aged 80', 25 June 207, holdthefrontpage.co.uk
6. Hylton 217–19
7. Kidd, *Manchester: A History* 206–8
8. Brian Harrison, 'Wilkinson, Ellen Cicely (1891–1947)', *Oxford Dictionary of National Biography*
9. *Manchester: 50 Years of Change – Post-War Planning in Manchester* (HMSO 1995), 24; Kidd and Wyke (eds), *Manchester* 339; Hylton 215
10. LP, *A Lancashire Lad* (Trailer 1972)
11. Hylton 215
12. Parkinson-Bailey 195
13. Parkinson-Bailey 195
14. Parkinson-Bailey 194–5, 209–12
15. Spinoza 7
16. Kidd, *Manchester: A History* 189–90
17. Paul Swinney and Elli Thomas, 'A century of cities', Centre for Cities, 4 March 2015, centreforcities.org
18. Paul Taylor, 'Manchester paid the price for Thatcher's modernising', *Manchester Evening News*, 8 April 2013
19. 'Obituary: Sir Harold Evans', bbc.co.uk, 24 September 2020
20. Kidd, *Manchester: A History* 192–3
21. Kidd, *Manchester: A History* 224
22. Spinoza 41–2
23. Spinoza 27
24. Spinoza 95
25. Kidd, *Manchester: A History* 235
26. Brian Robson in Kidd and Wyke (eds), *Manchester* 355–9
27. Trafford Council, 'Trafford Park Masterplan' 2008
28. Robson in Kidd and Wyke (eds), *Manchester* 379–80; Spinoza 100
29. Spinoza 167
30. Spinoza 98–101
31. *State of the City Report 2019* (Manchester City Council), 24, manchester.gov.uk
32. *Mancunian Gay*, 17 November 1984; Rose in Kidd and Wyke (eds), *Manchester* 202–5

33. 'Gay, Irish and radical – the invisible women who revolutionised Manchester', *Manchester Evening News*, 26 January 2020
34. 'Julia Grant: Transgender "pioneer" dies aged 64', 3 January 2019, bbc.co.uk; Spinoza 105, 107–8; 'How we made Queer as folk', *Guardian*, 6 January 2015
35. Spinoza 109
36. urbansplash.co.uk
37. Spinoza 164–7; Robson in Kidd and Wyke (eds), *Manchester* 359–62, 391
38. Hylton 228–9
39. Robson in Kidd and Wyke (eds), *Manchester* 363–4; Hylton 229–30
40. 'The abseiler and the turkey magnate', *Financial Times*, 29 November 2010; Spinoza 213–15
41. Kidd, *Manchester: A History* 247; Hylton 231–2

Chapter 15: Music

1. 'Elbow and the Hallé', *Guardian*, 9 July 2009
2. John Robb, *The North Will Rise Again: Manchester Music City 1976–1996* (Aurum 2009), 1
3. Dave Haslam, *Manchester, England: The Story of the Pop Cult City* (Fourth Estate 1999), xxviii
4. 'Sir Charles Hallé', halle.co.uk
5. Russell in Kidd and Wyke (eds), *Manchester* 268
6. Robert Roberts, *The Classic Slum: Salford Life in the First Quarter of the Century* (Penguin 1990, first published University of Manchester Press 1971), 151
7. Haslam 54–82; Brian Rust, 'Hylton, Jack (1892–1965)', *Oxford Dictionary of National Biography*
8. Evelyn Rothwell, *Life with Glorious John* (Robson 2002), 93–4; Michael Kennedy 'Barbirolli, Sir John', *Oxford Dictionary of National Biography*; Michael Kennedy, *Barbirolli, Conductor Laureate: The Authorised Biography* (MacGibbon and Key 1971), 224
9. 'Oldham's tribute for composer and most reluctant son', *Guardian*, 15 July 2002
10. 'Dirty old town – why Ewan MacColl wanted to take an axe to his neighbourhood', *Financial Times*, 29 June 2020; Haslam 26–7
11. Haslam 83–4
12. 'The Mancunian Way: Windrush 75', 22 June 2023, manchesterreveningnews.co.uk
13. Haslam 85–90
14. Haslam 91–6
15. Spinoza 106; Robb 14
16. Elton John, *Me: Elton John* (Macmillan 2019), quoted in Spinoza 25
17. Robb 7

18. Haslam 145–50
19. Haslam 107
20. Robb 35
21. Haslam 117; 'Sex Pistols gig: The truth', 24 September 2014, bbc.co.uk; 'They swear they were there: Sex Pistols at the Lesser Free Trade Hall', bbc.co.uk
22. David Scott, *Mancunians: Where Do We Start, Where Do I Begin?* (Manchester University Press 2023), 110–14
23. Graeme Thomson, *Cowboy Song: The Authorised Biography of Philip Lynott* (Hachette 2016), Ch. 8
24. 'It was the best party – ever', *Observer*, 3 March 2002; Spinoza 249; Haslam xxiii
25. Spinoza 40, 341
26. Spinoza 141–2, 253; Robb 178
27. Haslam 130
28. Spinoza 144–54
29. Haslam 175; Spinoza 130; 'Stark raving Madchester', *Newsweek*, 22 July 1990
30. 'Shaun Ryder says "nutty behaviour" was down to ADHD', *Manchester Evening News*, 29 May 2021
31. Scott 101–2; Haslam 206–7; 'Goldie leads tributes to Inner City Life singer Diane Charlemagne', *Guardian*, 28 October 2015; 'Denise Johnson: Primal Scream and New Order singer dies', 27 July 2020, bbc.co.uk
32. Spinoza 139–40
33. Robb 369
34. Scott 141
35. 'Troubled orchestra gets £3.8m fillip', *Guardian*, 21 June 2001; 'Kahchun Wong announced as new Principal Conductor and Artistic Adviser of the Hallé', 20 June 2023, halle.co.uk

Chapter 16: Twenty-first Century

1. Spinoza 283
2. 'Chancellor: We need a Northern Powerhouse', HM Treasury, 23 June 2014
3. Simon Jenkins, 'The secret negotiations to restore Manchester to greatness', *Guardian*, 12 February 2015
4. 'EU referendum: Brexit win amid Manchester's strong Remain vote', 24 June 2016, bbc.co.uk
5. 'Andy Burnham reveals his Top 5 Manchester bands – do you agree with his selection?', *Manchester Evening News*, 20 May 2017; Spinoza 285
6. Spinoza 300–1
7. 'I just sleep with a jacket to keep warm and woke up with no pants on this morning – it was freezing', *Manchester Evening News*, 5 December 2022
8. 'Manchester Arena inquiry: MI5 "profoundly sorry" for not stopping attack', 2 March 2023, bbc.co.uk

REFERENCES

9. ONS population estimates, nomisweb.co.uk
10. Multilingual Manchester 2010–21, University of Manchester, manchester .ac.uk
11. 'Life at the top: A look inside Manchester's tallest residential skyscraper which is like a 5-star hotel', *Manchester Evening News*, 2 December 2019
12. Spinoza 18
13. 'The death of Castlefield?', prideofmanchester.com; Spinoza 3
14. Paul Dennett, 'Sensible Socialism: The Salford Model', *Tribune*, 19 January 2021; 'Council's maiden: This City housing development starts on site', Manchester City Council, 5 July 2023, manchester.gov.uk
15. Adam Leaver, Richard Goulding and Jonathan Silver, 'Manchester offshored', Sheffield University Management School/University of Sheffield, 22 July 2022, Sheffield.ac.uk
16. Isaac Rose, 'Against the Manchester Model', *Tribune*, 25 November 2022
17. Sam Wheeler, 'Manchester needs change as much as it did in the 30s', *Morning Star*, accessed 15 August 2023, morningstaronline.co.uk
18. Daniel Timms, 'The billion pound Manchester question: Who has benefited from the city's breakneck growth?', *The Mill*, 29 July 2023, manchestermill .co.uk
19. *The English Indices of Deprivation 2019*, Ministry of Housing, Communities and Local Government, 26 September 2019
20. 'Unveiled: Transformative plans to turn area of Greater Manchester into "Atom Valley" with 20,000 new jobs and 7,000 homes', *Manchester Evening News*, 28 July 2022
21. 'The £1.7 billion plan to change the face of a Manchester city centre neighbourhood', *Manchester Evening News*, 22 June 2023; 'Joy in Manchester's cultural division as £211m arts centre opens', *The Art Newspaper*, 1 June 2023
22. Engels, *The Condition of the Working Class in England* 57

SELECT BIBLIOGRAPHY

Aikin, John, *A Description of the Country from Thirty to Forty Miles Round Manchester* (first edition 1795, republished by David & Charles 1968)

Allen, Robert C. , *The British Industrial Revolution in Global Perspective* (Cambridge 2009)

Arrowsmith, Peter, *Stockport: A History* (Stockport Metropolitan Borough Council 1997)

Aspin, C. and Chapman, S.D., *James Hargreaves and the Spinning Jenny* (Helmshore Local History Society 1964)

Aspin, Chris, *Lancashire: The First Industrial Society* (Helmshore Local History Society 1969)

Atkinson, Norman, *Sir Joseph Whitworth: 'The World's Best Mechanician'* (Sutton 1996)

Baines, Edward, *History of the Cotton Manufacture in Great Britain* (H. Fisher, R. Fisher and P. Jackson 1835)

Baker, Richard Anthony, *British Music Hall: An Illustrated History* (Pen and Sword 2014)

Bamford, Samuel, *Passages in the Life of a Radical* (1840–4, published initially in parts)

Bartley, Paula, *Emmeline Pankhurst* (Routledge 2002)

Boase, Tessa, *Mrs Pankhurst's Purple Feather: Fashion, Fury and Feminism – Women's Fight for Change* (Aurum 2018)

Bradburn, Jean and John, *A–Z of Manchester: Places, People, History* (Amberley 2019)

Bradshaw, L.D., *Visitors to Manchester: A Selection of British and Foreign Visitors' Descriptions of Manchester from c.1538–1865* (Neil Richardson 1987)

Bret, David, *Gracie Fields: The Authorized Biography* (Robson 1995)

Briggs, Asa, *Victorian Cities* (Penguin 1968, first published 1963)

Bruton, F.A., *A Short History of Manchester and Salford* (Sherratt & Hughes 1924)

Bull, Stephen, *'A General Plague of Madness': The Civil Wars in Lancashire, 1640–1660* (Carnegie 2009)

Burgess, Anthony, *Little Wilson and Big God* (Vintage 2012, first published 1987)

Busteed, Mervyn, *The Irish in Manchester c.1750–1921: Resistance, Adaptation and Identity* (Manchester University Press 2016)

Cardwell, Donald, *James Joule: A Biography* (Manchester University Press 1991)

Coase, Kathryn, *2000 Years of Manchester* (Pen and Sword 2019)

Cooper, Glynis, *Salford: An Illustrated History* (Breedon 2005)

Davies, Andrew, *The Gangs of Manchester: The Story of the Scuttlers, Britain's First Youth Cult* (Milo 2008)

Davis, Graham, *The Irish in Britain, 1815–1914* (Gill and Macmillan 1991)

Dickens, Steven, *Manchester's Military Legacy* (Pen and Sword 2017)

Disraeli, Benjamin, *Coningsby* (William Blackwood 1844)

Duxbury, Stephen, *The Brief History of Lancashire* (History Press 2011) 86–8

Endelman, Todd M., *The Jews of Britain 1656 to 2000* (University of California 2002)

Engels, Friedrich, *The Condition of the Working Class in England* (Oxford World's Classics)

Fisher, Michael H., Lahiri, Shompa and Thandi, Shinder, *A South-Asian History of Britain* (Greenwood 2007)

Fitton, R.S., *The Arkwrights: Spinners of Fortune* (2012 edition Derwent Valley Mills Educational Trust, first published 1989 Manchester University Press)

Fox, Kate, *Where There's Muck, There's Bras: Lost Stories of the Amazing Women of the North* (HarperNorth 2022)

Frangopulo, N.J. (ed.), *Rich Inheritance: A Guide to the History of Manchester* (Manchester Education Committee 1962)

Glinert, Ed., *Manchester Compendium: A Street-by-street History of England's Greatest Industrial City* (Penguin 2009)

Gregory, Richard, *Roman Manchester: The University of Manchester's Excavations within the Vicus 2001–5* (Oxbow 2007)

Hall, David, *Manchester's Finest: How the Munich Air Disaster Broke the Heart of a Great City* (Bantam 2008)

Haslam, Dave, *Manchester, England: The Story of the Pop Cult City* (Fourth Estate 1999)

Hazeldine, Tom, *The Northern Question: A History of a Divided Country* (Verso 2020)

Hochschild, Adam, *Bury the Chains: The British Struggle to Abolish Slavery* (Macmillan 2005, Pan 2006)

Hunt, Tristram, *Building Jerusalem: The Rise and Fall of the Victorian City* (Weidenfeld & Nicolson 2004, Phoenix 2005)

Hunt, Tristram, *The Frock-Coated Communist: The Revolutionary Life of Friedrich Engels* (Allen Lane 2009, Penguin 2010)

Hylton, Stuart, *A History of Manchester* (Phillimore 2003)

Inglis, Simon, *Played in Manchester: The Architectural Heritage of a City at Play* (English Heritage 2004)

Jackson, Lee, *Palaces of Pleasure: From Music Halls to the Seaside to Football, How the Victorians Invented Mass Entertainment* (Yale 2019)

James, Gary, *Manchester: A Football History* (James Ward 2008)

Jones, Barri, *Roman Manchester* (Manchester Excavation Committee, John Sherratt 1974)

Kay, James Phillips, *The Moral and Physical Condition of the Working Classes Employed in the Cotton Manufacture of Manchester* (Cass & Co. 1970, first published 1832)

Kennedy, Michael, *Barbirolli, Conductor Laureate: The Authorised Biography* (MacGibbon and Key 1971)

Kenyon, Denise, *The Origins of Lancashire* (Manchester University Press 1991)

Kidd, Alan, *Manchester: A History* (Carnegie 2006, first published 1993)

Kidd, Alan, *The Origins of Manchester: From Roman Conquest to Industrial Revolution* (Carnegie 2023)

Kidd, Alan and Wyke, Terry (eds), *Manchester: Making the Modern City* (Liverpool University Press 2016)

King, Ray, *Detonation: Rebirth of a City* (Clear Publications 2006)

Kirby, Dean, *Angel Meadow: Victorian Britain's Most Savage Slum* (Pen and Sword History 2016)

Lloyd-Jones, R. and Lewis, M.J., *Manchester and the Age of the Factory* (Croom Helm 1988)

MacColl, Ewan, *Journeyman: An Autobiography* (Sidgwick & Jackson 1990)

Maconie, Stuart, *Pies and Prejudice* (Random House 2008)

MacRaild, Donald, *The Irish Diaspora in Britain, 1750–1939* (Palgrave Macmillan 2011)

McNeil, Robina and Nevell, Michael, *A Guide to the Industrial Archaeology of Greater Manchester* (Association for Industrial Archaeology 2000)

Messinger, Gary S., *Manchester in the Victorian Age: The Half-Known City* (Manchester University Press 1985)

Miller, Ian and Wild, Chris, *A & G Murray and the Cotton Mills of Ancoats* (Oxford Archaeology North 2007)

Mokyr, Joel, *The Enlightened Economy: Britain and the Industrial Revolution 1700–1850* (Penguin 2009)

Musson, Albert and Robinson, Eric, *Science and Technology in the Industrial Revolution* (Manchester University Press 1969)

Nevell, Michael, *The Archaeology of Trafford* (Trafford Metropolitan Borough with University of Manchester Archaeological Unit 1997)

Nevell, Michael, *Manchester: The Hidden History* (History Press 2008)

Nevin, Charles, *Lancashire, Where Women Die of Love* (Mainstream 2004)

Nicholls, Robert, *The Belle Vue Story* (Neil Richardson 1992)

Ogden, James, *A Description of Manchester, 1783* (British Library reprint)

Olusoga, David, *Black and British: A Forgotten History* (Macmillan 2016)

Osborne, Roger, *Iron, Steam & Money: The Making of the Industrial Revolution* (Bodley Head 2013, Pimlico 2014)

Pankhurst, Emmeline, *Suffragette: My Own Story* (Solis 2015, originally published 2014)

Parkinson-Bailey, John J., *Manchester: An Architectural History* (Manchester University Press 2002)

Pevsner, Nikolaus, *The Buildings of England: South Lancashire* (Penguin 1969)

Phillips, C.B. and Smith, J.H., *Lancashire and Cheshire from AD 1540* (Longman 1994)

Pickstone, John (ed.), 'The History of Science and Technology in the North West', *Manchester Region History Review*, Vol. 18 (Manchester Centre for Regional History 2007)

Pollins, Harold, *Economic History of the Jews in England* (Associated University Presses 1982)

Poole, Robert, *Peterloo: The English Uprising* (Oxford 2019)

Pugh, Martin, *The Pankhursts* (Vintage 2008, first published Allen Lane 2001)

Purvis, June, *Emmeline Pankhurst: A Biography* (Routledge 2002)

Raffald, Elizabeth, *The Experienced English Housekeeper* (J. Harrop 1769)

Reid, Robert, *The Peterloo Massacre* (Windmill 2018, originally published 1989)

Riding, Jacqueline, *Peterloo: The Story of the Manchester Massacre* (Head of Zeus 2018)

Robb, John, *The North Will Rise Again: Manchester Music City 1976–1996* (Aurum 2009)

Roberts, Robert, *The Classic Slum: Salford Life in the First Quarter of the Century* (Penguin 1990, first published University of Manchester Press 1971)

Rohde, Shelley, *A Private View of L.S. Lowry* (Collins 1979)

Rose, Mary B. (ed.), *The Lancashire Cotton Industry: A History Since 1700* (Lancashire County Books 1996)

Ross, David, *George and Robert Stephenson: A Passion for Success* (History Press 2018)

Rothwell, Evelyn, *Life with Glorious John* (Robson 2002)

Russell, Dave (ed.), 'Sport in Manchester', *Manchester Region History Review*, Vol. 20 (Manchester Centre for Regional History 2009)

Sandbrook, Dominic, *Never Had It So Good: A History of Britain from Suez to the Beatles* (Little, Brown 2005, Abacus 2006)

Schofield, Jonathan, *My Guide to Manchester* (Manchester Books 2015)

Scott, David, *Mancunians: Where Do We Start, Where Do I Begin?* (Manchester University Press 2023)

Sherwood, Marika, *After Abolition: Britain and the Slave Trade Since 1807* (I.B. Tauris 2007)

Shotter, David, *Romans and Britons in North-West England* (Centre for North-West Regional Studies, University of Lancaster 2004, first published 1993)

Smith, Harold L., *The British Women's Suffrage Campaign* (Longman 2010, first published 1998)

Spinoza, Andy, *Manchester Unspun: Pop, Property and Power in the Original Modern City* (Manchester University Press 2023)

Swift, R. and Gilley, S. (eds), *The Irish in the Victorian City* (Croom Helm 1985)

Tait, James, *Medieval Manchester and the Beginnings of Lancashire* (Manchester University Press 1904)

Thomson, W.H., *A History of Manchester to 1852* (John Sherratt 1967)

Timmins, Geoffrey, *Four Centuries of Lancashire Cotton* (Lancashire County Books 1996)

Turing, Sarah, *Alan M. Turing: Centenary Edition* (Cambridge University Press 2012, first edition 1959)

Uglow, Jenny, *Elizabeth Gaskell* (Faber and Faber 1993)

Wadsworth, Alfred P. and de Lacy Mann, Julia, *The Cotton Trade and Industrial Lancashire, 1600–1780* (Manchester University Press 1931)

White, Jim, *Manchester United: The Biography* (Sphere 2009)

Wilkes, Sue, *Narrow Windows, Narrow Lives: The Industrial Revolution in Lancashire* (Tempus 2008)

Willan, T.S., *Elizabethan Manchester* (Manchester University Press 1980)

Williams, Bill, *Jewish Manchester: An Illustrated History* (Breedon 2008)

Williams, Joanna, *Manchester's Radical Mayor: Abel Heywood, The Man Who Built the Town Hall* (History Press 2017)

Williams, Joanna, *The Great Miss Lydia Becker: Suffragist, Scientist and Trailblazer* (Pen and Sword 2022)

Winchester, Simon, *Exactly: How Precision Engineers Created the Modern World* (William Collins 2018)

Woodman, Deborah, *The Story of Manchester* (Phillimore 2017)

Wroe, James, *Peterloo Massacre, Containing a Faithful Narrative of the Events which preceded, accompanied and followed the fatal Sixteenth of August 1819* (third edition, printed by James Wroe, Manchester 1819)

ACKNOWLEDGEMENTS

I owe a huge debt to all those who read and commented on my first book, *Northerners: A History, from the Ice Age to the Present Day*, which became a national bestseller. Your support, and that of all the booksellers who got behind it, and the societies and festivals that invited me to speak, has given me immense encouragement. How to follow such a wide-ranging work? The focus of *Made in Manchester* is a little narrower, yet it is a fascinating story of global significance. I have tried to make it accessible to the widest possible range of readers.

Massive thanks are due again to the brilliant team at HarperNorth, who have done so much to boost the publishing scene outside London since it was founded in 2020. Particular credit goes to Jonathan de Peyer, senior commissioning editor for non-fiction, who encouraged me to write about this topic and has guided me expertly through the publishing processes. Genevieve, Alice, Megan, Taslima and their colleagues have been tremendously supportive – thoughtful, constructive, kind and encouraging. My agent Andrew Lownie, a prolific historian and biographer, has been a rock.

This work owes a particular debt to my parents and my wider Manchester family, who gave me such a great start in life and imbued me with the kind of knowledge that you don't find easily in books. My parents made sacrifices that enabled me to become the first person in my family to go to university. Sadly they are not around to see the book, but I hope they would be pleased with the result.

Above all, I thank my wife Carola for her advice and for casting her novelist's eye over each chapter. I could not have done it without her. Thank you to all my family and friends, who have been patient me while I grappled with this project.

INDEX